Preserving Petersburg

T0311295

Preserving Petersburg

History, Memory, Nostalgia

Edited by
Helena Goscilo
and
Stephen M. Norris

Indiana University Press
Bloomington & Indianapolis

This book is a publication of

Indiana University Press
601 North Morton Street
Bloomington, IN 47404-3797 USA

http://iupress.indiana.edu

Telephone orders   800-842-6796
Fax orders   812-855-7931
Orders by e-mail   iuporder@indiana.edu

Library of Congress Cataloging-in-Publication Data

Preserving Petersburg : history, memory, nostalgia / edited by Helena Goscilo and
Stephen M. Norris.
    p. cm.
Includes bibliographical references and index.
ISBN 978-0-253-35142-5 (cloth : alk. paper) — ISBN 978-0-253-21980-0
(pbk. : alk. paper)   1. Saint Petersburg (Russia)—History.
    2. Saint Petersburg (Russia)—In literature.
    3. Saint Petersburg (Russia)—Civilization.
    I. Goscilo, Helena, date II. Norris, Stephen M.
        DK552.P73   2008   2007045267
            947'.21—dc22

1 2 3 4 5 13 12 11 10 09 08

Contents

Five
Petersburg in the Poetry of the Russian Emigration

Six
Multiethnic St. Petersburg: The Late Imperial Period

Seven
Leningrad Culture under Siege (1941–1944)

Eight
Cultural Capital and Cultural Heritage:
St. Petersburg and the Arts of Imperial Russia

Nine
Strolls Through Postmodern Petersburg: Celebrating
the City in 2003

Acknowledgements

The editors gratefully acknowledge the following people for their help with this volume's publication: Karen Dawisha, Director of the Havighurst Center for Russian and Post-Soviet Studies at Miami University; Anne Clemmer, June Silay, and Daniel Pyle at Indiana University Press; Candace McNulty, our outstanding copyeditor; and Melissa Cox Norris, who designed the original version of the beautiful cover. Helena thanks Steve for the pleasure of working with him, a feeling Steve reciprocates.

Introduction

Helena Goscilo and Stephen M. Norris

Vicissitudes of fortune, which spares neither man nor
the proudest of his works, which buries empires and
cities in a common grave.

EDWARD GIBBON, THE DECLINE AND FALL
OF THE ROMAN EMPIRE

The ravishing night
exudes joy and sensuality!
Heaven's northern daughter,
the night is mute
And light blue!

PETR VIAZEMSKII, "PETERSBURG NIGHT"[1]

The identity and status of cities inevitably changes with the years, though perhaps not in the perception of its residents, admirers, and detractors. Internationally, Rome continues to enjoy its long-standing (and tautological) reputation as the Eternal City, Paris remains the Center of Chic and Amour, and London, its current prices of apartments and houses notwithstanding, still impresses many as eminently Livable. By contrast, historical events as well as economic hardships have diminished the earlier significance of cities such as Berlin, Lisbon, and Warsaw. Perhaps no other European city, however, has experienced such a dramatic change in image as St. Petersburg, founded in 1703 as the country's Westward-oriented capital and as a visually stunning showcase of Russia's imperial ambitions.

In 2002, Petersburgers had the opportunity to publicly voice their views of what traditionally has been touted as Russia's Northern Palmyra when, as a prelude to St. Petersburg's 300th birthday the following year, the Russian edition of *Elle* magazine announced a contest for the best essay on "My Petersburg." The committee judging the entries included the well-known author Tatyana Tolstaya, and submissions came from a number of famous and not so famous Russians alike. Ultimately, Arkadii Ippolitov, a curator at the Hermitage, won. His essay, "The City in a Porcelain Snuffbox," argues that St. Petersburg no longer exists as a city, for it has become a museum piece, much like an eighteenth-century snuffbox. According to Ippolitov, St. Petersburg is an entity in storage, similar to materials and corpses in libraries and cemeteries—spaces where objects are arranged in a seeming order, yet places that seek to "act on the nerves, but produce a feeling of involuntary respect." As he argues, "In cemeteries, just as in museums, you understand acutely that there is no death. There is also no life." Ippolitov concludes that cemeteries, museums, and other depositories of culture store recollections as imprints of memory that "add to a repository of illusions and metaphors," which in turn create a sense of reality. In his view, "St. Petersburg" was "converted into a recollection and washed away by twilights, white nights, fogs, and hoarfrosts," thereby ceasing "to exist in reality; only the brittle porcelain of an ancient snuff-box preserved Petersburg." Ippolitiov's views correspond to a growing perception in Russia that St. Petersburg has become "museumified."[2] For those subscribing to this view, Petersburg is preserved in a way similar to other exotic phenomena that no longer have contemporary meaning, but function as objects of curiosity.

Ippolitov's essay explodes traditional views of St. Petersburg. For years scholars and writers have examined the city primarily through four lenses associated with canonized writers, according to which "Petersburg" is a place of great beauty, a supernatural space, an apocalyptic site, or a locus of spiritual endurance—specifically, the images created by Pushkin, Dostoevsky, Bely, and Akhmatova.[3] Vladimir Toporov argues that a study of the Petersburg Text, as this corpus is commonly called, reveals "the astonishing closeness the various descriptions of Petersburg bear to one another, both in the works of a single author and in those of diverse authors."[4] Thus the city might seem, in Julie Buckler's apt description, a place "composed exclusively of palaces and slums, populated entirely by pampered aristocrats, the desperate poor, and writers of genius who immortalized both in artistic masterworks."[5] Ippolitov explicitly rejects this "storied" view of the city in favor of other approaches. For him, Petersburg is best understood as a preservation piece, one inseparable from history, nostalgia, and constant recourse to memories of the past. Sentiment and desire have turned Petersburg into an immobile site of memory, much like an "old cemetery, a neglected library, and museum depositories." What links these locales is that "in them time is similar to a pond or a lake with standing water," where someone can step in more than once and experience the same sensations.[6] For a city intended as the stronghold of future-oriented ideas and projects, the image of stasis and regression represents a startling reversal.

That image of Petersburg intersects with the perspectives of scholars represented in this volume, who likewise maintain that the northern capital and its history have been shaped by ceaseless attempts at preservation and nostalgic yearning for a mythical Petersburg constructed over time. As William Brumfield's introductory chapter makes clear, Petersburg's story is above all one about survival. Brumfield focuses on the Winter Palace and the Admiralty, the two most important architectural symbols of Petersburg, and the concerted efforts to maintain the significance of these structures. At the same time, the buildings of St. Petersburg have prompted visitors and residents alike to focus on the unanticipated ramifications of the city's individual "identity." From the Marquis de Custine to Fyodor Dostoevsky, many observers maintained that the survival of the city's buildings created a sense of overwhelming artifice and power. Yet, as Custine noted, Petersburg's buildings were sites of memory invested with meanings that inspired successive generations to preserve them and the memories they contained. One might claim, then, that almost from the outset Petersburg was trapped between the progressive intentions of its founder and the preservationist passions of its residents and historians.

In her discussion of the city's history of preservation, Julie Buckler argues that Petersburg's empirical experience of repeated destruction and ruin has led writers to associate the former capital with a profound sense of loss. Over the course of the nineteenth century and well into the twentieth, St. Petersburg authors struggled to counteract this perceived evanescence with "cultural" excursions through the city intended to convey a feel for the "old Petersburg," and with the production of such texts as memorial plaques and gravestones that would "immortalize" city spaces. Tracing the history of these and other efforts at preservation reveals a great deal about the city's hidden history and the ways it has been both remembered and forgotten throughout the centuries of its existence.

As Helena Goscilo's chapter illustrates, images that helped to create a visual memory of the city simultaneously paralleled and subverted Petersburg's literary myths. Artists of the eighteenth century focused on documenting the city and its buildings, thereby providing historical evidence of "old Petersburg." Later artists such as Evgenii Lansere, Anna Ostroumova-Lebedeva, and Mstislav Dobuzhinskii depicted not only the city's imposing "sights"/"sites," but also its forgotten, less prepossessing nooks and crannies, complementing, reinforcing, and polemicizing with the famous literary renditions of Petersburg. Many of these neglected, often "unsaintly" images constitute attempts at preservation, but they themselves have largely fallen out of cultural memory. Whereas post-Soviet construction under Mayor Luzhkov's leadership has transformed sections of the medieval city of Moscow beyond recognition, eighteenth-century Petersburg, not unlike its custodians who prefer to forget the Soviet era, remains trapped in amber, preserved "as it should have been." The conviction that neither Revolution nor evolution should impinge on the city's "face" allies itself with aesthetics, while ignoring the political, social, and economic problems slowly undermining the life of the city, including the resplendent architecture that is its citizens' and preservationists' pride.

That project of preservation occupied various writers, including Osip Mandelstam in his poetry, as Zara Torlone shows in her chapter. Mandelstam lived through the years of revolution and civil war, which brought death and destruction on such a scale that his beloved city seemed "lost." Elaborating his own version of "Petersburg's soul," Mandelstam wrote poems about exile, memory, and loss associated with Petersburg (the name he favored over Petrograd) and compared it to Rome. For Mandelstam, the eternal city offered a readymade comparison to St. Petersburg, for by the 1920s he believed that Piter, like Rome, had become a decadent, moribund entity. In order to preserve a sense of this past, Mandelstam wrote wish-fulfillment odes that promised: "In Petersburg we shall meet again." Readers of this and other, similar poems might do well to remember that after his arrest Mandelstam not only never met fellow Petersburgers in the city, but perished in a Stalinist camp—a fate indicating the impossibility of separating or protecting art from politics and thus of keeping the city-snuffbox unblemished.

Mandelstam may have been the most famous poet who attempted to depict Petersburg as a forlorn, museum-like city, but, as Vladimir Khazan demonstrates in his chapter, countless other Russians attempted to preserve a vision of St. Petersburg after the events of 1917. For those Russians who found themselves abroad as a result of the Revolution, the city on the Neva ideally symbolized "old Russia" and "the Russia that we have lost." Nostalgia gripped exiled poets to such a degree that, Khazan argues, they succumbed to a "Petersburg syndrome." The fact that "Petersburg" no longer existed proved to be a ripe metaphor for poets experiencing a sense of loss, even those who had never set foot in Peter's city. These texts evidence the uncanny power of the Imaginary at the price of the Symbolic and partially illuminate Petersburg's gradual loss of status and current absence of an effective infrastructure that potentially could address the crime, poverty, and lack of adequate facilities blighting the city. In Marxist terms, the superstructure of elegiac romance and heightened emotions meant, at base, insufficient provisions, poor roads and transportation, and a moribund industry.

Any acts of preservation and remembering inherently involve acts of destruction and forgetting.[7] Noting that St. Petersburg has many forgotten histories, Steven Duke examines an aspect of the "Petersburg experience" that has escaped serious attention—its multiethnic character. Bringing to life some of the forgotten actors who helped to shape the history of the city, Duke contends that St. Petersburg should be understood as much from its forgotten aspects as from the literary and historical myths that have dominated its study. Multiethnicity is an aspect of the city that scholarship has largely ignored, even though buildings of its foreign communities and those constructed by its foreigners remain. Despite its international origins, contemporary Petersburg shares the rest of Russia's inhospitality or indifference to "aliens," particularly if they are dark-skinned, thereby aiding the process of historical amnesia against the comprehensive background of museumification.

In the midst of the Siege of Leningrad—one of the defining moments of the city's history—its residents, as Cynthia Simmons illuminates, also engaged in preservation. Fearful of the destruction that the war might inflict, Leningraders struggled to retain a sense of the city's "soul." For writers such as Lydia Ginzburg, that enterprise involved maintaining a diary of the city's activities under siege. Paradoxically, the war brought a renewed non-Soviet and thus Petersburg-like "freedom." Others took to reading about old Petersburg and thus communing with its spirit—an act that helped to fuel a culture of the siege that engaged Petersburg as much as Leningrad. Partly because of this turn back to Petersburg culture, the memories of the Siege became contested for the remainder of the USSR's existence, for the government attempted to preserve a more "Soviet" memory of World War II and of Petersburg's devastating horrors during the blockade. Not only official agendas attest to the role of politics in purportedly historical documents, for, paradoxically, much of the literature on the Siege, written by the intelligentsia, tended to slight other social groups, in a spirit of elitism consonant with the city's image of a High Culture Sepulcher.

The collapse of communism revived memories of Petersburg as a cultural capital as well as aspects of the city's history that had sunk into oblivion. Richard Stites argues that post-Soviet Petersburg has witnessed a memory boom of sorts, one that emphasizes a view of the city as a cultural center. This revival, however, involves its own destruction and forgetting. Touring some of the sites of memory where contemporary Petersburg culture is shaped, Stites shows how other features of the city's past remain obliviscent. In the attic of the Russian Museum, for example, hundreds of paintings that capture the daily life of times past remain in storage and therefore unseen, for they do not harmonize with a vision of the past that is useful or appealing to today's museum-goers. As in narratives of the Siege, the common place and the common people are shunted aside, so as to promote Petersburg as an elite museum.

As the city celebrated its tercentenary in 2003, it yet again strived to define itself. Stephen Norris guides us on a stroll through the celebrations within Ippolitov's "museum city," which packaged the past for its visitors, displaying it for their consumption. Aleksandr Sokurov's tercentenary gift of his film *Russian Ark* best represents this image of postmodern Petersburg, though numerous exhibits, tours, and pageantry presented the city as a porcelain snuffbox, a relic of bygone years. Given the grim aspects of the city's present and the uncertainty of its future, such an emphasis is psychologically understandable, however ill-advised from the standpoint of what Dostoevsky called "living life."

The chapters in this volume trace a process of preservation that stretches back nearly two centuries. Peter Fritzsche recently has written about how the nineteenth century led to new perspective on the past; as a result of the

Napoleonic Wars, the past became something lost and ruined—an object of mourning and desire. As Fritzsche argues, the "powerful apprehension of loss was the premise for a whole range of cultural activities with the debris of the past."[8] Indeed, the nineteenth century ushered in a new obsession with preservation, from collecting artifacts to folklore. At the same time, Fritzsche notes, "the debris of the past . . . spoke to contemporaries in a wide range of voices."[9] Many Europeans could look to the past with fondness or a sense of what might have been, while others conceived of it as merely a quaint relic. Regardless of how they were apprehended, the past and history became things to be possessed and, when the need arose, displayed in the manner of bibelots.

Petersburg proved to be a powerful symbol and site in the Russian version of this process. Over time, and concurrently with the development of the Petersburg literary myth, the city itself became viewed as a museum to be preserved. Shortly after the Napoleonic invasion of 1812, Konstantin Batiushkov's "A Stroll to the Academy of Arts" envisioned St. Petersburg as a living museum, ideal for imagining the past by musing about its buildings, which would inspire strolling spectators to "talk of times past."[10] Vissarion Belinsky carried this vision further, explicitly declaring in 1844, "Petersburg *itself* is a great historical monument."[11] As the nineteenth century drew to a close, artists and writers established the year 1815, or the end of the Napoleonic era, as the temporal boundary of "old Petersburg." Alexander Benois led this acceleratedly retrospective trend, encouraging Russians to view the monuments of "old Petersburg" (particularly suburban palaces) as something "truly good" and "eternally beautiful"—presumably as a contrast to contemporary markers of modernity. For Benois and his fellow members of the World of Art Movement, Petersburg was a unique and, in Emily Johnson's words, "supremely successful work of art."[12]

By the twentieth century, many Russians had singled out "Petersburg" as the city that preserved this imaginary old Russia. No group did more to promote the idea of Petersburg as a museum city than the preservationists, who were active in St. Petersburg during the early years of the twentieth century.[13] Responding to the changes unleashed first by modernization and then by the Bolshevik Revolution, preservationists such as Benois, Georgii Lukomskii, Petr Stolpianskii, and Nikolai Antsiferov all composed books about the "old Petersburg" in an effort to preserve its all too rapidly disintegrating past. Anatolii Koni, a representative of this cohort, wrote about a

Petersburg that contained "memories that have departed into the past of no return."[14] In 1921, the preservationists founded the Society for Old Petersburg, an organization dedicated to "the care of certain monuments, places, buildings, and things . . . to which the government could not extend [its efforts] . . . because it was not possible to preserve everything that should be preserved."[15] Then, as now, the past seemed a safe harbor of achievements and artistic glories, in contrast to the prospect of an at best uncertain future.

The Society disbanded in the late 1930s, but the belief that "Petersburg" had preserved the past continued, and gained renewed momentum after the Second World War. Alexander Solzhenitsyn in his 1960 poem "The City on the Neva" extolled the city as a site of "perfect, everlasting beauty." In a formulation implicitly contrasting the Northern Palmyra with Moscow, Petersburg, he claimed, had retained a sense of the old Russia, where "no wedding-cake skyscraper may elbow its way onto the Nevsky Prospect," making it "a pleasure . . . to stroll down [its] avenues."[16] Ultimately, "his poem evinces an unacknowledged desire to protect an imaginary authentic Petersburg"[17] and, perhaps more importantly, to anathematize the architectural transformation wrought by Stalinism in the capital. Indeed, the insistence on a legendary Petersburg served as an ill-disguised rejection of the Soviet regime, as is clear not only from Aleksandr Sokurov's 2003 film *Russian Ark* but also from Joseph Brodsky's earlier essay "Guide to a Renamed City." According to Brodsky, the Bolsheviks' abandonment of the imperial capital meant that the city "froze as if in total mute bewilderment before the impending era"—a process of museumification in its own right, for "the presence of Peter I's spirit is still much more palpable here than the flavor of the new [Soviet] epoch." Brodsky concludes that, owing to the Bolsheviks' actions, "the city itself was left to itself and to its reflections. [. . .] Petersburg, having nowhere to withdraw to, came to a standstill—as though photographed in its nineteenth-century posture."[18] Brodsky thus affirmed the widespread belief that "old Petersburg" still existed, for it was possible to visit the city and imagine it as a stronghold of the pre-revolutionary past. That perspective probably troubled a successful émigré writer in New York less than it would literati remaining in a city with few publishing houses and few prospects for anything more than eking out a minimal existence.

The accumulation of preservation memory in St. Petersburg created a city awash in heritage and nostalgia. When St. Petersburg reprised its original name in 1991, many critics interpreted this renaming as the final stage in its "museumification." Indeed, for some, "Petersburg" existed exclusively as a history museum or a nostalgic belief. Mikhail Kuraev, writing in 1996, asserted that the restoration of its original name rendered the city a "completed historical subject [*zavershennyi istoricheskii siuzhet*]" and "a finished artistic work [*zakonchennoe khudozhestvennoe proizvedenie*]."[19] Similarly, Aleksandr Skidan believes that post-Soviet Petersburg functions as the "sepulcher of imperial Russian culture," where "St. Petersburg" no longer is merely a name, but signals "museumification under an open sky [*muzeifikatsii pod otkrytym nebom*]."[20] Ippolitov's prize-winning essay thus represents only the most recent articulation of the notion that St. Petersburg has ceased to be a city, having metamorphosed into a museum where the past is carefully preserved.

Many doubtless find the "museumification" of Petersburg understandable in light of the tumultuous history of the city and the country that once commanded an empire. Thoughts of "old Petersburg" serve as a survival strategy, a place where any visitor—whether literal or figurative—can take refuge from both the Soviet past and the uncertain future. As David Lowenthal suggests about the contemporary study of history, "the new past is too chaotic to comprehend," while the "future, once embraced as a friend, becomes a fearsome foe."[21] In post-Soviet Petersburg, it may be safer and more comforting to visit a sanitized or romantic past than to confront many of the imponderables the future augurs. The idea of old Petersburg simultaneously represents a vision that allows one to forget the numerous streets, buildings, and spaces still desperately in need of preservation—even those institutionalized as museum sites, as anyone who has taken the Dostoevsky walking tour offered by any number of tourist agencies can testify.

Valery Gergiev, the preternaturally energetic director of the Mariinsky Theater, stumbled against sacrosanct tradition when he decided to build a second theater on land across a narrow canal from the historic Mariinsky. His insistence on modern architecture doubtless influenced the selection of the architect Dominique Perrault, who had designed the Bibliothèque Nationale in Paris, from among the competitors who submitted their proposals in 2003. Predictably, St. Petersburg traditionalists vehemently opposed Perrault's design, for it envisioned encasing the theater in "a translucent golden mass enclosure." Perrault's design eventually was modified to pacify the preservers of the city's architectural past.[22]

A threat more dire, however, was looming on the horizon. In 2006, Petersburg's consoling past, materialized in its beautiful though ravaged landscape, threatened to crumble. Gazprom, the state-controlled energy giant that is Russia's largest company, announced its intention to build a massive business center on the Neva River—a proposal that Petersburg preservationists predictably fought on the grounds that it would ruin "old Petersburg." Vladimir Popov, president of St. Petersburg's Union of Architects, claimed that the construction plan offered by Daniel Libeskind, Jean Nouvel, and other prominent international architects, would "kill the city." Mikhail Piotrovsky, the Hermitage director, noted that the city "needed development" but urged everyone who would listen, "Let's not destroy the old city." Aleksandr Margolis, head of the Charitable Fund for Saving Petersburg and Leningrad, claimed that the soaring towers envisioned by foreign architects would destroy a three-centuries-old "architectural harmony." An open letter circulated at the conference of St. Petersburg architects in June 2006 declared, "The building of a 300-meter tower will inevitably destroy the harmony of the Petersburg leitmotif, which took shape over centuries; it will cause irreparable loss to the fragile silhouette of the city."[23] Headlines featured such subtitles as "The 300 Meter Building 'Gazprom-City' Could Disfigure Petersburg by 2010."[24] Architectural Apocalypse, in other words, loomed on the horizon.

For its detractors, the very idea of a Gazprom City threatened to undermine the accumulated belief that Petersburg symbolized an irrevocably receding past that needed to be preserved, seemingly at all costs. As customary in debates about Petersburg, aesthetics and history (imaginary or otherwise) trumped all other considerations. For Petersburgers such as Piotrovsky, who had done much to refashion the Hermitage as a site of memory after 1991, such an aggressively modern and potentially lucrative venture involving architects from abroad was impermissible, "for this skyscraper would project opposite Rastrelli's Smolny Cathedral"—an unwittingly ironic statement that posthumously russified old Petersburg's favorite Italian architect and his works.[25]

Gazprom fought for its revolutionary project on different grounds, claiming that it reflected the original legacy of the city's founder. Like Peter, Gazprom officials argued, they embraced the West, progressive innovation, and foreigners. Nikolai Tanaev, a Gazprom director overseeing the enterprise, reminded critics, "We live in the twenty-first century, not the eighteenth." The deputy governor of Petersburg expanded on Tanaev's views: "There is a mistaken belief that St. Petersburg's center has remained unchanged since it was founded," concluding, "St. Petersburg should preserve its architectural traditions, but should not reject improvement."[26] Tellingly, even detractors admitted that the envisioned structure responded to contemporary needs and not those of "the Catherine era, in which we live."[27] As many proponents of the project pointed out, Peter the Great conceived his city as a symbol of Russian power; whereas in his era symbolic power meant the Admiralty, in the twenty-first century it meant gas. Gazprom's chief executive, Aleksei B. Miller, predicted that the building "will give birth to a new mentality for St. Petersburg, which lives in a new, modern civilization. And its citizens will feel the pulse of the new economy, the pulse of the contemporary world." After the British firm RMJM won the competition for designing the site, which lies outside the historic center recognized by UNESCO as a cultural landmark, Mikhail I. Amosov, one of the city's lawmakers, observed, "Eventually we are going to lose the shape of St. Petersburg that we inherited from previous generations." Valentina Matvienko, the Putin-supporting St. Petersburg governor, reasoned that Gazprom's business center would inject revenue into the city: "Without big companies coming, without turning the city into a financial and economic center, we shall never have these resources, and the unique architectural heritage in the center of the city will be quietly falling apart before our eyes."[28] As a city official, Matvienko, understandably, is more invested in filled coffers than imposing coffins—a priority that preservationists by definition cannot countenance.

The tricky problem of reconciling the city's traditions with new and potentially lucrative trends surfaced in a recent article by Matvienko, startlingly titled "St. Petersburg—the leader of Russian modernization." Matvienko prefaces hyperbolic claims for the city's "investment climate" as "the best in the country" and its "effective governance of the region" with the familiar image of it as "a world cultural treasure trove, a museum under the open sky."[29] She then proceeds to catalogue St. Petersburg's recent financial triumphs: a 40 percent rise in the investment rate in the city's economy in 2004–2005, and more than a threefold increase in foreign investments in the real economy during 2005, plus a series of large infrastructural projects, several with the participation of the Baltic States.[30] How all of these ventures will ameliorate the lives of the city's residents and how conservationists' responses to these initiatives will affect their implementation remains to be seen.

Gazprom City disturbs the reassuring but embattled heritage of Petersburg as a museum site, a sanctuary affording the opportunity to commune with the past and delectate the city's decaying splendor. Not only aesthetics, but centuries-old cultural habits will be violated by the installation of a towering spiral that doubles the size of St. Peter-Paul's spire, for it disrupts the hallowed process that the following essays document. As Luzhkov's economically successful but highly controversial introduction of new businesses and buildings into Moscow has demonstrated, many Russians resist novelties that demolish visible links with a revered past. Three centuries after Peter the Great seized Russia by the throat, forcing it willy-nilly into the modern age symbolized by the new northern capital, the powerful state once again is readying to actualize a bold and highly controversial plan for bringing Petersburg in line with contemporary life via a building that likely will cater to the elite while improving the city's finances. Whatever one's appreciation of aesthetics and tradition, the question implied by Matvienko's endorsement of such radical innovations as Gazprom City and the installation of Toyota, Nissan, and General Motors factories in the Palmyra of the North cannot be dismissed:[31] How do people who have to eat, clothe themselves, and educate their children survive in a museum? After all, even museums need subsidies, periodic upgrading, and personnel who work for wages. One cannot live by bread alone, but one indisputably needs bread in order to live.

Notes

1. "Peterburgskaia noch'": "Dyshit schast'em, Sladostrast'em, Upoitel'naia noch'! Noch' nemaia, Golubaia, Neba severnaia doch'!"

2. Arkadii Ippolitov, "Gorod v farforovoi tabakerke," in E. D. Shubina, *Moi Peterburg* (Moscow, 2003), 210–215.

3. For these categories, see Orlando Figes, "Tales of Petersburg," in Frank Althaus, Mark Sutcliffe, and Yury Molodkovets, eds., *Petersburg Perspectives* (London, 2003), 91–105.

4. Quoted in Julie Buckler, *Mapping St. Petersburg: Imperial Text and Cityshape* (Princeton, 2005), 17.

5. Buckler, *Mapping St. Petersburg*, 1.

6. Ippolitov, "Gorod v farforovoi tabakerke," 210.

7. See Paul Ricoeur, *History, Memory, Forgetting*, Kathleen Blamey and David Pellauer, trans. (Chicago, 2004), particularly 412–456.

8. Peter Fritzsche, *Stranded in the Present: Modern Time and the Melancholy of History* (Cambridge, MA, 2004), 214.

9. Ibid.

10. K. N. Batiushkov, "A Stroll to the Academy of Arts," online translation by Carol Adlam at http://hri.shef.ac.uk/rva/texts/batiushkov/bat01/bat01.html.

11. Quoted in Buckler, *Mapping St. Petersburg*, 241.

12. See Emily Denene Johnson, "How a Group of Books Gave Birth to a Discipline: Guidebooks, Excursions, and Literary Kraevedenie in Early Twentieth-Century Petersburg" (Ph.D. dissertation, Columbia University, 2000), 42–43.

13. Katerina Clark describes the preservationists' activities in *Petersburg: Crucible of Cultural Revolution* (Cambridge, MA, 1995), 57–65.

14. Buckler, *Mapping St. Petersburg*, 106–107.

15. Johnson, "How a Group of Books Gave Birth to a Discipline," 101.

16. Alexander Solzhenitsyn, *Stories and Prose Poems*, Michael Glenny, trans. (New York, 1970), 252–253.

17. Buckler, *Mapping St. Petersburg*, 37.

18. Joseph Brodsky, *Less Than One: Selected Essays* (New York, 1986), 69–94.

19. Mikhail Kuraev, "Puteshestvie iz Leningrada v Sankt-Peterburg," *Novyi mir*, no. 10 (1996).

20. Aleksandr Skidan, "O pol'ze i vrede Peterburga dlia zhizni," *Russkii zhurnal*, July 6, 1999. Available online at http://litpromzona.narod.ru/reflections/skidan3.html.

21. David Lowenthal, "The Past of the Future," *History Today* 56/6 (June 2006), 42–44.

22. George Loomis, "Gergiev's Opus: A New Concert Hall," *New York Times* January 9, 2007. http://www.nytimes.com/2007/01/09/arts/music/09mary.html?ei=507. Accessed January 9, 2007.

23. Quoted in Boris Vishnevskii, "Gazoskreb," *Novaia gazeta* 20 July 2006: http://2006 .novayagazeta.ru/nomer/2006/54n/n54n-s00.shtml.

24. Ibid.

25. Ibid.

26. This story made the front page of the *New York Times* in November 2006: Steven Lee Myers, "Russian Window on the West Reaches for the Sky," *New York Times*, November 28, 2006, 1.

27. Boris Vishnevskii, "Gazoskreb."

28. Steven Lee Myers, "A Russian Skyscraper Plan Divides a Horizontal City," *New York Times*, December 2, 2006. http://www.nytimes.com/2006/12/02/arts/design/02gazp .html?ei=5088&en=d44783da756cb3fb&ex=1322. Accessed December 16, 2006.

29. Valentina Matvienko, "St. Petersburg—the leader of Russian modernization." Pan-Eurasian Institute: *Baltic Rim Economies*, 28.2. 2007: 11.

30. Matvienko, *St. Petersburg*, 11–12.

31. Ibid., 12.

Preserving Petersburg

One

St. Petersburg and the Art of Survival

William Craft Brumfield

Dostoevsky's Underground Man called it "the most abstract and intentional city in the world." The Comte de Ségur spoke of it as a "monument to the victory of genius over Nature." For Andrei Bely, in his novel *Petersburg,* the city is a dot on the map of Russia, a dot without dimensions, whose existence is proclaimed by an endless stream of administrative circulars.[1] Even during the Soviet period, as the City of Peter became the City of Lenin, its perverse climate and monumental architecture served to remind one of an almost mythic imperial past—and of a capacity for survival against unthinkable odds.

For two centuries St. Petersburg was the capital of a vast and complex empire, a symbol of the implacable will that forged Russia into a modern European state. The city arose from a collision of two cultures, Muscovite and European, and the ensuing tensions formed one of the most persistent themes of a remarkable succession of writers, enthralled not only by the spirit of the city but also by its very appearance. And with reason, for the architecture of St. Petersburg—grandiose, overpowering at times, obsessed with a rational design—remains the clearest statement of purpose that Imperial Russia ever made: to measure, to build, to impose order at any cost.[2]

Even as the imperial capital oversaw this vast, multiethnic expansion, it also required a sense of stability, of historical continuity. In creating a myth of stability, architecture played a critically significant—albeit ambiguous—role. On the one hand the highly ornamental style of Muscovy, epitomized in its churches and monasteries, was resolutely discarded during the reign of Peter as the sign of Russia's backward, stagnant past. On the other hand a much younger Petersburg would strenuously appropriate the architectural values of another past, that of Europe's classical heritage which in turn suggested a still earlier, Roman empire as Russia's mythic model.

As Petersburg made Russian history, did its architecture endow the city with a sense of history—and in whose definition? As will be seen later in this chapter, the architectural commentary of de Custine and Dostoevsky (and Dostoevsky's comments on de Custine) are particularly apposite to the discussion of architecture as a primary—and most visible—means of projecting national identity in its dynamic vitality.

But what we see as the unique beauty of Petersburg—the city as a work of art—was seen by many, especially after the middle of the nineteenth century, as a deviation from "authentic" Russian culture. It is not by accident that for the first century and a half of its existence, Petersburg's imperial rulers demonstrated obsessive concern with the design and appearance of the city. Nonetheless, their sublime project always possessed a sense of a design imposed— on chaotic nature and a reluctant people. Whereas Moscow's plan possessed the "organic," irregular logic of a medieval center, gathering together its many roads from all directions, Petersburg's ordered ("logical") French plan seems paradoxically to have created a sense of self-enclosure—a bulwark placed in defiance of elemental forces—human and natural. Yet these forces would also play their essential role in creating and sustaining the myth of St. Petersburg, which displayed by turns a monstrous indifference to suffering and an ineffable sense of Russian—specifically Russian—pathos. How could any undertaking prosper in such an unpromising environment?

The city was built at the estuary of the River Neva (Finnish for "swamp"), and the flat terrain, marked with a network of canals and inlets, provided an effective setting for the visions of Petersburg's imperial architects. In both baroque and neoclassical styles, the monumentality of Petersburg architecture has a slightly stagy quality, and not all critics have been favorably impressed. As an ensemble, however, the city is one of the most imposing and best preserved in Europe. The regulated height, the dramatic use of columns and arches, and the vivid palette of colors for the stuccoed walls create an aura of fantasy in an environment that seems to be floating.

Early Survival

Peter the Great established the city in May 1703. Sankt Piterburkh was to be his Conduit to the West, as well as tangible evidence of his determination to transform Russia into a modern state.[3] But its immediate purpose was more limited: to serve as a strategic fortification at the point where the Neva River flows into the Gulf of Finland. Peter was then engaged in the Northern War, a protracted struggle with Sweden for control of northeastern Europe. Although the Swedish army, under Charles XII, was effectively destroyed at the battle of Poltava in 1709, the Baltic provinces—specifically the area around St. Petersburg—would not formally be considered Russian territory until the Treaty of Nystad in 1721.

The twenty thousand conscripted serfs and prisoners of war who labored to complete Peter's fortress in the fall of 1703 were soon followed by tens of thousands more. Many died from exposure and disease, but Russian history has shown scant concern for such costs, and the city began to take shape. Piles were driven, canals dug, marshes drained, streets paved, and craftsmen resettled by the thousands.[4] By 1712, after the victory at Poltava, the imperial court and much of its bureaucracy had been transferred from Moscow. Peter had become the first Russian emperor, and Petersburg was to be the seat of his empire. Noblemen were required to build houses in the city, foreign trading concerns were expected to do business through its port, and everyone entering Petersburg was required to bring a certain number of stones, since there were no quarries near the city. So that all available resources could be applied to the new capital, in 1714 masonry construction was prohibited for a time throughout the rest of the empire.

Like the real-estate developer he was, Peter laid a grid of canals and streets on Vasil'evskii Island, the largest of the estuary islands, but the canals soon silted, and building shifted south to the mainland, to the left bank of the Neva. The frequent use of the French word *"marais"* on early maps of the city reveals that Petersburg, like its contemporary New Orleans (founded in 1718), was designed according to a rigidly geometric French plan arbitrarily laid over a flood-prone swamp.[5]

One of Peter's major goals—one could even call it an obsession—was the creation of a Russian fleet, which, with a reorganized army, would serve as an instrument of Russia's rapidly expanding role in European politics. That aspect of Peter's achievement subsequently would be celebrated by such artists as Evgenii Lansere, as Helena Goscilo's chapter in the present volume argues. Petersburg, with its admiralty and its shipbuilding enterprises, was originally conceived to resemble the unpretentious Dutch seaports Peter had seen (and worked in) during an extended trip to Western Europe at the end of the seventeenth century.[6] His relatively modest, practical taste in architecture was soon superseded by a desire to build in a manner befitting the capital of a great power. Thus the architects entrusted with the design of the city's palaces, parks, and state buildings during the next century were to work on a monumental scale congenial to the tastes of their imperial patrons and patronesses.

Whatever their style—from the baroque of the Empresses Anna and Elizabeth to the neoclassical of Catherine the Great and Alexander I—the idiom was emphatically Western in origin, as were most of the architects: French, German, Scottish, and, above all, Italian. Of this group, the most imaginative and perhaps the most gifted was Bartolomeo Francesco Rastrelli (1700–1771), son of Count Carlo Bartolomeo Rastrelli, an architect and sculptor who entered Peter the Great's service in 1715. Little is known of the younger Rastrelli's education and travel in Europe, but it is obvious that he was familiar with the varieties of European baroque architecture, for in his palaces, pavilions, and churches he was to define the late baroque in Russia.[7]

Empress Anna Ioannovna and her Baltic German courtiers commissioned Rastrelli's early work in the 1730s. Little has survived from that period, since much of the building was done in wood, a material readily available in Russia and often used in the construction of "summer palaces." Rastrelli realized his greatest projects during the reign of Peter the Great's daughter by his second marriage, Elizabeth (reg. 1741–1761), whose generous purse and extravagant tastes gave free rein to the architect's imagination. His magnificent wooden Summer Palace—built in 1741 and demolished to construct a new palace for the emperor Paul I at the end of the eighteenth century (part of the fate met by countless stunning buildings in the city throughout its history, as Julie Buckler's chapter documents)—established a pattern that would be carried forward in his more solid masonry structures: grand proportions combined with a dramatic use of decorative detail. The theatrical effect was perfectly suited to Elizabeth's love of court spectacles and lavish masquerades.[8]

The Survival of the Winter Palace

During the two decades following the construction of the Summer Palace, Rastrelli occupied himself almost exclusively with the design of imperial residences: Peterhof and the Catherine Palace at Tsarskoe Selo, both gutted during World War II. Russian restorers subsequently devoted great effort to room-by-room restorations of both, part of the more comprehensive program to recover what had been demolished or neglected that Buckler discusses in chapter 2. Rastrelli's final imperial project was yet another version—by some counts, the fourth—of the Winter Palace. In each of these palaces the architect was ordered to carry out a massive expansion and reconstruction of a preexisting building, a task that imposed considerable limitations on his own concept of structural unity. The enormous facades (almost one thousand feet at the Catherine Palace) could not escape certain monotony, despite Rastrelli's valiant effort to break the horizontal with the use of columns, pilasters, caryatids, and the ingenious application of window detail.

The new Winter Palace, commissioned by Empress Elizabeth, was Rastrelli's grandest project. He had built an earlier version for Empress Anna, but Elizabeth desired a larger, more symmetrical design, in which the palace would convey the image of a great European power. Discussion of the project began in the early 1750s, and by 1753 Rastrelli had submitted the final variant of his plan. He operated under constraints similar to those imposed at Peterhof and Tsarskoe Selo: to incorporate a large existing structure (in this case Rastrelli's own Third Winter Palace) into the design of a still larger work, staggering in both size and cost. As construction proceeded during 1754, Rastrelli concluded that the new palace would involve not simply an expansion of the old, but would have to be built over its foundations, thus necessitating the razing of the previous structure.[9]

Rastrelli had no hope of meeting Elizabeth's expectations for constructing the Winter Palace within two years, yet he exerted his considerable experience in directing the vast project, organized to a degree unprecedented in Petersburg. Construction continued year round, despite the severe winters, and the empress—who viewed the palace as a matter of state prestige during the Seven Years War—continued to issue orders for its completion and requests for supplemental appropriations. Indeed, it is a telling comment on the state of Elizabeth's finances that the 859,555 rubles originally allotted for construction of the Winter Palace were to be drawn, in a scheme devised by her courtier Petr Shuvalov, from the revenues of state-licensed pothouses—frequented, no doubt, by Rastrelli's army of laborers, most of whom earned a monthly wage of one ruble.

Despite the huge sums designated for the Winter Palace, cost overruns were chronic, and work was occasionally halted for lack of materials and money at a time when Russia's resources were strained to the limit by involvement in the Seven Years War (1756–1763). Ultimately the project cost some 2,500,000 rubles, drawn from the alcohol and salt taxes placed on an already burdened population. Elizabeth did not live to see the completion of her greatest commission. She died on December 25, 1761. The main staterooms and imperial apartments were ready the following year for Tsar Peter III and his wife Catherine.

The plan of the Winter Palace resembles, albeit on a far greater scale, the perimeter concept of the Stroganov Palace, with a quadrilateral interior courtyard decorated in a manner similar to the outer walls. The exterior facades of the new imperial palace—three of which are turned toward great public spaces—can only be compared to those of the Catherine Palace at Tsarskoe Selo. On the river facade the palace presents from a distance an uninterrupted horizontal sweep of over two hundred meters, while the Palace Square facade is marked in the center by the three arches of the main courtyard entrance, immortalized by Sergei Eisenstein, who used the entrance to portray the storming of the Winter Palace. The west facade, overlooking the Admiralty, is the one area of the structure that contains substantial elements of the previous palace walls; and the decorative detailing of its central part of the facade, flanked by two wings, reflects the earlier mannerisms of Rastrelli's style.

Although a strict symmetry reigns in the articulation of the facades, each has its own formulation in the design of pediments and the spacing of attached columns, whose distribution provides an insistent rhythm to the horizontal expanse. The 250 columns segment some 700 windows (not including those of the interior court), whose surrounds are decorated in twenty different patterns reflecting the array of ornamental motifs—including lion masks and other grotesque figures—accumulated by Rastrelli over a period of three decades.[10] The three main floors of the Winter Palace are situated over a basement level, whose semicircular window surrounds establish an arcade effect that is followed in the tiers of windows above. The horizontal dimensions of the palace are emphasized by a string course separating the two upper floors from the first, and by the complex profile of the cornice, above which a balustrade supports 176 large ornamental vases and allegorical statues.

Changes have inevitably occurred in the structure and decoration of the Winter Palace. Above the balustrade the stone statuary, corroded by Petersburg's harsh weather, was replaced in the 1890s by copper figures; and the sandy color originally intended for the stucco facade has vanished over the years under a series of paints ranging from dull red (applied in the late nineteenth century) to the present green. This system of replacement and layering attests to preservationists' struggles to conserve while renovating, and its history may be read in guidebooks and verified in artworks of various decades.

The interior of the Winter Palace, with its more than seven hundred rooms, has undergone far greater modifications. Rastrelli's original designs used decorative devices similar to those of his earlier palaces: gilded plaster and wooden ornamentation, elaborate pilasters to segment the walls of large spaces such as the Throne Room, and intricate parquetry for the floors. Yet little of Rastrelli's rococo interior decoration has survived. Work on so elaborate a space was to continue for several decades, as rooms were changed and refitted to suit the tastes of Catherine the Great and her successors.

Far more damaging was the 1837 palace fire, which raged unchecked for over two days and destroyed the interior of the palace itself, although prompt and vigorous action prevented the fire from spreading to the adjoining Hermitage buildings, with their priceless collections of art.[11] During the reconstruction of the Winter Palace, most of the rooms were decorated in eclectic styles of the mid-nineteenth century or restored to the neoclassical style used by Rastrelli's successors in decorating the Winter Palace, such as Giacomo Quarenghi. Vasilii Stasov restored only the main, or Jordan, staircase (which plays a central role in Aleksandr Sokurov's film *The Russian Ark* [*Russkii kovcheg*]) and the corridor leading to it (the Rastrelli Gallery) in a manner close to Rastrelli's original design. Yet the Winter Palace remains, rightly, associated with the name of Rastrelli. For all of Elizabeth's apparent caprices and the problems inherent in a project of such scale, Rastrelli's genius succeeded in creating not only one of the last major baroque buildings in Europe, but also—in light of subsequent events—one of the central monuments in the history of the modern world.

Rastrelli's rococo genius is better revealed in his partially realized plan for the cathedral at the Smolny Convent of the Resurrection (1748–1764), a work whose sculpted, compact design provided a focus lacking in his larger palace structures. Intended for Elizabeth, who combined pleasure with piety and reportedly wished to retire to a convent that provided both, the ensemble represents an ingenious fusion of Russian Orthodox and baroque elements.[12] But it is the palaces, above all the Winter Palace, that define the spirit of Petersburg's imperial design. The height of the Winter Palace served as the city's standard, broken only by domes and spires, and when viewed across the Neva River, the horizontal mass of the palace dominates the sweep of the city's left bank. On closer inspection, the painted stucco facade with white columns and trim—repeated in many of Petersburg's imperial monuments—assumes a magnitude oddly at variance with the brilliant, almost frivolous, color scheme.[13]

Resurrecting the Admiralty

The Winter Palace, in all of its manifestations, is the most imposing example of the Russian court's ability to recognize architectural genius and provide it with almost unlimited support. Remarkably, this ability continued through another seven decades and fundamental changes in imperial taste. With the support of the Imperial Academy of Arts (Akademiia khudozhestv), talent was winnowed and brought to the attention of patrons whose awareness of European styles and sensitivity to the general design of St. Petersburg led to an unusual concord between patron and artist. The apogee of this imperial project occurred in a seemingly unpropitious project: the rebuilding of the Main Admiralty.

The docks and administrative center of the Admiralty were first built by Peter the Great and then rebuilt, in the 1730s, by Ivan Korobov.[14] Following a fire in 1783, there had been some thought of moving the Admiralty to the fleet base at Kronstadt, but this proposal was not implemented. The final remaking of this large, decrepit compound occurred only after advisors to Alexander I debated the wisdom of leaving this utilitarian ensemble, with its functioning shipworks, in the center of the capital—indeed, facing the southwest facade of the Winter Palace itself.

The planning commission ultimately gave approval in 1805 for a reconstruction of the Admiralty, thus preserving its critical importance both as a historical landmark and as a point of orientation for much of the city. The plans were created by Andreian Zakharov (1761–1811), son of a minor admiralty official. After graduating from the Imperial Academy of Arts, in 1782, Zakharov studied in Paris for four years under the direction of Jean François Thérèse Chalgrin, creator of the Arc de Triomphe. Zakharov also traveled extensively in Italy and after his return to Russia ultimately became chief Admiralty architect. Although he died long before the completion of construction in 1823, no significant changes were made in his design for the Admiralty.[15]

In reconstructing Korobov's partially destroyed building, Zakharov expanded its length from 300 to 375 meters, and he rebuilt two perpendicular wings almost half that long extending to the Neva River. From the perspective of the river, the Admiralty consisted of two pi-shaped buildings, one within the other, which were originally separated by a narrow canal. The inner building served the Admiralty dockyard, which it enclosed on three sides, and the outer contained administrative offices.

On the other side of the Admiralty was a large square—now a park—along the main facade. Its center is marked by a tower and spire, which envelop Korobov's original tower and preserve its importance as an urban dominant. The base of the tower is defined by the large open space of the arch, flanked by statues of nymphs supporting the globe (sculptor: Feodosii Shchedrin).[16] The tower's attic frieze portrays Neptune handing Peter the Great the trident, symbol of power over the seas. Above the attic corners are statues of Alexander the Great, Ajax, Achilles, and Pyrrhus. The base of the spire rests on an Ionic peristyle, whose cornice supports twenty-eight allegorical and mythological statues representing the seasons, the elements, and the winds. Not since the twelfth-century Cathedral of St. Dmitrii in Vladimir had architecture and sculpture combined so richly to proclaim temporal power and divine protection.[17]

Zakharov also understood the virtues of simplicity: On either side of the tower, a rusticated ground floor defines the base of the facade, above which are two rows of simply articulated windows—in sharp contrast to those of the Winter Palace (later in the nineteenth century, a third row of windows replaced the stucco frieze that had originally run along the upper part of the facade). At each end of the facade is a segment marked by a dodecastyle Doric portico with a pediment containing a sculpted frieze. This component is bounded by projections with six Doric columns.

Each of the perpendicular wings also has a Doric portico of twelve columns, with flanking hexastyle projections: and each culminates at the Neva in an end block, with a large rusticated arch flanked by Doric columns. The Admiralty end blocks have been called "essays in solid geometry," a radical attempt to achieve the monumental purity of volume idealized in French architecture at the end of the eighteenth century.[18]

In his design for the Admiralty, Zakharov had solved the problem of horizontal repetition by using classical orders at key points on simple geometric forms, whose surface provided a setting for his large rusticated arches and high-relief sculpture. The use of portico, pavilion, and spire, the restrained window detail, and the heroic sculpture on pediments and at the base of the spire produce, miraculously, a sense of both richness and simplicity.

The Winter Palace and the Admiralty, adjacent yet belonging to very different architectural sensibilities, epitomize the ability of imperial authorities to make sophisticated, effective decisions concerning the relationship between power and aesthetics in architecture. To be sure, the impact of the Admiralty's re-creation was vitiated in the latter half of the nineteenth century, when the area of the shipworks was filled and the land given to builders who erected three of Petersburg's most desirable apartment residences, thus obscuring most of the Admiralty from the Neva River. Yet the fact that the Admiralty remained in Petersburg at all shows an astute understanding of the need to render homage to history, to origins, to the driving impulses of the city's founder, who envisioned Russia as a sea power. But there was to be a third essential component to the imperial project on Palace Square: Carlo Rossi's Building of the General Staff.

"This Monument Must Be Eternal"

The equation of state and nation in imperial Russian architecture culminated in the late neoclassical monuments of Carlo Rossi, born in Russia and educated at the imperial estate of Pavlovsk. In 1805, having returned from a study tour of Europe (Italy in particular), the young Rossi submitted a proposal for the reconstruction of the Admiralty Embankment. The project never materialized and Rossi's drawings disappeared, but his note of explanation contains the following passage: "The dimensions of the project proposed by me exceed those accepted by the Romans for their structures. Indeed, why should we fear to be compared with them in magnificence? One should interpret this word not as an abundance of ornament, but rather grandeur of form, nobility of proportion, and solidity. This monument must be eternal."[19] Russia's greatness as a nation is here affirmed by a comparison to the heart of Western, Roman culture.

Rossi's greatest project, in terms of both size and conceptual daring, was to rebuild a warren of structures facing the south front of the Winter Palace. The enterprise—which began in 1819 and was completed in 1829—consisted of two parts: to construct an administrative complex for the General Staff of the Army and the Ministries of Finance and Foreign Affairs; and, in so doing, to create an imposing public square along the main front of the Winter Palace.

His solution called for the ministerial complex, subsequently known as the General Staff building, to take the form of a large arc facing the palace. The center of this main facade is dominated by a triumphal arch, surmounted by a chariot of victory. In his design of the arch, Rossi not only anchored the enormous facade, but also linked it to the surrounding area, particularly by the passageway through the triumphal arch that leads from Palace Square to Nevsky Prospect. The passageway is composed of three arches, the first two of which are located on an axis with the central gates to the Winter Palace, and the last follows the turn of the passage toward the Prospect. The light that enters between the arches enhances the perception of depth and illuminates the decorative detail of this unique procession of framed space toward the city's main square.

The Palace Square facade of the General Staff building—devoid of decoration except for a cornice frieze, a balustrade, and columns flanking the arch—forms the perfect complement to the baroque panoply of Rastrelli's Winter Palace. The color scheme for this and for most of Russia's other monuments was to be light gray with white trim, but later generations have preferred more assertive tones: yellow with white trim, and the metallic sculpture of military regalia painted black.

Yet more important than the color is the contour of the main facade, which not only imposes order over a vast urban terrain, but also channels movement within that space. The dramatic nature of that space in relation to massed humanity (military parades or demonstrations) has played a major role in the course of modern Russian history.[20]

Visitors and the Art of Survival

Not every visitor has approved of this imperial mixture of the baroque and neoclassical, of Western and Russian architectural exuberance. The Marquis de Custine, in *La Russie en 1839*, described St. Petersburg as "without character, more pompous than imposing, more vast than beautiful, filled with edifices without style, without taste, without historical significance."[21] As Sokurov's film establishes, de Custine's perception of Russia tended toward the condescendingly unsympathetic. Yet even the Marquis de Custine occasionally lapsed from his severe opinion and effusively praised the city and its setting.

Indeed, in the middle decades of the nineteenth century, Petersburg—not the medieval city of Moscow—served to validate Russia's position as a nation with a significant history. As Helena Goscilo notes (chapter 3), the architectural transformations imposed upon Moscow during the last decade have revived this image of St. Petersburg. This paradox is illuminated in Fyodor Dostoevsky's *Petersburg Chronicle* for June 1, 1847. Commenting on the advent of spring to the northern capital, the *flâneur* (the roving observer who is Dostoevsky's narrative persona) describes a city in the throes of growth: "Crowds of workers with plaster, with shovels, with hammers, axes, and other instruments dispose themselves along Nevsky Prospekt as though at home, as though they had bought it; and woe to the pedestrian, *flâneur*, or observer who lacks a serious desire to resemble Pierrot spattered with flour in a Roman carnival."[22]

Similar motifs of urban expansion and change reappear in the novelist's post-exile work, most notably *Crime and Punishment*, where they form an integral part of the psychological environment. The preceding passage, however, veers into a discourse on the built environment as history, a text whose decoding leads to the past as an expression of native identity. With summer approaching and cultured society leaving the town,

> [w]hat remains for those citizens whose captivity forces them to pass their summer in the capital? To study the architecture of buildings, to see how the city is being renewed and built? Of course this is an important occupation and indeed even edifying. Your Petersburger is so distracted in the winter, and has so many pleasures, business, work, card-playing, gossip and various other amusements—besides which there is so much dirt—that he would hardly have the time to look around, to peer into Petersburg more attentively, to

study its physiognomy and *read the history of the city and all our epoch in this mass of stones, in these magnificent edifices, palaces, monuments* [emphasis added]. After all, it would hardly come into anyone's head to kill valuable time with such an absolutely innocent and unprofitable exercise. [23]

The irony here is doubly ambiguous, since Dostoevsky's subsequent work uses architecture as an extension and reflection of the contemporary mental state of individual characters as well as entire collectives—hence the "Petersburg theme" developed in both nineteenth- and twentieth-century literature, which Goscilo discusses in chapter 3. Furthermore, by the time of Dostoevsky's early work, the city's architecture reflected only slightly more than a century of history, often in deliberate contrast to the cultural traditions of the pre-Petrine period. Although sensitive to the psychological impact of urban architecture, Dostoevsky showed little interest in architectural historicism as a means of reclaiming a sense of Russianness that presumably resided in pre-modern (i.e., pre-Petrine) history.

Dostoevsky's ambivalent—or highly selective—attitude toward history is developed in the subsequent passage of his June 1 entry in the *Petersburg Chronicle*. At this point Dostoevsky presents the historical approach to architecture through the comments on Russian monuments contained in *La Russie en 1839* by the Marquis de Custine. Although banned in Russia, the book was nonetheless widely known in intellectual circles and is the unmistakable source of Dostoevsky's references:

> Incidentally, a study of the city is really not a useless thing. We don't exactly remember, but sometime ago we happened to read a certain French book, which consisted entirely of views on the contemporary condition of Russia. Of course it is already known just what foreigners' views on the contemporary condition of Russia are worth; somehow up to now we stubbornly do not submit to being measured by a foreign yardstick. But despite that, the renowned tourist's book was eagerly read by all Europe. Among other things, it stated that there is nothing more lacking in character than Petersburg architecture; that there is nothing especially striking about it, *nothing national* [Dostoevsky's emphasis], and that the entire city is a hybrid caricature of several European capitals. And finally, that Petersburg, if only in an architectural sense, represents such a strange mixture, that one cannot cease to exclaim with amazement at every step. [24]

In Dostoevsky's paraphrase, de Custine portrays Petersburg as an instance of architectural hybridization: "Greek architecture, Roman architecture,

Byzantine architecture, Dutch architecture, Gothic architecture, architecture of the rococo, the latest Italian architecture, our Orthodox architecture—all this, according to the traveler, whipped up and shaped into a most entertaining form, and in conclusion not one genuinely beautiful building!"[25] Native Petersburgers, as Buckler argues, entertained a dramatically different notion of Petersburg's architecture.

In his *Diary of a Writer*, written during the 1870s, Dostoevsky would publish similar views on the hybrid nature of Petersburg architecture as a barometer of social confusion. Of more immediate interest, however, is his reaction to de Custine's claim that the architecture of Petersburg lacks an authentic, appropriate style. Despite his defensive maneuver ("we know what foreigners' views of Russia are worth"), Dostoevsky seems to revel in de Custine's description of the city's architectural palette. Although de Custine criticized the aesthetics of Petersburg, he was also amazed at the city's appearance, which combined stylistic variety with the monumental uniformity of an imperial capital.[26] In other words, the Roman aspects of the northern capital, which Zara Torlone assesses in her analysis of Mandelstam's poetry (chapter 4), did not elude the French visitor.

Furthermore, de Custine saw the building of Petersburg as both validated by history and anticipating it:

> Elsewhere great cities are made in memory of great deeds of the past. Or, while cities make themselves with the help of circumstances and history, without the least apparent cooperation of human calculation, St. Petersburg with its magnificence and immensity is a trophy elevated by the Russians to their power yet to come; the hope that produces such efforts seems to me sublime! Not since the Temple of the Jews has the faith of a people in their destiny wrested from the earth something more marvelous than St. Petersburg. And what renders this legacy made by a man to his ambitious country truly admirable is that it has been accepted by history. [27]

The reference to the Temple in Jerusalem is particularly apt in view of the Zion motif as a symbol of endurance and survival, of faith in the destiny of a people. Yet the more peculiar aspect of the preceding passage is its comment on Petersburg as a city both preparing for history and having been accepted by it. In the scheme presented by de Custine, there are two levels of history: a universal history of established civilization and culture, and the history of Russia, existing in tenuous relation to the former.

De Custine, like Dostoevsky, sees historical meaning in the stones of Petersburg. In commenting on the forbidding form of the Mikhailovsky Palace, in which the emperor Paul I was assassinated in 1801, de Custine notes in his ninth letter: "If men are silent in Russia, the stones speak and speak in a lamentable voice. I am not surprised that the Russians fear and neglect their old monuments: these are witnesses of their history, which more often than not they would wish to forget."[28] Yet there were, in fact, no "*vieux monuments*" in Petersburg: The Mikhailovsky Palace, for example, was completed less than four decades before de Custine's journey.[29] Furthermore, it is clear from subsequent parts of de Custine's narrative—particularly in Moscow—that much had indeed survived from Russia's distant, turbulent architectural past.

Throughout de Custine's account, the specific meaning of "*histoire*" can only be determined by context—in the preceding case, the recent political history of the imperial regime. In the same sense, no doubt, Dostoevsky in 1847 advised his readers to ponder the history of their city, whose imperial architecture—despite its recent provenance—could be defined as a historical text begun by Peter and decipherable by the contemporary resident or visitor (a deciphering urged by the preservationist movement on which Buckler's chapter focuses). Yet de Custine also describes Peter's great vision, whose tangible form derived from so many foreign sources, as an aggression directed toward the West ("contre l'Europe une ville . . . pour dominer le monde"). Even in its approach toward integration with Europe, even in its new Western-style capital, Russia is potentially hostile, alien, and separate.

As to the historical significance of St. Petersburg and its architecture, one can hardly blame the Marquis for lacking the gift of prophecy—only for his impatience. Few cities have witnessed more momentous historical events, and certainly none in the twentieth century. Although the storming of the Winter Palace as recreated in Eisenstein's *October/ Ten Days That Shook the World (Oktiabr'*, 1927) is myth, pure and simple, it is entirely appropriate—in a dramatic as well as a historical sense—that the palace that served as a symbol of the imperial order should also serve as the backdrop for two revolutions: one in 1917 and the other in 1991. Anyone who saw the crowds gathered on Palace Square in August 1991 would understand that great architecture has a way of creating its own destiny.

Notes

1. The quote comes from the conclusion of the novel's prologue, which reads:

> Kak by to ni bylo, Peterburg ne tol'ko nam kazhetsia, no i okazyvaetsia—na
> kartakh: v vide dvukh drug v druge sidiashchikh kruzhkov s chernoi tochkoiu v
> tsenter: i iz etoi vot matematicheskoi tochki, ne imeiushchei izmereniia,
> zaiavliaet on energichno o tom, chto on—est': ottuda, iz etoi vot tochki, nesetsia
> potokom roi otpechatannoi knigi; nesetsia iz etoi nevidimoi tochki stremitel'no
> tsikuliar.

Andrei Bely, *Peterburg* (Leningrad, 1981), 10.

2. For a detailed survey in English of the architecture of St. Petersburg, see William Craft Brumfield, *A History of Russian Architecture* (Cambridge, 1993).

3. A recent, authoritative Russian interpretation of the changes instituted by Peter the Great is Evgenii Anisimov, *Vremia petrovskikh reform* (Leningrad, 1989).

4. The standard account of the planning and construction of St. Petersburg in its first decades is contained in S. P. Luppov, *Istoriia stroitel'stva Peterburga v pervoi chetverti XVIII veka* (Moscow, 1957). On the process of amelioration, see 78–81.

5. See Samuel Wilson Jr., *Bienville's New Orleans: A French Colonial Capital* (New Orleans, 1968).

6. For an analysis of Peter's voyage to Europe as it affected his artistic tastes, see V. F. Levinson-Lessing, "Pervoe puteshestvie Petra I za granitsu," in G. N. Komelova, ed., *Kul'tura i iskusstvo petrovskogo vremeni* (Leningrad, 1977), 5–36. The considerable evidence of Peter's direct involvement in the design of Petersburg is presented in M. V. Iogansen, "Ob avtore general'nogo plana Peterburga petrovskogo vremeni," in T. V. Alekseeva, ed., *Ot Srednevekov'ia k Novomu vremeni* (Moscow, 1984), 50–72, and particularly 66–67.

7. There have been numerous surveys of Rastrelli's work, among which one of the most perceptive is B. R. Vipper, *Arkhitektura russkogo barokko* (Moscow, 1978), 65–94. Other studies include D. Arkin, *Rastrelli* (Moscow, 1954); and Iu. M. Denisov and A. N. Petrov, *Zodchii Rastrelli: Materialy k izucheniiu tvorchestva* (Leningrad, 1963), which includes a comprehensive listing of known Rastrelli graphic material in Russian, Polish, Swedish, and Austrian collections. A recent monograph is Iu. Ovsiannikov, *Franchesko Bartolomeo Rastrelli* (Leningrad, 1982).

8. On the construction of the Third Summer Palace, see Denisov and Petrov, *Zodchii Rastrelli*, p. 9 and figures 75–127.

9. The most authoritative recent history of the design and construction of the Winter Palace is Iu. M. Denisov, "Zimnii dvorets Rastrelli," in Piliavskii and Levinson-Lessing, eds., *Ermitazh: Istoriia i arkhitektura zdaniia* (Leningrad, 1974), 39–64.

10. S. B. Alekseeva provides a thorough analysis of the various sculptural elements of the Winter Palace, in terms not only of the plasticity of the facade, but also of their domination of the extensive space around the palace. See her "Arkhitektura i dekorativnaia plastika Zimnego dvortsa," in T. V. Alekseeva, ed., *Russkoe iskusstvo barokko: Materialy i issledovaniia* (Moscow, 1977), 128–158. Earlier variants of the plan had a weaker segmentation of an even greater number of windows on the facades. See Denisov, "Zimnii dvorets Rastrelli," 42–43.

11. The circumstances surrounding the Winter Palace fire are described in V. M. Glinka, "Pozhar 1837 goda," in Piliavskii and Levinson-Lessing, eds., *Ermitazh*, 107–118. On the rebuilding of the palace, V. I. Piliavskii, "Vosstanovlenie Zimnego dvortsa posle pozhara 1837 goda," ibid., 119–172. See also Richard M. Haywood, "The Winter Palace in St. Petersburg: Destruction by Fire and Reconstruction, December 1837—March 1839," in *Jarbücher für Geschichte Osteuropas*, 27 (1979): 161–180.

12. For an analysis of the adaptation of the traditional pentacupolar design in Russian baroque church architecture, see T. P. Fedotova, "K probleme piatiglaviia v arkhitekture barokko pervoi poloviny XVIII v.," in Alekseeva, ed., *Russkoe iskusstvo barokko*, 70–87. In view of the Italian origins of so many of Russia's architects, it is logical to assume, as Fedotova does, that seventeenth-century Italian churches (especially the work of Borromini) were influential in the Russian integration of baroque decoration with the concept of the central dome and surrounding towers. It must also be remembered that centralized church designs were very much a part of the Roman baroque, as is demonstrated in Rudolf Wittkower, *Architectural Principles in the Age of Humanism* (New York, 1971).

13. Boris Vipper noted that for all of the power and the variety of the Winter Palace, there is a certain "ambiguity" in Rastrelli's design that derives from the contradictions between the waning Baroque style and the rise of a neoclassical architectural aesthetic. Vipper, *Arkhitektura russkogo barokko*, 83.

14. On Korobov's Admiralty, see Brumfield, *A History of Russian Architecture*, 226–227.

15. A survey of Zakharov's work is presented in V. I. Piliavskii and N. Ia. Leiboshits, *Zodchii Zakharov* (Leningrad, 1963). See also N. Leiboshits, "Novye materialy ob A. D. Zakharove," *Arkhitekturnoe nasledstvo* 4 (1953):95–103; and V. K. Shuiskii, *Andreian Zakharov* (Leningrad, 1989).

16. E. Moskalenko, "Shpil' Admiralteistva i ego konstruktsiia," *Arkhitekturnoe nasledstvo* 4 (1953):177–188.

17. On the Cathedral of Saint Dmitrii, see Brumfield, *A History of Russian Architecture*, 52–60.

18. Hugh Honour, *Neo-classicism* (Harmondsworth, UK, 1968), 130. Honour relates this monumental simplicity of design to the late eighteenth-century philosophical search, embodied by Goethe's Altar of Good Fortune, for deep symbolism in simple universal forms. The ideological basis of an architecture of "geometric purism" or "geometric idealism," derived from natural laws of the universe (and especially prevalent in the work of Claude-Nicolas Ledoux), is discussed in Robert Rosenblum, *Transformations in Late Eighteenth Century Art* (Princeton, 1967), 120–127. See also Emil Kaufmann, "Three Revolutionary Architects—Boullée, Ledoux and Lequeu," *Transactions of the American Philosophical Society* vol. 42 (1952); and idem, *Architecture in the Age of Reason* (Cambridge, MA, 1955), 160–180, with brief reference to French stylistic currents in Russia, 179.

19. On the Admiralty Quay project, with Rossi's statement, see V. Kochedamov, "Proekt naberezhnoi u Admiralteistva Zodchego K. I. Rossi," *Arkhitekturnoe nasledstvo* 4 (1953): 111–114. For Rossi's description see ibid., 113. A general monograph on Rossi's life and work is M. Z. Taranovskaia, *Karl Rossi* (Leningrad, 1978).

20. Blair A. Ruble discusses the function of plazas in central Petersburg as an element enriching public space and the life of the city in "From Palace Square to Moscow Square: St. Petersburg's Century-Long Retreat from Public Space," in William C. Brumfield, ed., *Reshaping Russian Architecture* (New York and Cambridge, 1990), 10–12, 16–21.

21. See Le Marquis de Custine, *La Russie en 1839*, second edition (Paris, 1843), 1: 225–228.

22. "Peterburgskaia letopis'," in F. M. Dostoevsky, *Polnoe sobranie sochinenii v tridtsati tomakh*, vol. 18 (Leningrad, 1978), 23.

23. Ibid., 24.

24. Ibid.

25. Dostoevsky probably refers to the opening passage of de Custine's eighth letter, in which he presents his initial impressions of Petersburg. Similar views are presented in a description of the palaces and buildings of the central squares in the eleventh letter. Dostoevsky would likely have known the second, "corrected and expanded" edition of de Custine's work, which appeared in 1843 and was rapidly smuggled into Russia. See Dostoevsky, *Polnoe sobranie*, 18:226n24; also P. V. Annenkov, *Literaturnye vospominaniia* (Moscow, 1960), 256–257. The reaction of Vissarion Belinsky, Alexander Herzen, and Dostoevsky to de Custine's work is analyzed in E. I. Kiiko, "Belinskii i Dostoevsky o knige Kiustina 'Rossia v 1839'," G. M. Fridlender, ed., *Dostoevskii. Materialy i issledovaniia*, vol. 1 (Leningrad, 1974), 189–199.

26. De Custine, *La Russie en 1839*, 1: 225–228; 344–349.

27. Ibid., 267–268.

28. Ibid., 259.

29. On the design and construction of the Mikhailovsky Palace, see V. K. Shuiskii, *Vinchentso Brenna* (Leningrad, 1986), 120–164.

FIGURE 1.1. Peter-Paul Fortress, Winter Palace, Cathedral of St. Isaac, the Admiralty.
William Craft Brumfield; reproduced by permission.

FIGURE I.2. Winter Palace. Palace Square Façade.
William Craft Brumfield; reproduced by permission.

FIGURE 1.3. Palace Square, Building of the General Staff, Alexander Column, Cathedral of St. Issac. William Craft Brumfield; reproduced by permission.

FIGURE 1.4. Winter Palace, Jordan Staircase.
William Craft Brumfield; reproduced by permission.

FIGURE I.5. Winter Palace, Jordan Staircase, Atlantes.
William Craft Brumfield; reproduced by permission.

FIGURE 1.6. Small Hermitage, Marble Hall.
William Craft Brumfield; reproduced by permission.

FIGURE 1.7. Winter Canal Arch and Small Hermitage.
William Craft Brumfield; reproduced by permission.

FIGURE 1.8. Theban Sphinx in front of the Academy of Arts, University Quay.
William Craft Brumfield; reproduced by permission.

FIGURE 1.9. West Pavilion, Mikhailovsky Palace Ensemble.
William Craft Brumfield; reproduced by permission.

FIGURE 1.10. Mikhailovsky Palace, Church of the Archangel Michael.
William Craft Brumfield; reproduced by permission.

FIGURE 1.11. Bourse (Stock Exchange), Colonnade. William Craft Brumfield; reproduced by permission.

FIGURE 1.12. Cathedral of the Kazan' Icon of the Mother of God, Colonnade.
William Craft Brumfield; reproduced by permission.

FIGURE 1.13. Cathedral of the Kazan' Icon of the Mother of God, Dome Interior.
William Craft Brumfield; reproduced by permission.

FIGURE 1.14. The Admiralty. Main Façade and Tower.
William Craft Brumfield; reproduced by permission.

FIGURE 1.15. The Admiralty. Central Tower and Peristyle.
William Craft Brumfield; reproduced by permission.

FIGURE 1.16. Cathedral of St. Isaac, Dome Interior.
William Craft Brumfield; reproduced by permission.

FIGURE 1.17. Cathedral of St. Isaac. William Craft Brumfield; reproduced by permission.

FIGURE 1.18. Church of the Resurrection of the Savior. William Craft Brumfield;
reproduced by permission.

FIGURE 1.19. Griboedov Canal, House No. 56. William Craft Brumfield;
reproduced by permission.

FIGURE 1.20. Main Choral Synagogue, Aron Ha-Kodesh.
William Craft Brumfield; reproduced by permission.

Two

The City's Memory: Texts of Preservation and Loss in Imperial St. Petersburg

Julie Buckler

Petersburg's chroniclers have long been preoccupied with the young city's history and memory, or, to put it another way, these chroniclers have underscored Petersburg's paradoxes of preservation and loss. Count Francesco Algarotti was among the first to observe this curious conflation of old and new, noting the dilapidated state of the city's grand palaces, hastily constructed by courtiers whom Peter the Great compelled to establish residency in the new capital: "Their walls are all cracked, quite out of perpendicular, and ready to fall. It has been wittily enough said, [sic] that ruins make themselves in other places, but that they were built at Petersburg."[1] William Kinglake, who visited Petersburg in the mid-1840s, scornfully advised travelers to admire the city by moonlight so as to avoid seeing, "with too critical an eye, plaster scaling from the white-washed walls, and frost-cracks rending the painted wooden columns." Comparing Peter's project to Solomon's obstinacy in creating Tadmor, Kinglake evoked the city's "huge, staring masses of raw whitewash," which, to him, had "the air of gigantic models, abandoned on the site intended to be hereafter occupied by more substantial structures."[2]

Algarotti and Kinglake viewed the ruined aspect of the Russian imperial capital with the critical assessing gaze of foreign visitors, as an inadvertent admission of Petersburg sham and scam.[3] The image of Petersburg in ruins more famously reflects the eschatological thinking in literary works and discussions within contemporary scholarship on the "Petersburg mythology."[4] What is less often acknowledged, however, is that this imagery also responds to real historical processes of urban destruction and reconstruction.

Although imperial Petersburg was not an old city, by the nineteenth century its urban topography constituted a much-overwritten and rewritten cultural text, subject to cycles of overlay long before the well-known early-Soviet and post-Soviet remapping projects. The quintessential twentieth-century Petersburg project of replacing, renaming, and reclaiming city structures finds many counterparts in nineteenth-century literature that illustrate the continuous remapping—that is, the intertwined process of forgetting and remembering—that constitutes both the life and death of the city.

Beginning in the nineteenth century, Petersburg's memory has been maintained by diverse institutions, events, and practices. Monuments and memorial plaques around the city physically figure a past proposed to contemporary viewers as simultaneously present and absent. The Museum of Old Petersburg and its successors, as well as the city's historical archives, have provided paper repositories for memory, while cemeteries preserve both inscriptions and material "remains," albeit not very reliably. Written and material tributes memorialize aspects of city life that fell victim to the gradual passage of time, as well as those erased in a single day by disasters such as flood and fire. This sort of remembering is necessarily selective and mythological, however, and it is also true that in imperial St. Petersburg old structures were intentionally destroyed to make way for the new. During the Soviet period, of course, extensive changes of this sort were imposed on the city by the Bolshevik government. The ongoing project of remapping Petersburg has thus often resembled a kind of willed amnesia, occasioned by imperial caprice, political revolution, and rehabilitative efforts that can be by turns cynical, simply expedient, or quixotic. Petersburg proves the counterintuitive but ancient rule that writing, a seemingly ephemeral medium, offers the most reliable material for building an enduring monument to the past. Still, all of this writing about imperial Petersburg also requires the physical resources of the city for its continued preservation in libraries, museums, and archives.

Cemeteries: The Trope of Permanence

In the 1990s, the writer Aleksandr Skidan acknowledged Petersburg's primary function as the "sepulcher of imperial Russian culture." The "museum principle" as everywhere manifested in Petersburg "gives rise to the nauseating sensation of unceasing *déjà vu*."[5] Even the most recent of events are "conserved," "surrendered before our eyes into an archive," and transformed into "reminiscence" and "petrified ruins." Petersburg's dead, fixed quality could be attributed to the Bolsheviks' neglect of the imperial capital, compounded by the lack of funds during the post-Soviet period for renovating shabby palaces and formerly grand apartment houses. For many imperial-era commentators, however, Petersburg was already a city of loss, a cemetery-like site of much-regretted change and destruction. In Petersburg cultural history, even the cemetery topos itself—elsewhere a metaphorical site of memory and a repository of urban history—is often linked to the threat of encroaching oblivion. There have been moments in Petersburg's pre-revolutionary history when the city as a whole could be seen as a tombstone marking its own grave: for instance, the interlude following Peter the Great's death, when the capital temporarily shifted back to Moscow (1728–1731), as well as the years after the 1881 assassination of Alexander II, when both Alexander III and Nicholas II preferred to reside in Moscow and at the Gatchina and Tsarskoe Selo palace-parks outside of Petersburg.[6]

As Lewis Mumford points out, "Mid the uneasy wanderings of paleolithic man, the dead were the first to have a permanent dwelling." Since the site of ancestral graves provided an incentive for the living to form a settlement, "The city of the dead antedates the city of the living . . . is the forerunner, almost the core, of every living city."[7] In the Petersburg text, the cemetery provides one of the most common figures for the city's memory, as well as a favorite subject for cultural historians, who use tombstones to document city life. Aleksandr Kobak and Iurii Piriutko term the Petersburg cemeteries "a chronicle of the city, which preserves thousands of names of government officials, military men, scholars, performers, writers, artists, and musicians."[8] Vladimir Saitov in his massive project of 1907–1911 took precisely this approach to Petersburg cemeteries within the city territory and its environs, compiling more than 40,000 epitaphs from fifty-seven different burial places in a four-volume reference that he termed a "dictionary of individuals."[9] Petersburg's cemeteries also collectively compose a cultural text that speaks to phenomena such as the haphazard nature of cemetery planning in eighteenth-century Russia, the uneven evolution of cemeteries' relationship to the nineteenth-century city, and the post-revolutionary relocation of individual graves to the "Masters of Art" cemetery (*Nekropol' masterov iskusstv*) and the Volkovo "Writers' Footway" (*Literatorskie mostki*)—museum-like collections of dead Russian cultural luminaries. In 1939, all of the city sculpture, including monuments and memorials inside cemeteries, came under the supervision of the "Museum of City Sculpture"—an abstraction more than an institution that signaled the increasingly museum-like quality of St. Petersburg as a whole.

Despite well-developed burial practices, the explicit transformation of selected Petersburg cemeteries into museums during the 1930s occasioned an immense loss of gravemarkers from the imperial period. These "cemetery-museums" oddly represent at once an acknowledgement and, simultaneously, a violation of hallowed cultural ground. Up to this time, logical "groupings" of graves—according to family ties, close friendships, area of residence, professions, and circumstances of death—had evolved in many of the city's cemeteries.[10] Many literary and cultural luminaries of the imperial period had been interred in the Lazarevskoe cemetery at the Alexander-Nevsky monastery as a result of organically evolving burial practices.[11] The 1930s plan in then-Leningrad, however, sought to establish a formal pantheon of dead Russian cultural heroes modeled after Paris, and to this end the Lazarevskoe and Tikhvinskoe cemeteries at the Alexander-Nevsky monastery and the Volkovskoe cemetery in the city's southern territory were reconceived and remapped.[12] While tombstones of the greatest historical and artistic interest were transferred from various graveyards to the new cemetery-museums—often without the human remains whose location they marked—many other markers were destroyed in the process of liquidating old burial grounds throughout the city.

The Masters of Art cemetery was opened on the grounds of Tikhvinskoe in 1937, and, in 1939, the "Cemetery of the Eighteenth Century" (*Nekropol' XVIII veka*) was established on the territory of Lazarevskoe. The Eighteenth Century cemetery houses the graves of the writers Lomonosov and Fonvizin, the architects Quarenghi, Starov, Voronikhin, Zakharov, Toma de Thomon, and Rossi, and the painter Borovikovskii, among others. The Masters of Art cemetery includes the graves of the writers Karamzin, Zhukovskii, Gnedich, Krylov, Baratynskii, Viazemskii, and Dostoevsky, the

composers Glinka, Serov, Dargomyzhskii, Mussorgsky, Rubinstein, Borodin, Tchaikovsky, and Rimsky-Korsakov, the sculptor Klodt, and cultural
notables such as the critic Vladimir Stasov and the actress Vera Komissar-
zhevskaia. It is true that many of these luminaries *were* originally buried in
the Lazarevskoe cemetery, but their numbers were significantly augmented
by new arrivals during the 1930s. As a 1970s guidebook to the Museum
of City Sculpture explains, "[T]he cemetery was liberated of monuments
that possessed no artistic value or historical significance. At the same time . . .
many gifted prominent figures were transferred here from other cemeteries
in Leningrad." The cemetery was converted into a "shady park with wide alleys" and well-tended vegetation. As a rule, continues the guidebook, "the
graves are grouped according to the principle of the intellectual and creative
affinity between the interred: writers, musicians, representatives of the theater, and masters of the plastic arts. This particularity of the necropolis significantly facilitates the study of its historical-artistic collection."[13] In a
lengthy piece from the late 1930s titled "Thought Describing a Circle" (*Mysl',
opisavshaia krug*), Lydia Ginzburg contemplated the new cemetery-museum
at the monastery. Where poorly preserved monuments or lesser personages
have been removed to make the cemetery-museum less crowded, she noted
the presence of identifying markers on sticks, "like those used in botanical
gardens," whose textual presence mirrors and supplements the job of the
tour-guide. "What constitutes the exhibit of this museum?" asks Ginzburg.
"The monument, the name, or the empty space, on which it is written that
here a particular (historical) person turned to ashes?" Our incomprehen-
sion of death is so immense, she argues, that it overpowers the habits of professional museum-workers, who know that, in general, explanatory text
with no accompanying exhibit object does not enlighten, and merely irri-
tates the public. In this case, however, respectful visitors fill these marked
empty spaces with their "cultural baggage."[14] Graveside memorials, just like
the museum's absurd markers of absence, may include text engraved or inscribed on their physical surfaces, but these objects are no more than place-
holders for a different kind of writing—the invisible, pervasive, and shared
cultural text of commemoration.

The transfer of tombstones and human remains effected a rearrange-
ment of the Petersburg cultural text, making it at once more coherent and
historically less accurate. Conveying mortal remnants to a new location to
underscore their emblematic cultural significance, not to mention the

import of their new resting place, parallels Peter the Great's 1724 decision to transfer the relics of thirteenth-century Prince Alexander Nevsky from a monastery in Vladimir to the Petersburg Alexander-Nevsky monastery, in commemoration of this Russian hero's 1240 victory over the Swedes at the confluence of the rivers Izhora and Neva.[15] Like the "translation" of religious relics, the resettlement of Petersburg's dead writers and artists established a place of pilgrimage and a locus of moral and cultural authority. The cemetery-museums of the 1930s also suggested the extent to which the imperial era as a historical and literary construct had become the property of the Soviet cultural establishment.

The Writers' Footway of the Volkovo cemetery constitutes Petersburg's other cemetery-museum of the imperial era, also officially established during the 1930s. Beginning with Radishchev's burial at Volkovo in 1802 (although the precise site of his grave has been lost), there evolved a tradition of burying Petersburg's "civic-minded" writers in a community of their literary brethren. Belinsky was buried at Volkovo in 1848, and Dobroliubov in 1861.[16] Also buried in the Writers' Footway now are Saltykov-Shchedrin, Leskov, Goncharov, Pomialovskii, Grigorovich, Pisarev, Reshetnikov, Mamin-Sibiriak, Garshin, and Gleb Uspenskii.[17] As in the Alexander-Nevsky cemetery-museums, a considerable number of literary luminaries had originally been buried in this same part of the Volkovo cemetery; other writers, Turgenev and Kavelin among them, were transferred during the 1930s from liquidated sections of Volkovo and from other city cemeteries slated for destruction. As a twentieth-century institution, the Writers' Footway appropriated and augmented a nineteenth-century development that proved fortuitously convenient for the Soviet establishment—the canonization of Russian literature's "Belinsky line."[18] In this sense, Soviet cultural policy might be said to have fulfilled the wishes of the Petersburg democratic intelligentsia of the latter nineteenth century, as expressed in their writings.

In Nikolai Nekrasov's "Morning Stroll" (*Utrenniaia progulka*), the first part of his long poem "About the Weather" (*O pogode*, 1859), the morose narrator happens upon a funeral procession. He idly follows the lonely coffin being conveyed by a dray-cart hearse to the Volkovo cemetery, where he searches for the "inconspicuous grave" that constitutes the resting place of "a great force" (Belinsky, dubbed the "raging," or *neistovyi*, Vissarion). The cemetery watchman cannot tell him where Belinsky lies, but advises him on navigating the cemetery: crosses mark the graves of the petty-bourgeoisie, officers, and lower gentry; tombstone slabs stand above the graves of government officials, while such slabs cover the ground over teachers' burial-places. The watchman concludes, "Where there is neither a slab nor a cross/ There, most probably, lies a writer (*sochinitel'*)."[19] Nekrasov's poem fashions itself as a substitute gravemarker for Belinsky, whose resting place the narrator fails to find.

Vsevolod Garshin, who would himself be buried in the Writers' Footway, described a stroll through Volkovo in his "Petersburg Letters." Explicitly echoing Pushkin's 1836 poem "When pensive, I stroll outside the city . . ." (*Kogda za gorodom, zadumchiv, ia brozhu . . .*), Garshin goes to the cemetery for a quiet walk, noting that city cemeteries such as Smolenskoe, Mitrofanievskoe, and Volkovo still accept new "residents," even though the dead have already been stacked one on top of another and in tight rows.[20] "Cemeteries are the shadiest parks in the city," declares Garshin with dark humor, because vegetation grows beautifully in the "rich soil."[21] He evokes the Poets' Corner in Westminster Abbey as a reproach to his own countrymen: "We do not take care of our great dead as the English do. We do not take care of them even while they are alive." Petersburg's own "Poets' Corner" is not, in fact, a corner for poets, observes Garshin, but, rather, houses "journalists" (*publitsisty*) such as Belinsky, Dobroliubov, and Pisarev. These great men inhabit their cramped corner, "surrounded by a numberless crowd of obscure names . . . The crowd, which they loved and taught and which suffocated them, has not left them in peace even after death, and has crowded and constricted their little corner so that there was no place for a new friend to lie down . . ."[22] Belinsky is now forgotten, mourns Garshin, and not a single wreath adorns his simple black granite tombstone, in shameful contrast to ornate surrounding monuments erected to merchants. Visitors from long ago have simply inscribed their own "naïve prose with expressions of love and grief" on the wooden railings around the writers' graves. Garshin's emphasis on Russian prose and journalism, as opposed to English verse, implicitly proposes his own "Letters" as the true monument to Belinsky, even as he deplores this poverty of physical commemoration.

The eulogy "Oration on Lomonosov" (*Slovo o Lomonosove*) that concludes Alexander Radishchev's *Journey from Petersburg to Moscow* (*Puteshestvie iz Peterburga v Moskvu*, 1790) represents a significantly earlier contribution to such meditations on public memory—one that proves oddly prescient about the post-revolutionary fate suffered by Petersburg cemeteries. Radishchev describes an evening stroll to the Alexander-Nevsky monastery, where he finds the 1765 grave of Mikhail Lomonosov, whose marble tombstone erected by Count Vorontsov bears inscriptions in both Latin and Russian. In contrast to Garshin, Radishchev disputes the power of a graveside monument (mere "cold stone") to preserve cultural memory, arguing that such majestic structures merely commemorate human vanity. "A stone with your name inscribed will not carry your fame into future centuries," intones Radishchev. "Your words, living always and forever in your creations, in the words of the Russian tribe, made new again by you in our language, will fly on a people's lips beyond the boundless horizon of the centuries." He adds, "Let the elements, raging together, open the earthly abyss and swallow this splendid city, from which your great song resounded to all of the corners of vast Russia . . . but as long as the Russian language can be heard, you will be alive and will not die."[23] Radishchev's evocation of the Petersburg apocalypse notwithstanding, he could hardly have anticipated the neglect and indignities that the later nineteenth century, not to mention the twentieth, would inflict upon the city's cemeteries, and the extent to which we now must rely on written accounts of "dead Petersburg."

Although burial sites represent a primary institution of memory, Petersburg has had to make special efforts to remember its cemeteries and markers, Saitov's immense catalogue among them. Early twentieth-century preservationists, most particularly Nikolai Vrangel' in his famous 1907 piece, "Forgotten Graves" (*Zabytye mogily*),[24] protested the disrepair into which many historical cemeteries had fallen. Thirty years before the establishment of the Masters of Art cemetery, Vrangel' wrote passionately of the destruction wrought by time, the elements, and vandals on the expressive Lazarevskoe tombstone sculpture created by Petersburg Academy artists such as Mikhail Kozlovskii, Ivan Martos, and Dominique Rachette. Vrangel' pointed out the painful irony in the motifs of remembering that pervade the epitaph verse on these forgotten graves, and warned that the ongoing neglect would lead to the loss of historical knowledge about Petersburg's burial practices. Thirty years later, however, the 1930s saw the destruction of entire cemeteries in a mass exercise in historical forgetting. During the 1970s, several more imperial-era cemeteries were liquidated, resulting in the loss of thousands of gravesites and hundreds of marble tombstones, not to mention the handmade decorative metalwork fencing that surrounded them. This process was halted only after the intervention of prominent city intellectuals headed by Academic Dmitrii Likhachev.

During the early years of the twentieth century, Saitov and Vrangel' worked to capture on paper the collective memory that a cemetery, with its monuments and inscriptions, is intended to preserve. The more recent efforts of cemetery historians have extended this pre-revolutionary project, and perhaps this is only proper. As Pushkin's famous "Monument" poem (by way of Horace and Derzhavin) asserts, material commemoration is doomed to fail in its goal of guarding against the loss of memory. Only writing, that seemingly fragile but well-developed Petersburg practice, can hope to succeed where the monument fails.

Cultural Memory and Monumental Loss

In his 1844 essay "Petersburg and Moscow" (*Peterburg i Moskva*), Belinsky challenged the image of Petersburg as a city without a history, allegedly evidenced by its lack of ancient historical monuments. "Yes, dear sirs, there are no such monuments in Petersburg, and there can be none because Petersburg has existed since the day of its founding for only 141 years," he granted. Even so, "Petersburg *itself* is a great historical monument" in the extraordinary fact of its existence.[25]

Yet a city is *not* a very apt visual analog for either individual or cultural memory. As Sigmund Freud took pains to show in *Civilization and Its Discontents*, forgetting is an operation quite distinct from destroying, since any idea once formed in the human mind can in theory be retrieved or reconstructed. To support his point, Freud offered an elaborate metaphor, hypothesizing that if Rome were a human consciousness "with just as long and varied a past history," it would look quite different from the modern city by that name:

> This would mean that in Rome the palaces of the Caesars were still standing on the Palatine and the Septizonium of Septimius Severus was still towering to its old height; that the beautiful statues were still standing in the colonnade of the Castle of St. Angelo, as they were up to its siege by the Goths . . . But more still: where the Palazzo Cafferelli stands there would also be, without this being removed, the Temple of Jupiter Capitolinus, not merely in its latest form, moreover, as the Romans of the Caesars saw it, but also in its earliest shape,

when it still wore an Etruscan design and was adorned with terra-cotta antifixae. Where the Coliseum stands now we could at the same time admire Nero's Golden House; on the Piazza of the Pantheon we should find not only the Pantheon of to-day as bequeathed to us by Hadrian, but on the same site also Agrippa's original edifice; indeed, the same ground would support the church of Santa Maria sopra Minerva and the old temple over which it was built. And the observer would need merely to shift the focus of his eyes, perhaps, or change his position, in order to call up a view of either the one or the other. [26]

For Freud, this metaphor proves that mental life cannot be adequately rendered by visual representation, since only one structure can occupy a given space in an artistic depiction. What Freud does not acknowledge—although he performs this very operation in elaborating Rome as metaphor—is that in theory, at least, a city's memory, like the memories of a person, may be fully represented in writing. The seemingly infinite contemporary Petersburg project of textual commemoration strives for precisely this articulation, in its never-ending reconstruction of the city's past. While a city may not be an adequate analog for the human mind, text serves very well as a model of the city. Structures such as libraries, archives, and museums make this connection explicit, realizing in physical form the "containers for the documents that represent the memory of a civilization," no less than architectural monuments do.[27] Architectural models of memory are common in treatises dating back to the ancient Greeks, who first articulated the practice of mnemonics, mentally creating *loci* for objects, concepts, and events to be remembered.[28] Thus the creation of textual as well as physical architecture aids greatly in developing the faculties of memory.

A certain amount of change and loss in a cityscape over time is to be expected. Few Petersburg residences from the early baroque period have survived except for the Menshikov Palace on the University Embankment and the restored Kikin house not far from the Tauride Palace. The beautiful Stock Exchange building by Thomas de Thomon (1805–1810) replaced Giacomo Quarenghi's partially completed Stock Exchange from the 1780s. The present St. Isaac's cathedral is actually the *fourth* cathedral by that name constructed in more or less the same place—the first two dating to the first half of the eighteenth century, and the third designed by Antonio Rinaldi during the reign of Catherine the Great and completed by Vincenzo Brenna under Paul. Similarly, there were four different Winter Palaces. The third and fourth Winter Palaces were built by Bartolomeo Rastrelli, the former for Anna Ioannovna during the 1730s, and the latter for Elizabeth during the 1750s.[29] Catherine's Tsaritsyn Meadow became Paul's Field of Mars. Elizabeth's Summer Palace was torn down to make way for Paul's Mikhailovsky Palace. Petersburg cultural historians have treated these major architectural "rewritings" as a normative, if regrettable, part of the city's history during the eighteenth century and the first part of the nineteenth century. In contrast, the later nineteenth-century destruction of small homes and other buildings dating from the eras of Catherine the Great and Alexander I in order to make room for eclectic-style apartment buildings enraged many of Petersburg's most prominent cultural commentators, most notably the preservationists.

Beginning with the final years of the nineteenth century, Petersburg lost a number of its major architectural "monuments" owing to unfortunate decisions by city officials. The neoclassical Bolshoi Theater by Thomas de Thomon was almost entirely demolished and turned into a conservatory of music, with nothing to recommend it architecturally. Torn down in 1898 to make room for an apartment building, the famous Stroganov dacha on Chernaia rechka is preserved only in the well-known painting by the architect Andrei Voronikhin that hangs in the Russian Museum. In like fashion, the Iakovlev residence by the Obukhov Bridge, built in the 1760s by Rastrelli, was torn down in 1901 to accommodate the expansion of the Haymarket. The greater part of Trezzini's early eighteenth-century Gostinyi Dvor on Vasilievskii Island was destroyed to make room for the construction of the Academy of Sciences library during the 1910s in a clear manifestation of presumed cultural precedence that might well be questioned today.

During this late-imperial period, Petersburg preservationists actively protested the "vandalism" of the capital's older buildings, initially in the journal *World of Art* and particularly in the journal *Past Years* (*Starye gody*, 1907–1916), which considered saving Russia's architectural legacy one of its primary missions.[30] A 1907 article in *Past Years* mourned Petersburg's old chain bridges, the Panteleimonovskii and Egipetskii bridges across the Fontanka, both dating from the last years of Alexander I's reign and defunct by the first decade of the twentieth century.[31] A 1915 article deplored the disappearance of gardens adjoining various palaces.[32] The preservationist movement—a union of artists and architectural specialists—made major textual contributions to the cult of "Old Petersburg" in the form of books, articles, and catalogues, and sponsored public lectures and exhibitions.[33]

In its fusion of literature and architecture, the preservationists' work at the end of the imperial period was consummately Petersburgian. Like the journal *Past Years*, the Museum of Old Petersburg—eventually incorporated into the City Museum, and later called the Museum of the History of Petersburg—dates from the late 1910s. A repository for a large collection of original architectural drawings and photographs, it had many homes over the years, including the residence of Count Siuzor, the Anichkov Palace, the Rumiantsev house on the English embankment, and the Peter-Paul Fortress.[34]

For the preservationists, "Old Petersburg" was not simply a quaint place of memory, the setting for entertaining stories told by elderly residents. Rather, this fragmentary, necessarily partial and non-contiguous locus spoke to the riches of cultural legacy that were more lasting than reminiscence, as embodied by specific architectural structures, both defunct and provisionally extant. The preservationists provided their readers with time tours that performed virtuoso synchronic elaborations of individual locales, excavating beneath the contemporary surface to reach aspects of St. Petersburg that now led an exclusively textual life. Readers of these works depended on the immensely knowledgeable narrator for this information, nowhere visible on the city's surface. Unlike traditional guidebooks, which turn complex urban environments into legible cultural topography, empowering tourists by placing knowledge literally in their hands, the preservationists' studies showed readers how much they did not and could not know. The preservationists estranged readers from their city even as they attempted to win new converts to their cause. Following the tradition of the many "memory," "archive," and "legacy" journals such as *Russian Archive* (*Russkii arkhiv*, 1861–1917), *Russian Antiquity* (*Russkaia starina*, 1870–1917), and *Historical Herald* (*Istoricheskii vestnik*, 1880–1917), the preservationists continued the project of constructing an entire city out of printed material. The "physical" Petersburg contemporary to their writing projects was revealed to be only a ghost of its former self.

The cult of Old Petersburg established during this era continued through the 1920s. Among the longest-lived efforts to preserve Petersburg's memory of itself were the excursionist school of Ivan Grevs and Nikolai Antsiferov, specializing in the study of local lore, and the Old Petersburg Society (1921–1938).[35] Both groups survived the early Soviet era by focusing on the cultural enrichment of city workers, in a departure from the elitist orientation of the pre-revolutionary organizations.

Antsiferov's work represents the culmination of nineteenth-century guidebook literature and preservationist studies, while also serving as the basis for many Soviet and post-Soviet guides to St. Petersburg. Antsiferov perfected the humanitarian excursion that combined architectural and literary history—a format prefigured by poetry-citing nineteenth-century guidebooks. This genre of cultural tour treated literary referents associated with urban topography while exploring the physical city itself. An excursion of this type also exhibited its *guide*, who had mastered the network of cultural connections that linked text and terrain. As one of Antsiferov's contemporaries declared, "A brilliant memory helped him to preserve and at the necessary moment to extract verse and prose excerpts, which he used to corroborate his conclusions."[36] Antsiferov's body of work crystallizes the essential connections between excursion text and physical city, invoking the persistent textual metaphors for urban culture that infuse the entire tradition of writing about St. Petersburg.

With the onset of the Stalinist 1930s, the collective project of remembering and preserving imperial Petersburg was largely put aside, although energies were newly directed at remembering and preserving revolutionary and Leninist sites. Many of the city's most beautiful buildings were turned into functional headquarters for Bolshevik organs, while others became Soviet museums, veterans' hospitals, and "cultural centers" for teachers. Toward the end of the Soviet period, however, the remembering project that had been broken off by the 1930s resumed. The 1988 exhibition catalogue *Lost Architectural Monuments of Petersburg-Leningrad* (*Utrachennye pamiatniki arkhitektury Peterburga-Leningrada*) accompanied brief descriptions of defunct structures with images from old photographs and postcards in order to commemorate approximately 150 vanished civil structures and church buildings, monuments, engineering projects, and minor architectural forms such as bridges, gates, and railings from the imperial period. The compilers of the catalogue conceded that all cities are subject to an ongoing and organic process of change, but they distinguished this inevitable work of time from "malevolent" forces that degrade the cityscape. The center of then-Leningrad, they argued, should be considered a cultural "preserve" (*zapovednik*).[37] To this proposed city-museum, *Lost Architectural Monuments* therefore added in textual and photographic form those structures that should have remained intact.

While the nineteenth-century construction of apartment housing caused the demise of old homes and dachas, the early Soviet period flattened church buildings in an attempt to change the essential face of the city. Among the churches destroyed were Znamenskaia, torn down to make way for the metro station opposite the Moscow railway station; Pokrova Bogoroditsy, invoked by Pushkin in his poem "A Little House in Kolomna" (*Domik v Kolomne*); Uspenskaia, dating from the mid-1700s and called Spas-na-Sennoi during the nineteenth century; the Church of St. Matvei, built in 1720 to commemorate the 1704 Russian victory at Narva on that apostle's day; Preobrazhenskaia, erected during Peter's reign on the left bank of the Neva; and the Troitskii Cathedral, which dated from the very earliest period in the city's history, although it had burned down and been restored more than once. The Sergievskaia, Voznesenskaia, Rozhdestvenskaia, Vvedenskaia, Vladimirskaia, Ekaterininskaia, and Panteleimonovskaia churches were similarly demolished, the Ekaterininskaia ignominiously pulled down to make way for a movie theater. Most of these churches in their earliest wooden forms dated from the eighteenth century, and, although over the years they all had undergone remodeling and rebuilding, most had retained their original period style and appearance.

After the October Revolution of 1917, busts depicting Russia's imperial rulers were removed from their places in front of public institutions such as the Obukhovskaia and Mariinskaia hospitals and the Alexandrovskii lyceum. Several sculptures of Peter the Great erected for Petersburg's bicentennial celebration in 1903 were moved to unobtrusive places in the city or destroyed. The large statue of Alexander III on Znamenskaia Square was moved to a courtyard of the Russian Museum. One major sculptural monument was entirely demolished—the 1880s victory column in front of the similarly defunct Troitskii Cathedral, commemorating Russian soldiers and officers of the Izmailovskii regiment who fought in the 1877–1878 war with Turkey. As shown in period postcards, the monument was constructed from dozens of captured Turkish cannons, forming five vertical "rings" and crowned with a winged Nike. Photographs, drawings, and written accounts are all that remain of this victory monument, however, despite its vivid emphasis on the material spoils of war. In such a case, reading the cityscape—a task of much Petersburg literature from the imperial period—thus becomes an exclusively textual practice.

Along with the catalogue of *Lost Architectural Monuments*, memorial plaques affixed to buildings and other landmarks are among the Petersburg commemorative practices that offset the losses of time, telling stories that such plaques literally inscribe upon the cityscape. Memorial plaques thus qualify as both literature and sculpture. It has been said that literature may be, at its origins, a lapidary object or an inscription.[38] Literary language of a sort is often inscribed upon an architectural work in decorative symbols, narrative bas-reliefs, dedications, and proclamations, and the existence of an architectural object is entwined with the various texts that are written before, in, around, and about it.[39] In fact, an edifice is by nature "forgetful," and can only reacquire its lost meaning through the agency of historians' studies, guidebooks, and plaques. As evidenced by a substantial body of secondary literature, Petersburg memorial plaques dating back to the eighteenth and nineteenth centuries themselves now constitute an object of study—an exercise of meta-recollection—within the larger project of reconstructing cultural memory.[40]

It is hard to miss the irony and paradox that infuse the history, preservation, and loss of cultural memory in St. Petersburg. The memory journals of the nineteenth century, like all periodicals, were easily lost, destroyed, or preserved as incomplete series. The Museum of St. Petersburg, with its dizzying succession of names and locations, scarcely resembles a permanent institution. The Museum of City Sculpture, in transferring graveside monuments and human remains from all over Leningrad, and in converting the city's oldest cemetery into a cultural park, violates the notion of a final resting place. Some of the most serious and sustained efforts at preserving the past, or at least its memory, have been made by *temporary* exhibitions, such as those staged by the preservationists through the Society of Architect-Artists during the early 1910s, or by the Lost Architectural Monuments project of the 1980s. To a great extent, the continuity in the project of preserving Petersburg's cultural memory comes most demonstrably from the frequency with which new efforts have been mounted.

Ever since the restoration of its historic name in the early 1990s, St. Petersburg—the "city without a history"—has been eager to remember as much as possible, and this project expanded at an accelerating rate as the 2003 tercentenary year approached. The collective project of recollection, which went underground during the Soviet era, becoming the province of individual eccentrics and intelligentsia research-workers, was back in full swing.

Notes

1. Francesco Algarotti, "Letters from Count Algarotti to Lord Hervey and the Marquis Scipio Maffei," Letter IV, June 30, 1739. (London, 1769; Reprint in Goldsmiths'-Kress Library of Economic Literature no. 10500).

2. William Kinglake, "A Summer in Russia," *The New Monthly Magazine and Humorist* 2 (1846): 278–279.

3. For a discussion of the impressions conveyed by the Marquis de Custine in his mid-nineteenth-century account of a visit to Petersburg, see the first chapter by William Brumfield in the present volume. Brumfield also discusses Dostoevsky's response to Custine.

4. See the third chapter by Helena Goscilo in the present volume for a comprehensive overview of Petersburg mythology as conveyed in literature and the visual arts.

5. Alexander [Aleksandr] Skidan, "O pol'ze i vrede Peterburga dlia zhizni," http:// www.russ.ru/krug/99-07-06/skidan.html. Like Brodsky, Skidan declares that the Bolsheviks are to be thanked for the city's transformation into a cemetery-museum after the transfer of the capital back to Moscow.

6. For details on the latter period, see Richard Wortman, "Moscow and Petersburg: The Problem of Political Center in Tsarist Russia, 1881–1914," in Sean Wilentz, ed., *Rites of Power: Symbolism, Ritual, and Politics Since the Middle Ages* (Philadelphia, 1985).

7. Lewis Mumford, *The City in History: Its Origins, Its Transformations, and Its Prospects* (New York, 1961), 7.

8. A. V. Kobak and Iu. M. Piriutko, "Ot sostavitelei," *Istoricheskie kladbishcha Peterburga: Spravochnik-putevoditel'* (St. Petersburg, 1993), 5. For a historical survey of Petersburg's cemeteries, see their "Ocherk istorii peterburgskogo nekropola" in the same volume.

9. V. I. Saitov, Introduction to *Peterburgskii nekropol'* (St. Petersburg, 1912–1913), t. 1–4.

10. Iu. M. Piriutko, "Leningradskii panteon," *Antsiferovskie chteniia: Materialy i tezisy konferentsii* (Leningrad, 1989), 162.

11. For detailed historical information about Lazarevskoe, see the section on "Kladbishcha Aleksandro-Nevskoi lavry" by Iu. M. Piriutko in *Istoricheskie kladbishcha Peterburga*. See also Iu. M. Piriutko, "Lazarevskaia usypal'nitsa—pamiatnik russkoi kul'tury XVIII—XIX vv.," *Pamiatniki kul'tury. Novye otkrytiia* (Moscow, 1989).

12. Note that the Paris Panthéon was established in an eighteenth-century church that was secularized during the French Revolution (although it twice reverted to being a church during the nineteenth century) and dedicated to the memory of great French citizens. The Panthéon contains the remains of Voltaire, Jean-Jacques Rousseau, Victor Hugo, Émile Zola, and Marie Curie, among others. The Père-Lachaise cemetery, opened in 1804, contains the remains of dozens of famous Frenchmen and Frenchwomen. London's Westminster Abbey provides another example of this phenomenon, housing the tombs and memorials of famous British subjects such as Sir Isaac Newton, Geoffrey Chaucer, Ben Jonson, John Dryden, and Robert Browning.

13. G. D. Netunakhina and N. I. Udimova, *Muzei gorodskoi skul'ptury: Kratkii putevoditel'* (Leningrad, 1972), 109–110.

14. Lidiia Ginzburg, "Mysl', opisavshaia krug," *Zapisnye knizhki. Vospominaniia. Esse* (St. Petersburg, 2002), 557–558.

15. For a description of the official ceremonies accompanying the transfer of the relics, see M. I. Pyliaev, *Staryi Peterburg* (Leningrad, 1990), 23.

16. Note also the parallel tradition of burying nineteenth-century radical thinkers (Vera Zasulich among them) in the Literatorskie mostki. For a description of the notorious funeral of populist Pavel Chernyshev at Volkovo, see Tom Trice, "Rites of Protest: Populist Funerals in Imperial St. Petersburg, 1876–1878," *Slavic Review* 60/1 (Spring 2001).

17. Note that the Literatorskie mostki is also home to the gravesites of Petersburg cultural historians Mikhail Pyliaev and Petr Stolpianskii—a characteristic detail of Petersburg's meta-commentary upon its own history.

18. For a historical survey, see A. I. Kudriavtsev and G. N. Shkoda, "Pravoslavnoe kladbishche i nekropol'-muzei Literatorskie mostki" in *Istoricheskie kladbishcha Peterburga*. For a Soviet-era description, see *Leningrad: Putevoditel'* (Leningrad, 1988), 194–195.

19. N. A. Nekrasov, *Polnoe sobranie sochinenii i pisem*, t. 2 (Moscow, 1949), 64.

20. Most scholars concur that the site of Pushkin's famous stroll through a depressing "public cemetery" took place at the Blagoveshchenskoe cemetery on Kamennyi Island, since the poem was written during the author's visit to this island. The notion has also been advanced that this poem captures the impressions of a visit to his friend Anton Del'vig's grave at the Volkovo cemetery, known for its diverse mix of representatives from the Petersburg population. See M. P. Alekseev, *Pushkin i mirovaia literatura* (Leningrad, 1987), 148.

21. Vsevolod Garshin, "Peterburgskie pis'ma," *Rasskazy*, kn. 3 (St. Petersburg, 1902), 62–64.

22. This last is a reference to the writer Afanas'ev-Chuzhbinskii, who had requested that he be buried near Belinsky and Dobroliubov, but was laid to rest at some distance from them due to a lack of space.

23. A. N. Radishchev, *Puteshestvie iz Peterburga v Moskvu*, V. A. Zapadov, ed. (St. Petersburg, 1992), 115. Ironically, in 1783 Radishchev had composed an epitaph for his late wife and wished to have it inscribed upon her tombstone at the monastery cemetery, but was forbidden by the authorities on the grounds that the verses showed "insufficient certainty in the immortality of the soul." See A. N. Radishchev, *Sochineniia* (Moscow, 1988), 650.

24. N. N. Vrangel', "Zabytye mogily," *Starye gody*, February 1907.

25. V. G. Belinsky, "Peterburg i Moskva," *Peterburg v russkom ocherke XIX veka*, M. V. Otradin, ed. (Leningrad, 1984), 89.

26. Sigmund Freud, *Civilization and Its Discontents*, Joan Riviere, trans. (New York, 1930), 17–18.

27. See, in this regard, V. N. Zaitsev, "Bibliotechnoe-informatsionnoe prostranstvo Sankt-Peterburga," *Fenomen Peterburga*, Iu. N. Bespiatykh, ed. (St. Petersburg, 2000).

28. For a detailed historical exposition of these practices from antiquity up to Leibniz, see Frances Yates's classic study of "mnemotechnics" in *The Art of Memory*, vol. 3 in *Selected Works* (London, 1966). For a fascinating particular case, see "Building the Palace" (chapter 1) in Jonathan D. Spence, *The Memory Palace of Matteo Ricci* (New York, 1984).

29. For a detailed discussion of Rastrelli's final Winter Palace, see the first chapter in the present volume by William Brumfield.

30. Alexander Benois's best-known articles in this regard are "Zhivopisnyi Peterburg," *Mir iskusstvo* no. 1, 1902; "Krasota Peterburga," *Mir iskusstvo* no. 8, 1902; and "Vandalizmy," *Mir iskusstvo* no. 10, 1904. For a brief historical sketch of *Starye gody*, see F. M. Lur'e,

"Golosa 'Serebrianogo veka': knigi, zhurnaly, vystavki," *Fenomen Peterburga*, 183–187. For a memoiristic account of the founding of *Starye gody* written during the mid-1920s, see M. A. Vitukhnovskaia, "Vospominaniia P. P. Veinera o zhurnale 'Starye gody,'" *Pamiatniki kul'tury. Novye okrytiia. Ezhegodnik 1984* (Leningrad, 1986).

31. S. Troinitskii, "O tsepnykh mostakh Peterburga," *Starye gody* March 1907.

32. V. Kurbatov, "Unichtozhenie petrogradskikh sadov," *Starye gody* January–February 1915.

33. For an overview of preservationist activities, see Katerina Clark, *Petersburg, Crucible of Cultural Revolution* (Cambridge, MA, 1995), 59–65.

34. Sources on the Museum include *Muzei goroda: k Oktiabriu 1927 g.* (Leningrad, 1928); A. M. Blinov, "Muzei 'Staryi Peterburg', 1907–1918 g.," *Leningrad ves' na ladoni 1990*; A. N. Andreeva, "Muzei goroda," *Peterburgskie chteniia 96* (St. Petersburg, 1996); and R. I. Shpiller, "Gosudarstvennyi muzei istorii Leningrada (1918–1985 gg.)," *Muzei i vlast': Iz zhizni muzeev: Sbornik nauchnykh trudov* (Moscow, 1991).

35. See A. M. Konechnyi, "Obshchestvo 'Staryi Peterburg—Novyi Leningrad,'" *Muzei* no. 7, 1987.

36. Ia. A. Veinert, "Vospominaniia o Nikolae Pavloviche Antsiferove." *Mashinopis'.* 1958 (sobranie M. B. Verblovskoi). Cited in A. M. Konechnyi and K. A. Kumpan, "Peterburg v zhizni i trudakh N. P. Antsiferova," in N. A. Antsiferov and M. B. Verblovskaia, *Nepostizhimyi gorod* (Leningrad, 1991), 14.

37. V. V. Antonov and A. V. Kobak, eds., *Utrachennye pamiatniki arkhitektury Peterburga-Leningrada* (Leningrad, 1988), 4.

38. Philippe Hamon, *Expositions: Literature and Architecture in Nineteenth-Century France*, Katia Sainson-Frank and Lisa Maguire, trans. (Berkeley, 1992), 4.

39. Hamon, *Expositions*, 45–50.

40. See V. N. Timofeev, E. N. Poretskina, and N. N. Efremova, sost., *Memorial'nye doski Sankt-Peterburga: Spravochnik* (St. Petersburg, 1999), and B. N. Kalinin and P. P. Iurevich, sost., *Pamiatniki i memorial'nye doski Leningrada: Spravochnik* (Leningrad, 1979).

Three

Unsaintly St. Petersburg?
Visions and Visuals

Helena Goscilo

Though according to Shakespeare's *Romeo and Juliet* alternate names for a rose would not diminish its seductive scent, the history of Russia's occasional capital attests to the enormous political and psychological weight of nomenclature: Originally St. Petersburg, briefly Petrograd in 1914–1924, Leningrad from 1924, and now once more St. Petersburg—though in danger of becoming Putinburg—the city seems determinedly Petered, and, as recent reports on its physical condition intimate, petering out.[1] Indeed, one journalist in 2002 summed up a widespread perception of Petersburg when she characterized it as "a gracefully decaying bastion of Imperial Russia."[2] In light of the city's ailing transportation system, the conspicuous disrepair of its buildings, and the parlous state of its hospitals, schools, institutes, and museums, the princely sum of sixty billion rubles allegedly spent on its extravagant, maximally publicized tercentenary in 2003 inevitably evokes the specter of the Potemkin village, by now a rather tired metaphor for the nation's habit of camouflage through glitter.[3]

During the last decade, St. Petersburg's reputation as Russia's crime capital and hotbed of corruption has tarnished its vaunted image as the nation's citadel of architectural splendor for anyone not invested in preserving a moribund past or prepared to confront an unsettling present. Part of the city's surreal atmosphere today, in fact, derives from the indivisibility of its internecine conflicts in business, politics, and culture. As the astute journalist Iuliia Latynina maintains, "That's the kind of city St. Petersburg is. Deputy governors are killed over money, and crime bosses are killed over politics."[4] Yet the ostensible contradiction of aesthetic splendor and vicious violence inheres in the city's very origins and long-standing traditions, as William Brumfield's discussion of the city's founding (chapter 1) makes all too clear.

The proliferation of names for the northern capital has bred a bewildering chaos that reflects the zigzags of Russia's history: Current newspapers refer to "Petrogradskoe upravlenie vnutrennikh del" (the Petrograd Administration of Internal Affairs, presumably, on the "oblast"/"raion" level); the church diocese is "Leningradskaia eparkhiia," while the city itself bears the formal label "Sankt-Peterburg," as well as the colloquial, intimate sobriquet of Piter.[5] Each variant, needless to say, evokes culturally freighted associations with turning-points in the nation's tumultuous and richly documented past.[6] Collectively, the time-specific appellations attest to the city's image as a palimpsest to be read and "interpreted" from diverse viewpoints—precisely the endeavor described in detail by Julie Buckler (chapter 2) and referenced by practically all other contributors to the present volume.

The Petersburg Myth

Russian -*burg* (from the Dutch for "town/city") lacks the pejorative connotations of its English equivalent, which dictionaries define neutrally, but American colloquial usage equates with torpid, regressive non-being ("This is a burg"). As Russia's challenge to West European elegance, scale, and panache, Petersburg was envisioned by its conceptual father in utopian, hyperbolic terms, as a challenging, resplendent showcase of Russia's bounties within a progressive European context. That the city for most of its existence has borne its founder's name merely observes international conventions of denomination. But . . . what of the "Saint/Sankt," especially when conjoined with the name of a tsar deemed demonic by numerous subjects, contemporaries, and generations of Slavophilic Russians? After all, the city's renowned literary image sooner privileges ominous darkness over sunny sanctity, despite, and frequently because of, the White Nights that seem a violation of nature, and especially the specific, complex makeup of human nature.[7]

The copious scholarship on the literary myth of Petersburg has ana-lyzed various texts' inscription of its imposing grandeur—coupled, how-ever, with a psychological and moral destructiveness, an inhumane dedica-tion to flamboyant display at the cost of Christian values, to which the metropolis seems eerily indifferent. A speedy glance at three centuries of major literary statements about Petersburg reveals three different hypos-tases of varying complexity, which roughly may be categorized as positive, negative, and mixed.

First, the city as an aesthetically spectacular creation and the new seat of a progressive imperial power appears in the eighteenth-century ode, which, as Mark Al'tshuller's first-rate article argues, exalts Petersburg's magnificence in terms surprisingly undifferentiated and scant in descrip-tive particulars. That image dominates the following, far from exhaustive, list of works: Vasilii Trediakovskii's "Praise to the Izherskii Land and the Reigning Town of St. Petersburg" ("Pokhvala Izherskoi zemle i tsarstvui-ushchemu gradu Sankt-Peterburgu," 1752); Mikhail Lomonosov's "Sol-emn Ode to Catherine Alekseeva on Her Accession to the Throne, 28 June 1762" ("Oda torzhestvennaia Ekaterine Alekseevne na eia vosshest-vie na prestol iiunia 28 dnia 1762 goda");[8] Mikhail Murav'ev's verses "To the Goddess of the Neva" ("Bogine Nevy," 1794); and Petr Viazemskii's classical poem "Petersburg" ("Peterburg," 1818).[9] The quasi-odic sections of Pushkin's *Bronze Horseman* (*Mednyi vsadnik*, 1833) extend this line, but inasmuch as the narrative poem simultaneously spotlights the brutal im-perviousness to individual human life associated with the city's construc-tion, it launched the dual myth of Petersburg. The sustained and unre-solved ambivalence of Pushkin's narrator—also of Osip Mandelstam's later verses, as Zara Torlone argues in chapter 4—communicates itself through the contrast of such impassioned apostrophes as "I love you, Pe-ter's creation" ("Liubliu tebia, Petra tvorenie")[10] with a lexicon of destruc-tive force and mayhem, plus the elegiac tone identified with the "alas and alack" Evgenii line in the narrative poem. In short, Petersburg resembles the fin-de-siècle phallic woman, who both seduces through beauty and dooms through cruelty or indifference.[11]

Second, the metropolis as an "unnatural," malevolent locus of ambi-tion, insanity, and fantastic visions figures not only in Pushkin's *Bronze Horseman*, but also in his "Queen of Spades" ("Pikovaia dama") and *Eu-gene Onegin* (*Evgenii Onegin*). This productively portentous image acquires a spectral, other-worldly dimension in Gogol's "Nevsky Prospect" ("Nevskii Prospekt"), "The Nose" ("Nos"), and "The Overcoat" ("Shi-nel'"), which construe the metropolis as a demonic, phantasmagoric do-main, in terms blending fascinated horror and uncomprehending hatred (the Devil, in Gogol's bizarre synthesis of pagan and quirkily Orthodox beliefs, lights the lamps on the major thoroughfare of Nevsky). Gogol's bleak view of Petersburg as "all deceit, all dreams," in turn, finds richly psychologized elaboration in Dostoevsky's *Poor Folk* (*Bednye liudi*), *The Double* (*Dvoinik*), and *Crime and Punishment* (*Prestuplenie i nakazanie*)—the last famously characterizing Petersburg as the most abstract and in-tentional of cities, one conducive to hallucination, mental disintegration, and murder.[12]

Third and finally, a complexly synthetic image of Petersburg emerges in Andrei Bely's intricate novel *Petersburg* (*Peterburg*, 1913–1914/1922), which, like Andrei Bitov's *Pushkin House* sixty-odd years later (*Pushkin-skii dom*, wr. 1970, pd. 1978), offers an encyclopedic, deconstructive sum-mary of the city as a cultural repository inseparable from its philosophi-cal and literary treatments. Bitov's narrative absorbs in an archeological mode the wealth of conceptual and aesthetic attributes in which the verses of Alexander Blok, Anna Akhmatova, Osip Mandelstam (who wrote, "Living in Petersburg is like sleeping in a coffin"),[13] and Joseph Brodsky had haloed the city.

The cumulative effect of these inscriptions has predisposed critics to speak not of Petersburg, but of its myth, as though its literary image super-sedes its phenomenological and ontological identity—and, as Vladimir Khazan's chapter lavishly illustrates, such indeed has been the case for for-mer Petersburgers languishing in emigration. Tellingly, Bitov, who volun-tarily moved from the northern city to the capital, once observed, "We read Leningrad like a book."[14] A cryptic site of phantoms, delirium, and delu-sion, in literature Petersburg also functions as a hostile sanctuary for insen-tient bureaucrats impervious to individuals and their needs, serving as an irresistible topic for writers seemingly addicted to contributing their input into the city's evolving mythology.[15] Studies by Nikolai Antsiferov, Leonid Grossman, Nils Ake Nilsson, Donald Fanger, Robert Maguire, and others have habituated us to conceive of Petersburg as a profoundly literary and literarized locus, and this strand of scholarship, frankly, has worn rather thin through tireless iteration.[16]

Visual Petersburg

Slavists' conservative attachment to the logocentric trough largely ignores three equally sumptuous repositories of images—first, music, such as Shostakovich's Seventh/ "Leningrad" Symphony, the operas *Nose* (Shostakovich) and *The Queen of Spades* (Tchaikovsky), and songs by the rock group Aquarium, with Boris Grebenshchikov as frontman, and by the vastly popular rock group Leningrad; second, film, notably Sergei Eisenstein and Grigorii Aleksandrov's *October* [*Ten Days that Shook the World*] (*Oktiabr'*, 1927), *The End of St. Petersburg* (*Konets Sankt-Peterburga*, 1927) by Vsevolod Pudovkin and Mikhail Doller, and, most recently, Aleksei Uchitel''s *Stroll* (*Progulka*, 2003) and Aleksandr Sokurov's *Russian Ark* (*Russkii kovcheg*, 2002), as well as adaptations, including Grigorii Kozintsev and Leonid Trauberg's *Overcoat* (1926) and sundry screen versions of Dostoevsky's novels; and third, art, produced by Russia's foremost painters, set designers, and graphic artists. These visuals, which constitute an understudied heritage in which literature not infrequently serves as a reference point or mediator, are the focus of my condensed commentary.

Given Russia's cult of Pushkin—cleverly ironized in Iurii Mamin's subversive film *Sideburns* (*Bakenbardy*, 1990)—the originator of the city's myth predictably remains not only the most illustrious but also the most illustrated author. Even a minuscule sampling of the graphics and set designs devoted to Pushkin's texts and their adaptations encompasses a broad array of works, among them Alexander Benois's illustrations not only of "The Queen of Spades" (1905), but also of *The Bronze Horseman* (1916–1922). The latter convey, with an impressive economy of means, Evgenii's existential terror amid the vast, deserted stretches of the flooded city, with its insignia of Empire and the colossal figure of its omnipresent creator, whose single-minded will transformed remote, unpopulated marshlands into a modern metropolis.[17] N. V. Kuz'min's lesser-known illustrations to *Eugene Onegin* (1933), which suggest the influence of Pushkin's own sketches crowding the margins of his manuscript and Mstislav Dobuzhinskii's graphics, which accompanied three editions of the printed text (1938, 1939, and 1943), eloquently contextualize the arrogant, overly polished protagonist in the impersonal urban landscape at decisive junctures in the narrative.[18] A similar stylistic diversity distinguishes the set designs for Tchaikovsky's *Queen of Spades*, which range from the dramatic, intensely dark blue structures by

FIGURE 3.1. One of Alexander Benois's illustrations in ink, brush, and charcoal pencil (1916–1922) for an edition of A. Pushkin's *The Bronze Horseman*, showing the statue of Peter I pursuing Evgenii through the deserted streets of the metropolis.

Mikhail Vrubel' (1901) recalling the palette of his *Demon* series, softened in V. Dmitriev's bluish shading of the snowy streets for a later production (1932), to the particularized neutrality of Dobuzhinskii's more realistic, meticulous design (1933). The last shares with countless portrayals of Petersburg a focus on the Peter-Paul Fortress—a structure associated with both culture and torture: Compressing key aspects of the city's early history, it played a grisly role in the civic-minded Nikolai Chernyshevsky's biography: Arrested in 1862 for his revolutionary activities, he was incarcerated there until his exile to Siberia in 1864.

Gogol likewise attracted several skillful artists, notably Boris Kustodiev, whose illustrations for "The Overcoat" (1905) show Akakii Akakievich as Petrovich's suitably nondescript supplicant, and, more expressively, as a lone, anonymous figure engulfed in his larger-than-life cloak amid the swirling darkness of the St. Petersburg night, poorly illuminated by a distant streetlight. By contrast, D. Kardovskii's sepia frontispiece to "Nevsky Prospect" captures the daytime's jostling crowds swarming along the city's main thoroughfare, which seems barely capable of accommodating the throngs and thus conveys the aura of chaotic excess in Gogol's story.

FIGURE 3.2. Mstislav Dobuzhinskii's illustration for an edition of Pushkin's *Eugene Onegin* (1938), capturing Lenskii and Onegin en route to the Larins' house: "Visiting the Neighbors."

FIGURE 3.3. Mstislav Dobuzhinskii's set design for a production of Tchaikovsky's opera *Queen of Spades* (1933), focusing on the history-steeped Peter-Paul Fortress.

FIGURE 3.4. Boris Kustodiev's illustration of Akakii Akakievich's solitary walk along the city's streets for the 1905 edition of Gogol's "Overcoat."

In the sense that they attempt to visualize what printed texts verbalize, these works cannot avoid collusion with the "originals" that by definition relegate their visual counterparts to secondary status, for the latter's function is illustration, not independent creation. Awareness of, and resistance to, this relegation informed the World of Art's credo for graphic design, which posited the book as a single "integral decorative and graphic entity, whose every component was linked in overall style and rhythm."[19] The chronological primacy of the word, however, cannot be gainsaid, forcing the graphic artist responsible for the visual accompaniment to adjust his or her imagination to the conceptual parameters of the literary text. Such a constraint, however, imposes a discipline that may well account for the superlative achievements of graphic artists affiliated with the World of Art.[20]

Fascinatingly, images of Petersburg unrelated to literature tend to be what linguists call less "marked": They frequently convey the atmosphere or the topography/look of the city's sundry areas in a relatively neutral or mixed manner. If the verbal myth of St. Petersburg instantly conjures up

FIGURE 3.5. Detail of D. Kardovskii's frontispiece for the 1904 edition of "Nevsky Prospect," emphasizing the milling crowds along the city's main thoroughfare.

the names of Pushkin, Gogol, Dostoevsky, Bely, and Bitov, then the roster of primary image-producers in art embraces Alexander Benois, Vladimir Favorskii, Evgenii Lansere, Anna Ostroumova-Lebedeva, Mstislav Dobuzhinksii, Pavel Shillingovskii, and Il'ia Glazunov. While instantly recognized by specialists, many of these figures, unlike their literary counterparts, have fallen out of popular memory—part of the forgetting discussed throughout this volume. St. Petersburg as a cultural museum, in other words, functions only to the extent that its population wishes to retain contact with the treasured artifacts. Eventually, the financial constraints imperiling all aspects of high culture, as well as the younger generations' unabating enthusiasm for (mainly imported) pop culture, may fatally compromise this nostalgic aspect of the city's identity, which is heavily invested in immobility and the backward glance. The heated controversy over the envisioned plans for Gazprom City—an enterprise that promises to swell the city's budget but ruin its prized aesthetics—symptomatize the dilemma of choosing between "baksy" and beauty.

Paradoxically, retrospection rules Peter's city of the future. The metamorphosis undergone by the image of Petersburg once it gains independence from the verbal text in the late nineteenth and early twentieth centuries reprises the aesthetics and agenda of an earlier era—notably, the eighteenth century. Works of the latter period possess, above all, documentary value, for in the absence of photography they alone provide concrete information about the city's appearance at a specific moment in history. The etchings of Aleksei Zubov (1682–1750), the period's premier master of the genre, epitomize this historical bent, while also emphasizing stability.[21] Part of his series titled *Panoramas of Petersburg, The Palace of Peter the Great* (1716) is an exercise in grand symmetry, the huge three-story palace occupying more than half the available space, flanked by identical one-story wings, with the groupings of people in front of it and the boats in the foregrounded water placed so as to fit into the almost mathematical composition of all the elements. His *View of St. Petersburg* (1727) exudes a kindred imperturbable solidity in the blocked tri-partite structure, dominated by the more than half-dozen ships in the river occupying the center, projected boldly against the official-looking buildings in the distance and dwarfing the human figures walking or riding along the embankment. Both etchings combine harmony with controlled activity, contrasting with the greater dynamism achieved by the diagonal that rules the otherwise similar triple arrangement of M. Makhaev's *Third Winter Palace* (1750–1853), executed in pen, ink, and brush. While these placid, flat renditions suggest the stolid immovability of state power, later decades favored more atmospheric, psychologically infused images, especially of the Falconet statue of Peter I unveiled in 1782 and rendered immortal by Pushkin's verses, as in Vasilii Surikov's blue-saturated *A View of the Monument to Peter I* (1870).

Much of nineteenth-century Russian culture, whether out of humane considerations or political convictions, polemicized with or recoiled from the radical innovations forcibly instituted by Peter's visionary pragmatism. As the century neared its close, however, the prolific, cosmopolitan representatives of the World of Art movement, which advocated a European, modernized Russia, revived the spirit of the Petrine era, perhaps most dramatically concretized in the symbolic northern capital. The World of Art

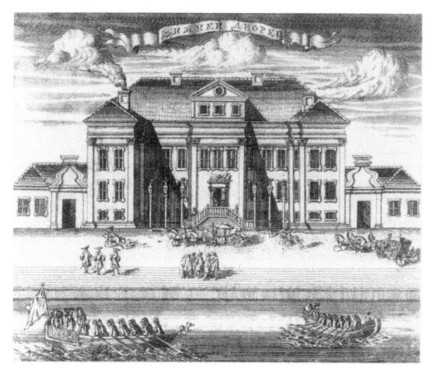

FIGURE 3.6. Aleksei Zubov's etching of the Palace of Peter the Great (1716)
belonged to his series *Panoramas of Petersburg.*

constituted a loose collective, united in its search for innovative forms and
an aesthetic that combined retrospection and novelty, as amply evident in
the collaborative publications of the 1900s that displayed its members' technical proficiency and sophistication.[22] Within this extraordinarily talented
and heterogeneous group, Evgenii Lansere, Anna P. Ostroumova-Lebedeva,
and Mstislav Dobuzhinskii attained renown for their numerous representations of the city, mainly in a historical mode, though one not entirely devoid
of partisanship. Their substantial differences notwithstanding, their works
share three major traits: first, a focus less on the showcased resplendence of
the city than on little-known and smaller-scale areas within it (a tendency
shared by Georgii Lukomskii's guidebook *Old Petersburg* [1917]); second, a
striking dearth of people in the urban landscape—few if any human figures
fracture the spatial continuity, as if the artists conceived of St. Petersburg
as an unpopulated terrain or, perhaps, one quintessentially resistant or

FIGURE 3.7. Aleksei Zubov's *View of St. Petersburg* (1727).

FIGURE 3.8. Vasilii Surikov's intensely atmospheric *View of the Monument of Peter I* (1870).

inimical to human presence; and third, a diversity of artistic media, spanning the gamut from gouache and canvas painting to lithograph. This proliferation of visual media likewise accorded with the broad range of verbal genres devoted to "capturing" or "preserving" the city: Poetry and such prose genres as novels, stories, sketches, guidebooks, and histories all colluded in the massive "museum" enterprise that marks the city and, as we contend in our introduction, may be equated with it.

Evgenii Lansere's Petersburg

Son of the sculptor Evgenii Lansere, grandson of the architect Nikolai Benois, and nephew of the Versailles-enthralled Alexander Benois, whose creative principles exerted a decisive influence on his artistic development, Evgenii Lansere (1875–1946) nurtured a fascination with Peter I and the city he founded—a passion reflected in the wealth of works that he devoted to the "larger than life" tsar. A prolific adept at the historical genre so popular with the World of Art, in drawings, paintings, and lithographs Lansere strived to convey the aura of the Petrine era, and particularly the colossal changes it had ushered in through foreign borrowings, which Lansere implies by the persistent presence of ships. Boats in general, while part of Lansere's detailed, often apparently static renditions of the cityscape, metonymically inscribe mobility, cultural interaction, and imperial expansion—the goals of Peter's comprehensive program of modernization. If juxtaposed with Lansere's many paintings of Peter abroad, these visuals acquire a dynamism that celebrates the vigor and enterprise invested in the creation and accelerated development of the northern Palmyra. For instance, *At the Old Nikol'skii Market* (1901) intimates plenitude through the laden boats clustered in front of the market, in a style of saturation that approximates cinema's "closed form." Less locally and in a manner spatially paralleling cinema's "open form," the painting *Early-18th-Century Petersburg* (1906) depicts a corner of Vasilievskii Island, with the building of the Twelve Colleges running perpendicular to the Neva. Several single-story buildings and the masts of ships skirting the island are visible in the distance as the city goes about its everyday commercial life. The overcast sky and rolling gray waves suggest the battle with the elements that has been a perennial motif in the history of St. Petersburg[23] but that here sooner resembles an

FIGURE 3.9. Evgenii Lansere's *At the Old Nikol'skii Market* (1901), in gouache and watercolor on cardboard, depicts Kolomna, an area rendered memorable by Pushkin's narrative poem *The Little House in Kolomna* (*Domik v Kolomne*, wr. 1830; pd. 1833).

invigorating challenge rather than a fatal, disastrously ungovernable force of arbitrary nature.

No other representative of the retrospective tendency within the World of Art group (Valentin Serov,[24] A. Benois, Konstantin Somov) matched Lansere's enthusiasm for the Petrine era, its beauty, vitality, and accomplishments. And few paintings contradict the literary image of St. Petersburg as forcefully and directly as his portrayal of an amorous couple gaily strolling along the city's sunlit pier in a mood of carefree enjoyment. Above all, Lansere's treatment of space accounts for the ebullience of his vision. Whereas Gogol conveyed the desolation of the city's endless streets and Dostoevsky dwelled on the claustrophobia resulting from poverty-stricken isolation in soul-destroying tenements, Lansere joyously opened up the city to the free expanse of the sea, which promised adventure and liberating participation in the larger world outside the nation's borders. To ally Lansere's emphasis on

FIGURE 3.10. Evgenii Lansere's *Early-Eighteenth-Century Petersburg* (1906),
in tempera on paper, conveys the city's vitality.

the new capital's zest and vibrant promise with the "saintly" line aspect of Petersburg would be misguided, however, for the sheer energy and mobility he
ascribes to the imperial center (moreover, in finely-detailed representations of
concrete phenomena) could not be more remote from the Imaginary of the
literary images eulogizing beauty and the museum project contrived to preserve high culture. In a manner paradoxically reminiscent of the earthbound
Henry Fielding, Lansere engages the vertical and horizontal axes through the
metaphorical metonyms of sea and ship so as to celebrate Petersburg as the
potential for a more intense and ample life of experience, embracing not only
Russia, but all the countries to which Peter's reforms and naval innovations
provided a conduit. Lansere may have painted horizons, but his works imply
an exciting, shoreless world awaiting discovery, and a tsar eager to explore the
world behind the horizon so as to gain a foothold in international culture and
affairs, or, as current jargon has it, "to globalize."

Anna Ostroumova-Lebedeva's Vision

To an even greater extent St. Petersburg dominates the thematics of the
graphic artist and engraver Ostroumova-Lebedeva (1871–1955), whose sizable gallery of city scenes profited from the extensive collaboration between

FIGURE 3.11. Evgenii Lansere's *Promenade on a Pier* (1909), in tempera on cardboard, captures an informal moment on a sunny day.

the World of Art and the Society of St. Eugenia (1896–1920). A publishing house and subsection of the St. Petersburg Committee of the Red Cross, the Society of St. Eugenia was founded in 1881 under the leadership of I. Stepanov.[25] As part of its entrepreneurial agenda, it published guidebooks to Petersburg museums and Russian towns, albums and monographs on modern artists, table-calendars, and illustrated editions of Russian classical literature, such as Pushkin's *Bronze Horseman* with Benois's illustrations (1923). Members of the World of Art who helped to design the Society's printed materials included Ivan Bilibin, Boris Kustodiev, Ostroumova-Lebedeva, Dobuzhinskii, and many others. The chief and ultimately most lucrative item produced by the Society was its black and white or multi-colored postcard, printed with a variety of techniques—color and tinted lithography, xylography (engraving on wood, one of Ostroumova's specialties), phototype, zincography, and helio-engraving. Indeed, if the exuberant, fast-changing 1920s in Russia pioneered the film poster, the 1900s witnessed the rapid rise of the postcard, in large part owing to the indefatigable efforts of the Society of St. Eugenia, which printed catalogues of postcards, mounted exhibitions of them, and in 1904 released a special magazine titled *The Postcard*. During a twenty-year period the Society issued more than six thousand postcards.[26]

A student of Il'ia Repin's, with a two-year stint (1898–1899) in the Parisian studio of the American painter James Whistler, Ostroumova-Lebedeva chose Petersburg as the chief subject of her professional work, primarily realized in the media of watercolor and the easel woodcut. Her engravings of the city, like Dobuzhinskii's watercolors, enjoyed immense popularity when disseminated in the new genre of the postcard, which originated in Western Europe during the 1870s and made its way to Russia probably in the 1890s.[27] The symbiosis between the Society of St. Eugenia and the World of Art, activated through Benois's vigorous exertions, made the Russian picture postcard both a commercially viable item and a cultural genre that eventually benefited from advances in the fast-developing field of photography.

Ostroumova's oeuvre features both "large" and "small" Petersburg, encompassing such imposing settings and structures as Falconet's renowned Peter, the Summer Garden, the Kazan Cathedral, and the Admiralty, on the one hand, and on the other, bridges, sections of the Neva River glimpsed between columns, boats near Biron's palace, pillars lapped by the river, and the like. Her tirelessly reproduced color woodcut of *The Summer Garden* (1902) in winter manages to convey the "hushed softness" of new-fallen snow through delicate hues—the white subtly shading into the pale gray of the surroundings, with the sky a muted gold—and the illusion of an intimately self-contained cushioning: Denuded black trees, their branches intermingled, arch over a woman with two children, also realized in black, creating the impression of the small-scale figures' place in expansive but controlled nature, projected against the background of a solid edifice whose immovable weight emphasizes the contrasting transience of seasons. The juxtaposition of miniature human forms and the magnificent architectural structure superbly catches a moment of "protected," domestic/familial intimacy within a ruptured space, where the bucolic "garden" is installed in the all too public city, whose dimensions are suggested not only by the imposing building, but also by the receding lines of the path within the garden. The image, remarkably free of bathos and self-congratulation, inscribes an experiential oasis, unobtrusively documenting the contradictions of the northern capital, which for decades showcased the lavishness of its architecture and grand art, yet

FIGURE 3.12. Anna Ostroumova-Lebedeva's engraving of *The Summer Garden* (1902), her first color xylograph of the cityscape.

FIGURE 3.13. Anna Ostroumova-Lebedeva's colored woodcut, *Perspective of the Neva* (1908).

during the blockade approximated the skeletal appearance of its ravaged, war-worn residents.

Between 1908 and 1910 Ostroumova produced a series of colored woodcuts of the city's famous, central spots, as well as its obscure, neglected nooks, and she continued to "record" the city from different perspectives, under diverse conditions, at various times of day until the end of her life. She returned to some locations, such as the Summer Garden, more then once, to catch nuances and transformations unnoticed by the average eye.[28] Her illustrations for Vladimir Kurbatov's book *St. Petersburg* (1912) comprised black-and-white engravings that "fixed" the appearance of various, often ostensibly unprepossessing, locations from diverse vantage points. Similar engravings by her illustrated the 1922 edition of Antsiferov's *Soul of Petersburg (Dusha Peterburga)*, a fundamental "city text" for culture mavens seeking orientation around the city and particularly intent on retracing its web of literary associations.

Stylistically nothing significant distinguishes Ostroumova's delineation of Petersburg from her depiction of Venice or Paris. Unlike Lansere, committed to the vision of a vital, youthful city teeming with opportunities, or Dobuzhinskii, whose cityscapes transmit his unease at the alienating aspects of modern technology, Ostroumova eschewed both endorsement and opprobrium, focusing instead on documentation in an objective key in multiple media. While some may find her cityscapes bland by comparison with Dobuzhinskii's, the dimensions and quality of her output testify to her status as Petersburg's principal, and most steadfast, visual chronicler. Ultimately, Ostroumova remained independent of the interplay between saintly and unsaintly Petersburg, her passion for time-sensitive documentation removing her from the partisanship that characterized the literature and, to an appreciably lesser extent, the visual art of her contemporaries.

Mstislav Dobuzhinskii's City

The foremost and certainly the most versatile of the three artists was Dobuzhinskii (1875–1957), to whom the young Vladimir Nabokov, who took private drawing lessons from him, dedicated one of his Petersburg poems, "*UT PICTURE POESIS*" (April 1926).[29] Dobuzhinskii's urban images extend beyond Russia to include Wilno [now Vilnius], Naples, London, Bruges, and other locales. Like many members of the World of Art, Dobuzhinskii in his graphics practiced the art of the silhouette, so popular in the eighteenth century, but in his more experimental stage designs during the latter half of his career (in emigration in Lithuania, then in England and the United States), he anticipated future trends. Though his numerous renditions of the northern Russian capital made such an impact that people spoke of "Dobuzhinskii's city," they were remarkably diversified in genre and mood, comprising self-standing images, literary illustrations, and set designs for plays and operas.[30]

Dobuzhinskii's attitude toward cities in general and Petersburg in particular was productively complicated. Emotionally attached to the urban centers (and especially Petersburg) in which he spent most of his life, he nonetheless realized the potential devastation of the human psyche by the increasing industrialization and mechanization rapidly transforming modern cities into depersonalized spaces for automatons. His oeuvre richly reflects that ambivalence. Whereas his lithographs executed for postcards published by the Society of St. Eugenia, such as *The Alexandrine Theater*

АЛЕКСАНДРИНСКІЙ ТЕАТРЪ

FIGURE 3.14. Mstislav Dobuzhinskii's *Alexandrine Theater* (1902), a lithograph
created for a postcard published by the Society of St. Eugenia.

(1902), *Fontanka, Peter I's Summer Palace* (1902), and *The Moika by the New
Admiralty* (1903), offer neutral, elegant images of noteworthy monuments,
produced in a linear-rhythmic pattern on a flat surface, many other works
focus on what Alla Gusarova refers to as the city's "seamy side."[31] Acknowl-
edging Dostoevsky's influence on his artistic perception of the imperial capital, Dobuzhinskii captured its "non-imperial" aspects—"the outskirts, dimly
lit, empty, and sad. In [. . . his] works, Petersburg's walls, roofs, and chim-
neys formed fantastic landscapes filled with anxiety and anticipation."[32] The
artist confessed, "Those sleepy canals, endless fences, dark wells of
courtyards—it all astonished me with its sharply drawn, even eerie features.
Everything seemed extraordinarily original, imbued with bitter poetry and
mystery."[33] As Gusarova astutely observes, Dobuzhinskii sought in city
streets motifs that would express the essence of his time, collecting what he
called the city's "grimaces and oddities"—its bizarre, incoherent elements,
materialized in the fences, roofs, yards, signboards, small back-streets, and
vast bare walls,[34] with vagrants sprawled on an embankment, dwarfed by
their surroundings.

FIGURE 3.15. Mstislav Dobuzhinskii's *An Embankment in St. Petersburg* (1908), showing its less illustrious residents.

Dobuzhinskii's seventeen drawings of 1922 for Dostoevsky's *White Nights* (*Belye nochi*), realized in a graphically austere fashion, rhythmically alternate white paper with patches of black ink and virtuoso linear drawings,[35] starkly creating an atmosphere of quiet despair.[36] Desolate stretches of water and streets emphasize the loneliness of the individual in the modern city.[37] Like his illustrations for Nikolai Antsiferov's *Dostoevsky's Petersburg* (*Peterburg Dostoevskogo*, 1923), they contrast with Benois's to *The Bronze Horseman*, for they privilege not the wide squares and the Neva, but the outlying districts, dead-end lanes with rickety streetlights, dank courtyards, and dark, "meandering canals in which the reflections of the surrounding tenements tremble and collapse."[38] In that respect they succumb to and reproduce the atmosphere of the literary source.

Bleakness and understated horror suffuse Dobuzhinskii's cityscapes of the 1920s, particularly the eerie, almost surrealistic *Petrograd in 1920* (1920), which stylistically recalls Evgenii Zamiatin's "The Dragon" ("Drakon," 1918), "Mamai" (1921), and "The Cave" ("Peshchera," 1922), modernist prose cameos of stark terror, grounded in matrix metaphors for atavism in the New World of post-revolutionary Russia. Dobuzhinskii's *Night in St. Petersburg* (1924) likewise projects an existential abyss through the ominous illusion that inanimate objects have acquired a life in the empty, dark streets of the alienating city. The painting recalls his earlier Hoffmannesque *Hairdresser's Window* (1906), in which mannequins with well-defined faces contrast with a shadowy, anonymous passerby under an uncannily arachnoid street lamp.[39] These images offer twentieth-century reprisals of Gogol's nightmarish cityscapes.

Dobuzhinskii's album of autolithographs, *St. Petersburg in 1921* (1923), which became a classic of Russian printed graphic art,[40] represented his farewell to the city, which, as he later recalled in emigration, "was dying before my eyes with a death of incredible beauty, and I tried to capture as best I could its terrible, deserted, and wounded look."[41] In short, Dobuzhinskii's vision of Petersburg, not unlike the poet Mandelstam's, darkened with the years, partly in response to Russia's seemingly endless historical convulsions: World War I, the revolutions of 1917, and the Civil War, which not only cost numerous human lives, but eliminated a fundamental sense of stability within a country and a city decimated by relentless struggle and strife. In that sense, Dobuzhinskii's art of the later period embraces the unsaintly tendency in Petersburg's inscriptions.

FIGURE 3.16. Mstislav Dobuzhinskii's illustration for Dostoevsky's *White Nights* (1922).

FIGURE 3.17. Mstislav Dobuzhinskii's illustration for Dostoevsky's *White Nights* (1922).

FIGURE 3.18. Mstislav Dobuzhinskii's chilling *Petrograd in 1920* (1920),
in gouache and pencil on cardboard.

Conclusion: *Plus ça change* ... or the Shrinking Head and Its Mega-Concept

In June 1991, shortly before Leningrad recovered its old name of St. Petersburg, a new monument to Peter the Great was unveiled at the Peter-
Paul (Petropavlovskaia) Fortress, which figures so prominently in visual
representations of the city. Crafted by the émigré artist/sculptor Mikhail
Shemiakin, now a resident of the United States, the statue is unusual in
that for the wigless, disproportionately small head Shemiakin reached back
into history, so as to cast a life mask of the tsar made by Rastrelli in 1719.[42]
That head, we might recall, conceived of "the window onto Europe." Petersburgers reportedly have named the monument "Bronze-Stay-at-Home" and
"Peter IV," since the structure is the fourth monument to Peter the Great in
the city.[43] A scant four months after its official installation, following impassioned debate and the failed coup against Gorbachev, the city Peter
founded once more became St. Petersburg. Brodsky hailed the event with
the words, "Returning the city's previous name is a means of at least hinting
at continuity, if not establishing it. [...] It is much better for those [who
will be born in St. Petersburg] to live in a city that bears the name of a saint

FIGURE 3.19. Mstislav Dobuzhinskii's eerie *Hairdresser's Window* (1906), in watercolor, gouache, and charcoal on paper, evokes the fictional worlds of Gogol and E.T.A. Hoffmann.

than that of a devil."[44] Brodsky's evocation of the devil stirs Gogol's shade, just as the circle of nomenclature closes.

The year 2003, which marked St. Petersburg's tercentenary, completed another circle—that of ritualistic activities and their chroniclers. Amid the "no holds barred" celebrations during the summer that transformed the city's streets into a noisy kaleidoscope of living color, television cameras captured festivities recalling previous eras rendered familiar by the visual historian of Russian "types" and seasonal rituals, Boris Kustodiev. Contrary to its intentions, not unlike Sokurov's *Russian Ark*, continuously screened during the 2003 celebrations, Kustodiev's *Night Gala on the Neva* (1923) provides a salutary reminder of how a visually stunning city, originally oriented to the future, with the passage of time metamorphoses into a weather-beaten museum of artistic treasures accumulated in its distant past. Ironically, owing to the radical makeover of Moscow during Iurii Luzhkov's extended mayorship, Russians now view not the capital, but Petersburg, with its crumbling edifices, peeling paint, and all too visible lack of renovation, as the repository of Russia's national traditions. That status seemed confirmed in the Russian Museum's exhibit, "St. Petersburg: Portrait of a City and Its Citizens (Sankt-Peterburg: Portret goroda i gorozhan)," during the tercentenary celebrations, which predictably displayed works by all three artists, who remain the city's "visual historians." Peter the Great's bold vision of the future, in other words, has devolved into a casket of former glories for inert contemplation, not catalytic inspiration.

Notes

1. On the emotional impact of the changes in the city's name, see the chapters by Khazan and Torlone in the present volume.

2. Susan Glasser, "St. Petersburg Fights Rap as Crime Capital," *Washington Post* (October 15, 2002). Despite recent increases in salaries, Sibneft's plans to transfer tax registration from Omsk to Petersburg (Teagarden), the construction of a new General Motors plant in the city (Dranitsyna), and the controversial plans for building the monumental Gazprom City skyscraper on the Neva (Myers), only a fervent optimist would judge Petersburg's current status hope-inspiring. See Michael Teagarden, "Sibnest to Change Name as Petersburg Becomes Home," *The St. Petersburg Times* (April 4, 2006). http://www.sptimes.ru/index.php?action_id=2&story_id+17213. Accessed 12 December

2006; Yekaterina Dranitsyna, "GM Unveils Petersburg Plans," *The St. Petersburg Times* (June 2, 2006). http://www.sptimes.ru/index.php?action_id=2&story_id=17769. Accessed 9 December 2006; Steven Lee Myers, "A Russian Skyscraper Plan Divides a Horizontal City," *The New York Times* (December 2, 2006). http://www.nytimes.com/2006/12/02/arts/design/02gazp.html?ei=5088&en=d44783da756cb3fb&ex=1322. Accessed 10 December 2006.

3. For a vivid critique of the celebrations, see the excellent study by Elena Hellberg-Hirn, *Imperial Imprints: Post-Soviet St. Petersburg* (Helsinki, 2003), chapter 13 and epilogue.

4. Yulia Latynina, "St. Pete's Criminal-Business-Political Elite," *Moscow Times* (June 4, 2003).

5. E-mail message on SEELANGS by Alina Israeli, October 4, 2002.

6. For an imaginative and highly selective encapsulation of that past one can do no better than to see Aleksandr Sokurov's original and justly acclaimed though ideologically blinkered film, *Russian Ark* (2002).

7. Moreover, the Russian tradition ups the ante by almost invariably, it seems, contrasting the intellectual, abstract, and forced origins of the new capital with the more provincial but organic development of Moscow. During the post-Soviet era, however, the seismic changes in budget-rich Moscow increasingly have marginalized Petersburg into a museum piece in dire need of renovation.

8. See also Semen Bobrov's "Torzhestvennyi den' stoletiia ot osnovaniia grada Sv. Petra maiia 16 dnia 1803." Bobrov added a note to the poem's title: "Izvestno, chto S.-Peterburg zalozhen v nachale proshlogo veka, t.e. 1703 goda, na takom meste, gde po nizkoi i topkoi pochke kazalos' by nevozmozhnym postroenie stol' prekrasnogo goroda, kakov on nyne" (Sinel'nikov, *Peterburg*, 38). For three centuries of poetry about the city, see Mikhail Sinel'nikov, ed., *Peterburg, Petrograd, Leningrad v russkoi poezii* (St. Petersburg, 1999).

9. Mark Altshuller, "Peterburg glazami odopistsev XVIII veka," in Roger Bartlett, Gabriela Lehmann-Carli, eds., *Eighteenth-Century Russia: Society, Culture, Economy* (New Brunswick, London, 2007), 3–16.

10. The line recalls the seventh stanza of Murav'ev's poem, which opens, "Ia liubliu tvoi kupal'ny. . . ." (Sinel'nikov, *Peterburg*, 36).

11. On the ubiquity of this figure in the literature and art of this era, see Bram Dijkstra, *Idols of Perversity: Fantasies of Feminine Evil in Fin-de-Siècle Culture* (New York/London, 1986).

12. On Dostoevsky's fraught attitude toward St. Petersburg, see chapter 1 by Brumfield.

13. Solomon Volkov, *St. Petersburg: A Cultural History* (New York, 1995), 447.

14. Cited in Ibid., 526.

15. One of the most recent additions is Tatyana Tolstaya's profoundly visual gnomic sketch, titled "Snow in St. Petersburg," which opens with the Hemingwayesque sentence, "St. Petersburg has one sea, 101 islands, and endless rivers." Tatyana Tolstaya, *Pushkin's Children: Writings on Russia and Russians* (Boston, 2003), 214.

16. Volkov's erudite and disarmingly readable cultural history of St. Petersburg impresses all the more against the rather lackluster background of narrower studies that tend to repeat their forerunners. See also Katerina Clark's ambitious, fact-packed

Petersburg: Crucible of Cultural Revolution, published the same year by Harvard University Press (1995). For a handy collection of poems about Petersburg, see *Peterburg v russkoi poezii*, comp. M. V. Otradin (Leningrad, 1988).

17. The incommensurate proportions of Evgenii at decisive moments in the narrative vis-à-vis his surroundings and the emperor's statue materialize the concept of what subsequently became called the alienation of the "little man" in the big city.

18. The formidably prolific Dobuzhinskii also provided illustrations for the 1905 edition of Pushkin's "Stantsionnyi smotritel'" and for dozens of other literary works by sundry authors.

19. Alla Rosenfeld, "The World of Art Group: Book and Poster Design" in Alla Rosenfeld, ed., *Defining Russian Graphic Arts, 1898–1934: From Diaghilev to Stalin* (New Brunswick, NJ, 1999), 79.

20. Ivan Bilibin's considerable fame, for instance, rests almost exclusively on his illustrations, principally of folklore.

21. Zubov's etchings graced the pages of the city's paper *Vedomosti*, and he worked as an official visual chronicler of the city's developments. His older brother, Ivan, likewise documented the city through etchings.

22. For sensitive, thorough analyses of the history and aesthetics of the World of Art, see the following lavishly illustrated volumes: Vsevolod Petrov and Alexander Kamensky, eds., *The World of Art Movement in Early 20th-Century Russia* (Leningrad, 1991); Evgeniia Petrova, ed., *The World of Art/Mir Iskusstva* (Helsinki/St. Petersburg, 1998–1999).

23. Quite apart from the literary preoccupation with the floods, inclement weather, and obfuscating mists endemic to the city, book illustrations and artists' depictions of St. Petersburg also tended to portray the city in the midst of rain. See, for instance, Evgeniia Petrova, ed., *The World of Art/Mir iskusstva*, to whose excellent commentaries I am indebted.

24. On Serov's portrayals of Peter I, see Petrov and Kamensky, *The World of Art Movement*, 84–90.

25. Rosenfeld, "The World of Art Group," 87.

26. For detailed information about the development of the postcard in Russia, see the copiously illustrated studies by Iurii Kombolin, *Pozdravitel'naia otkryka v Rossii (konets XIX—nachala XX veka)* (St. Petersburg, 1994); and M. Chapkina, *Khudozhestvennaia otkrytka: K stoletiiu otkrytki v Rossii* (Moscow, 1993).

27. Kombolin, *Pozdravitel'naia otkryka v Rossii*, 14, 16.

28. In this respect, she resembles Claude Monet and his repeated renditions of the same water lilies, cathedral, haystacks, and so on, in an attempt to discover and convey the effects of changing light on phenomena.

29. Another Nabokov lyric about Petersburg, titled "K rodine" (December 1924), intriguingly conflates the poet's body with the city's ("Tak vse telo—tol'ko obraz tvoi,/ i dusha—kak nebo nad Nevoi" (Sinel'nikov, *Peterburg*, 403).

30. The foremost contemporary specialist on Dobuzhinskii is Alla Gusarova, author of a first-rate monograph, *Mstislav Dobuzhinski*, Moscow, 1982.

31. Ibid., 9.

32. Volkov, *St. Petersburg*, 225.

33. Ibid., 224.

34. Gusarova, *Mstislav Dobuzhinskii*, 10.

35. Elena Petinova, "The Graphic Culture of the World of Art," in Petrova, ed., *The World of Art/Mir Iskusstv*, 195.

36. Volkov, *St. Petersburg*, 225.

37. Rosenfeld, "The World of Art Group," 89.

38. Petinova, "The Graphic Culture of the World of Art," 195.

39. For the horrors of urban existence Dobuzhinskii exploited the trope of the spider in highly inventive ways, also resorting to variations on the spider web to convey entrapment. See, for example, his illustration for Konstantin Bal'mont's cycle of poems "Khorovod vremeni" (Circle Dance of Time) for the journal *Zolotoe runo* (1907) and the sketch titled "Flying" for his series *Gorodskie sny* (City Dreams 1909).

Gusarova refers to Dobuzhinskii's image of the "octopus-city" or "spider-city." Gusarova, *Mstislav Dobuzhinskii*, 18.

40. Ibid., 211.

41. Volkov, *St. Petersburg*, 224.

42. Ibid., 544.

43. For information on the monument, see "Monument to Peter the Great" at http://www.saint-petersburg.com/monuments/peter-1st-mikhail-shemiakin.asp, accessed August 9, 2005.

44. Volkov, *St. Petersburg*, 544.

Four

A Tale of Two Cities: Ancient Rome and St. Petersburg in Mandelstam's Poetry

Zara Torlone

St. Petersburg as Rome

An Italian architect who helped to shape the imperial image of St. Petersburg, Carlo Rossi viewed the city as another Rome and drew his chief inspiration from the grandeur and opulence associated with the ancient empire. In 1802 the twenty-six-year-old Rossi, son of an Italian ballerina who retired to the suburbs of St. Petersburg, studied in Rome under the tutelage of the famous architect and designer Vincenzo Brenna, whose work was greatly influenced by Roman palatial interiors. Rossi returned to the Russian capital intending to create a new architectural style that would "surpass that which the Romans [had] considered sufficient for their monuments."[1] He fulfilled his dream by creating numerous buildings, among these the Mikhailovsky Palace, which blended the ancient style with Rossi's own vision.

Subsequent Russian artists and intellectuals likened St. Petersburg to Rome, often admiringly, sometimes pejoratively, while an energetic debate continued over which of Russia's two capitals, Moscow or St. Petersburg, should be considered true heir to the classical tradition that connected Russia to the West. Since "Moscow symbolized everything national," and was embedded in religious tradition deriving from Constantinople, it came to be seen as the Third Rome and a rightful heir to a long tradition.[2]

The city built by Peter the Great changed that perception in the minds of Russian intellectuals. As the Russian court gradually migrated from Moscow to St. Petersburg, the city became the center of everything sophisticated, refined, and trendy. Moscow suddenly seemed a merchants' capital, unlike the magnificent city on the Neva River to which Western aristocrats, architects, and fashion-conscious courtiers flocked, mesmerized by its sprawling grandeur and limitless wealth. Paradoxically, the new city introduced the meaning of ancient cultural legacy into Russian society[3] and materialized the nation's desire to be part of the Western heritage. As Dmitrii Likhachev aptly observed, ultimately, "Petersburg is not between the East and the West, it is the East and the West simultaneously."[4]

While Slavophiles saw the city as an alien, Westernized locus that drained the country's lifeblood and created unprecedented slums ridden by poverty and disease,[5] for the majority, St. Petersburg became not only the "window onto Europe," as Alexander Pushkin phrased it, but also the only Russian city culturally connected to Greco-Roman antiquity and a larger Western heritage. For many, Mikhail Kozlovskii's statue of the renowned eighteenth-century general Aleksandr Suvorov erected on the Field of Mars evoked the statue of Marcus Aurelius on the Capitoline Hill in Rome. Indeed, according to Ryszard Przybylski, "All the great architects of Russian Classicism—Rastrelli, Quarenghi, and Zakharov—attempted to make the city on the Neva look like the Eternal City on the Tiber."[6] Russian poets likewise identified St. Petersburg with Rome, through a loaded metaphor that enabled them to present their city as a victory over fate, time, and space.

The Acmeist poet Osip Mandelstam, especially influenced and fascinated by classical antiquity and the legacy of Rome, saw in the ancient seat of empire not only a symbolic representation of perennial culture, but also a means of understanding his own city and his own time within the limits of the Russian and then the Soviet empires. This chapter examines the significance of Rome in Mandelstam's poetry and analyzes his St. Petersburg poems so as to gauge the extent to which his treatment of Rome and Roman themes converges with his view of the "New Rome."

Such a comparison reveals Mandelstam's ambivalent perception of his own city. On the one hand, he depicts Petersburg, with its imperial facades and architecture, as a proud heir of the classical heritage. On the other, he conceives of the northern capital as the wounded, tortured city of loss and sorrow. Mandelstam's unusual background, rich in connections with the classical world, illuminates not only his identification of Petersburg with Rome, but also his contradictory attitude toward both imperial capitals and the values they represented.

The Poet and His Times

That background and his early experiences account for much of Mandelstam's cosmopolitanism, his capacity to make connections across national boundaries. The poet was born in Warsaw (January 15, 1891) to the family of a merchant who descended from Spanish Jews and was fascinated with European culture. The family moved to St. Petersburg, where in 1900 Mandelstam entered the Tenishev School, one of the best institutions in pre-revolutionary Russia, where education included the study of foreign languages, classical and European history, art and sciences. The Tenishev School by its untraditional encouragement of creative thinking unquestionably helped the future poet to conceive of culture in universal terms—as a unified entity not divided by the borders of geography, customs, or language. Moreover, after graduation, Mandelstam spent several years abroad, especially in France and Italy, and in 1909–1910 studied philosophy and philology at Heidelberg University, then a major center of classical philology. His passionate interest in the ancient world, which developed there, led to, and further intensified with, his participation in the so-called "Tower" (Bashnia) of the poet and classical scholar Viacheslav Ivanov. Evenings at Ivanov's home (the Tower) functioned as a creative laboratory of sorts for the St. Petersburg poets and artists who gathered there to find new modes of artistic expression.

In this milieu, Mandelstam soon allied himself with the poetics of Innokentii Annenskii, which heralded the Acmeist movement. Spearheaded by Mandelstam, Anna Akhmatova, and Nikolai Gumilev, Acmeism adopted a "longing for world culture" as part of its credo. These changes in the orientation of Russian poetry coincided with dramatic political changes that culminated in the October Revolution of 1917. While many elected to emigrate in the aftermath of the Revolution, Mandelstam—whose poems focus not on the contemporary, but on the timeless, and strive to unite Russian culture to the ancient world—opted to stay. Indeed, some of his poems, like Boris Pasternak's, welcomed the Revolution,[7] though he remained loyal to the principles of Acmeism and explored the theme of classical antiquity in his verses.

Mandelstam's life and his poetry make clear that he never adjusted to the new Soviet reality, and his few attempts at politically conscious poetry proved feeble and unconvincing. As the lyrical "I" arrogantly declares in his poem "Net, nikogda, nichei ia ne byl sovremennik" (1924):

> I was never anyone's contemporary, no,
> That kind of honor's not right for me. [8]

Such notable exceptions as Nikolai Nekrasov and Vladimir Mayakovsky notwithstanding, poets are rarely the contemporaries of the events that pass outside their windows. Certainly, Mandelstam considered himself a contemporary of the world and its culture. His stance did not mean, however, that he did not acutely feel an affinity with the events transpiring in Russia. He simply preferred to view them against the larger picture of the history of the world. For him every great city had to be viewed in the context of his own. This "uncommon visage"—to invoke Joseph Brodsky's words—made him somewhat of a pariah in his own society, but also made him an influential, eloquent spokesman for the feelings of loss and nostalgia among the intelligentsia unleashed by the 1917 October Revolution. During his lifetime, however, this indifference and dismissal of the Revolution and its new ideology did not win him popularity with the new government. Along with many intellectuals Mandelstam was arrested in 1938 and disappeared into the abyss of the GULAG. He died of hunger and unbearable conditions in December of the same year somewhere in the concentration camps near Vladivostok.

Mandelstam and Rome

Mandelstam's interest in classical themes is obvious. Yet the many manifestations of his Hellenism did not include frequent, explicit reference to any cities or provinces of ancient Greece in his poetry, while a significant number of his poems are devoted to the city of Rome.[9] Mandelstam's approach to ancient Rome is remarkably consistent. The eternal city is not material. It exists as an idealized entity, an unbroken focal point of human existence, a timeless symbol rather than a network of streets and buildings. Furthermore Mandelstam limits his idealized perception of Rome only to the ancient city. Medieval or contemporary Rome and Italy do not emerge in his poetry in the same haze of unreality as the city of the Caesars, which in his verses acquires a mythical dimension. The poet's understanding of Rome as a symbol is best expressed in a poem written in 1917:

> Let all the flowering city-names
> Stroke the ear with their tiny, brief importance.
> It's not Rome, as a city, that lasts forever,
> But man's place in the universe.
>
> Kings try to take it,
> Priests use it as an argument for war,
> and without it houses, and altars,
> are contemptible rubble, pitiful, wretched.[10]

This poem glorifies the human ability to conquer nature and create culture. Though it is a place of houses and altars—the places of life and worship—what makes these constructions important is the human creator. The mighty of the world—kings and priests—oppose the creative force of man. Pagan Rome thus for Mandelstam is a unified and wholesome body that embraces the entire civilization created by brutality, greed, and conquest.[11]

Mandelstam makes this symbolic view of Rome explicit in another poem composed in 1917 "Priroda tot zhe Rim" ("Nature is Roman, and mirrors Rome"):[12]

> Nature is just like Rome, and is reflected in it.
> We see its images of civic grandeur
> In the transparent air as in a blue circus,
> In the forum of the fields and in the colonnades of groves,
>
> Nature is just like Rome, and again it seems
> Inane for us to trouble the gods,—
> There are entrails of those sacrificed to fathom war,
> Slaves to be silent and stones with which to build.[13]

Here Mandelstam expresses an idea that persists throughout his poetry: the controversy produced by culture when man attempts to impose his order and artifice on the spontaneity of nature.[14] In this respect his perception of ancient Rome is rather unusual, differing significantly from the ancient poets' view of their own city. Horace, for instance, viewed Rome's urban invasion into nature as corrupting and destructive. In Mandelstam's vision of ancient Rome there is no urban defilement of nature's serenity. Instead, Mandelstam links three representative elements of Roman urban culture: the circus, forum, and colonnade, with three aspects of nature: blue sky, fields, and groves. This harmony of nature and culture, this "natural city" creates a harmonic locale for the man who feels like a citizen of the world within it.

The dichotomy between nature and culture is resolved in this poem through the simple solution of declaring Rome as the city where everything has its proper place and purpose. The controversy that troubled the human spirit for centuries—man's guilt over destroying nature while creating culture—is defused by Mandelstam with one word: Rome. Neither Mandelstam's questions nor his answers are new.[15] Rome derives its might from having followed the perfect model: nature. The circus is created in the image of the sky, the forum "copies" wide-open fields, and the colonnades "mirror" sacred groves. "Man's place in the universe" is clearly defined by Mandelstam in this poem, which posits the attainment of a perfect symbiosis between nature and culture, epitomized by Rome.

Ryszard Przybylski offers another interpretation of the lines cited above.[16] He argues that that if Rome is created in nature's image, then the city, like any living organism, must obey the laws existent in nature. These laws are often cruel and governed by the power of the stronger species that subjugates and destroys the weak. Since the founders of Rome were suckled by a she-wolf, making the citizens of Rome wolf cubs, Rome is a ruthless creature unconcerned with morality. Rome's foundations rest on conquests and brutal force far removed from ethical considerations. Thus, the "natural" of Rome is amoral. In my view, Mandelstam never saw Rome as a city that deems itself beyond ethics and morality. In one of his essays, Mandelstam reveals his approach to antiquity: "Poetry as a whole is always directed toward a more or less remote, unknown addressee, whose existence a poet cannot doubt unless he doubts himself."[17] Rome for Mandelstam was precisely that kind of addressee, idealized and remote, a universal idea rather than a city whose streets he walked and in whose buildings he dwelled. In his Roman themes he is very much a romantic in the manner of Vasilii Zhukovskii, who perceived antiquity as a life-affirming, bright world, now lost forever. That nostalgic vision of Rome as a powerful locus of ruined glory, the grave of sublimity, also reflected the sense of irrevocable loss that some Russians felt after the dramatic changes of 1917. For Mandelstam, at least in this poem, Rome is the metaphor for a might and power that are not enforced but natural, hence the equation between Rome and nature. The poem makes no mention of the cruel laws of nature, the survival of the fittest, to which Przybylski refers, because for Mandelstam these considerations are irrelevant. Whatever the ruthlessness of nature, Mandelstam views human laws as much more ruthless.

While Mandelstam mentions no Greek cities in his poetry, Rome challenges St. Petersburg as the poet's most frequent addressee, for the Rome of the Caesars is a "paradise lost" for Mandelstam, an imagined entity opposed yet kindred to the reality of his own city. Mandelstam conceives of Rome and his own city as almost the same civilization, with the former transformed and moved to the North.

That feeling of the lost, ideal city led Mandelstam to yet another Roman theme that reflected his relationship with Petersburg: the theme of separation and, consequently, a nostalgia of the poet separated from his city. Mandelstam's Rome poems addressing the theme of exile can easily be mapped onto his attempt to hold onto the "old" Petersburg, reflecting his nostalgia and pain for the "dying" city as it becomes Petrograd, the alien and foreign entity bred by the Revolution.[18]

The theme of separation from Rome is thoroughly explored in the poems that evoke Roman poet Ovid's exile by Octavian Augustus from the city he never ceased to miss.[19] The last stanza of Mandelstam's poem "About Simple and Crude Times" (1914) ("O vremenakh prostykh i grubykh,") specifically evokes Ovid's separation from Rome as a possible analogy for his own yearning:

> Like Ovid, his love turning
> stale, blending Rome and snow in his songs,
> singing ox carts
> in the barbarians' plodding lines.[20]

This poem offers the traditional image of Ovid as a man oppressed by misery, mourning the loss of the only city suitable for living. It echoes to some degree Pushkin's evocation of Ovid, written during his exile in Moldova (1820–1823). In the poem "To Ovid" (1821) Pushkin's depiction of Ovid's plight corresponds to Ovid's own pleas in his exile poetry *Tristia* (*The Poems of Sadness*) and *Epistulae Ex Ponto* (*Letters from the Sea*), where he portrays with disdain the region of Tomi, the place of his exile near the Black Sea. Pushkin accepts the general tone of Ovid's sadness about being away from his homeland but replaces the Roman poet's treatment of the Getae country with a much warmer depiction. The idea of exile, however, remains mournfully Ovidian even if brightened by Pushkin's optimistic stanza encouraging Ovid to be happy with his unrivaled poetic immortality. Mandelstam also adopts the lamenting tone in his 1918 poem titled *Tristia* ("Ia izuchil nauku rasstavan'ia"/"I have learned the science of separation"), which evokes Tibullus as well as Ovid, and translates the theme of exile into that of separation from the object of love.[21]

The poem that explicitly and curiously alludes to Ovid, written in 1915, completely reconfigures Ovid's exile as a tragic event:

Horses graze, neighing happily,
and the valley takes on a Roman rust;
time's transparent rapids sweep away
the dry gold of classical spring.

I'll think of Caesar's fine features,
this autumn, trampling oak leaves
thick on deserted paths—
that feminine face, that crafty little nose-hook!

Here, far from Capitol and Forum,
where Nature withers, peaceful,
I hear Augustus' name and, on the world's edge,
hear years rolling like a majestic apple.

Let sorrow be lucid, in my old age:
I was born in Rome, Rome is mine again.
Cheerful old Autumn was my she-wolf
and Caesar's month, August, smiled at me.[22]

Despite the obvious absence of Ovid in this poem, and its first-person singular authorial persona, the allusion to Ovid's exile can hardly be missed. The poem functions as a farewell letter to Rome and to Ovid's nostalgia for her. Old age has come to the poet who is banished from the city of his youth, but the resultant "sorrow" becomes "lucid" and the autumn of his life becomes a nourishing she-wolf. However, the poem can be also viewed as

Mandelstam's own perception of Rome as the city that never leaves its off-spring, no matter where they go.

Ovid, of course, was born not in Rome, but in Sulmona. Moreover, in his poetry he never expressed any particular fondness for the month of August or for the autumn. Thus *mesiats tsezarei* ("the month of Caesars") does not make much sense in an Ovidian context, though it makes sense in the context of another exile, Petr Chaadaev, with whom Mandelstam was preoccupied during the same time.[23] In Mandelstam's article on Chaadaev we read: "And so in August of 1825, in a little seaside village near Brighton, a foreigner appeared whose bearing combined the solemnity of a bishop with the correctness of a worldly mannequin."[24] As Victor Terras points out, this is the only mention of the month in the whole article, and "it refers to an event of import and *ulybnulsia* does not seem out of place to describe it."[25] In the same poem Mandelstam combines two different levels of consciousness linking together the stories of two exiles, just as he links throughout his poetry the "tales" of Rome and St. Petersburg. Mandelstam's choice of Ovid, particularly Ovid in exile, reveals not only an attempt on Mandelstam's part to re-center and reinterpret the present through the past, but through a past that was itself radically de-centered and self-alienated.[26]

In Ovid's poetry of exile, the country of the Getae, the land of his banishment, is a barren terrain deprived of trees and the joy of bountiful nature. But Mandelstam depicts a very picturesque landscape, with Ovid wandering amid fallen oak leaves while horses graze peacefully in pastures. Mandelstam transforms the landscape that Ovid himself described as the place of his exile to render his Ovid inseparable from Rome. The second stanza also echoes Ovid's *Epistolae ex Ponto* II, 8, which describes the portraits of the imperial family that he recently received from Rome. Though exiled by the emperor Augustus and sentenced to the outskirts of the empire, he remains unwavering in his loyalty to Augustus. The only line that suggests animosity is the reference to Augustus' "feminine face" and his "crafty" nose, which nonetheless are called "prekrasnye cherty" ("fine features"). Another remarkable aspect of this poem is that the poet does not return to his beloved city; it is the city that returns to him. The poet ultimately triumphs over his fate, inasmuch as a sovereign cannot truly banish the poet from the city that defines him. Whoever is a creation of Roman culture always possesses a degree of *Romanitas*, even in miserable Tomi, "on the world's edge." This poem about Ovid's plight as an exile is dauntingly optimistic and can be interpreted through Mandelstam's relationship to his own Rome—St. Petersburg. Indeed, Mandelstam returns to the theme of exile and nostalgia in his poems on St. Petersburg ("Ia vernulsia v moi gorod" and "V Peterburge my soidemsia snova").[27] His "rewriting" of Ovid's historical exile helps us to better understand how Mandelstam felt about his own "internal" exile from post-revolutionary St. Petersburg.[28]

Mandelstam's St. Petersburg

One of the many Russian poets to become infatuated with St. Petersburg, Alexander Pushkin immortalized its image in his *Bronze Horseman* by showing the most magnificent as well as the deeply devastating aspects of the mighty polis (see Helena Goscilo's commentary on the poem in this collection). In the Russian poetry of the twentieth century, St. Petersburg emerged as a "Third Rome," not in a Muscovite, Christian sense, but rather as a seat of a new, vigorous, and, more importantly, secular empire. Mandelstam, whose poetry is imbued with images of Greco-Roman antiquity, wanted to see his own city of St. Petersburg as another Rome of Caesars. Yet for him Peter's city, unlike Rome, was not an immaterial, idealized entity. Anna Akhmatova observed that he "managed to be the last writer about Petersburg mores— precise, vivid, dispassionate, and unique. In his writing, the half-forgotten and many times vilified streets reappear in all their freshness."[29]

Whereas Rome for Mandelstam was an eternal ideal of harmony with nature, he changes the relationship between his city and his poetic text as the imperial St. Petersburg transforms into the city of loss and nostalgia. The city, forever changing, underwent numerous transformations in his poetry, particularly after 1917. In this fluctuating image of the city one can see Mandelstam's contribution to the "Petersburg mythos" which emerged in the art of the early twentieth century.[30] The St. Petersburg "syndrome," as Goscilo argues in her contribution to this volume, was perpetuated in paintings by Mstislav Dobuzhinskii and Alexander Benois, poems by Alexander Blok, and Andrei Bely's novel, all of whom, each in his own way, re-created the myth of St. Petersburg. In contrast to the gloomy St. Petersburg of Blok ("Night, street, street light, pharmacy" ["Noch'. Ulitsa. Fonar'. Apteka."]) and the tragic visions of Dobuzhinskii, Mandelstam's "Petersburg Stanzas" creates a St. Petersburg of power and splendor:[31]

A snowstorm whirled over yellow
government buildings, and whirled on,
and the lawyer climbs back into the sleigh,
pulling his coat closed with a broad sweep.

Ships are wintering. In direct sun
thick cabin-glass lights up.
Monstrous, like a docked battleship,
Russia rests, heavily . . .

Thick discomfort presses down on a northern snob
Onegin's ancient boredom;
out on Senate Square—a snowdrift,
bonfire smoke, faint cold of bayonets . . .

Skiffs ladle water, gulls
visit the hemp warehouse
where muzhiks straight off the opera stage
ramble, selling hot honey teas and rolls.

Cars fly in a line, into the fog;
a finicky, frugal pedestrian—
type of eccentric Evgenii—is ashamed of poverty,
breathes gasoline and curses at fate![32]

The calm diction of Mandelstam's "Petersburg Stanzas" seems to be born of the city's imperial, classical architecture. In the slow, flowing lines of the poem Mandelstam captures the width of the Neva and the magnificence of imperial buildings. Yet the language of the poem is very modern and full of descriptive details that emphasize the classical tone of the work. St. Petersburg in this poem closely resembles Mandelstam's Rome: the city is unpalatable, unembraceable, and intimidating, but at the same time idealized. The landscape captured in this poem and others is authentic (the Senate Square, the riverbanks near the Winter Palace), but it is not merely a sketch of what the poet beholds, for the whole picture is permeated with history, including cultural history through the references to Pushkin's *Bronze Horseman* and his novel in verse, *Eugene Onegin*. Connecting the past (Peter the Great's ships, the bayonets evoking the Decembrist uprising) with the present (cars, gasoline), the poem reflects the end of an epoch.

The atmosphere of tranquility in "Petersburg Stanzas," however, is unstable, for "the Senate Square" and the "docked battleship" not only allude to the past, but also foreshadow social change and war. Though short, the work is replete with meaning and metaphor, evoking the historical role of the city as "a window onto Europe," albeit with delayed industrial development: the sleds and the *muzhiks* trading their goods. The dreamy quiet of government buildings in the falling snow also starkly contrast with the only feature of industrial progress, cars. Allusions from a proud literary tradition in this poem intermingle with important historical events: the Decembrist uprising on Senate Square, connected here somewhat obliquely with Onegin's famous boredom, and the tragedy of the small man, Evgenii, from *The Bronze Horseman*. This detailed scene is built around the Bronze Horseman as a metaphor for a decisive moment in Russia's history—a metaphor materialized in the famous statue that is conspicuously unnamed but clearly present.[33]

In the same year (1913) Mandelstam composed "Admiralty," another poem about St. Petersburg that contains a stanza crucial for Mandelstam's understanding of humankind's place in the metropolis:

Boat of air, a touch-me-not for a mast,
Serving as a yardstick to Peter's heirs
It teaches: beauty is not the fancy of a demigod
But the simple carpenter's predatory eye.[34]

Jane G. Harris argues that this poem "is another fine example of Mandelstam's Acmeist principles, applied in this instance to his beloved St. Petersburg, emphasizing its place in the cosmos."[35] In this poem, not only the image of the city is idealized, but so is the work of the builders who made the city's magnificence possible. Peter the Great's Admiralty is depicted as a complex and vital structure towering majestically over the Neva River and beckoning the open sea. Symbolized by the Admiralty, the city emerges as a ship that originated not in semi-divine inspiration, but in a carpenter's hands. Mandelstam here pays tribute to human creativity in terms that are specific and concrete, but also acknowledges the historical import of empire, for the elongated, needlelike spire of the Admiralty tower appears in the poem as a ship's untouchable mast, a metaphor that conveys the poet's perception of the city as the empire's preeminent port.

In these poems Mandelstam glorifies St. Petersburg in the same way he idyllically pens imperial Rome, with its bold streets and its haughty buildings. For the poet, Petersburg is an unforgettable city of dreams not yet destroyed by revolution. However, unlike his treatment of Rome as *caput mundi* and the perfect symbiosis of nature and culture, Mandelstam idealizes his own city only until the reality of the streets and common buildings enters the verse. In other words, his poetic view is not limited to magnificent imperial edifices, but takes into account the gray fog and sorrow-ridden quarters whose inhabitants experience life's trials. Written on the eve of the October Revolution of 1917, "Admiralty" is full of melancholy foreboding, following the "unsaintly" line of literary depiction by identifying the city as a locus that kills rather than engenders life:

> We shall die in transparent Petropolis
> Where Proserpina rules over us.
> With each breath we drink the air of death,
> And each hour is a year of death for us.[36]

This city, even then viewed as the "cradle of revolution," struggles with mutiny and discord. Proserpina, the Roman name of the Greek goddess Persephone, is the wife of Hades, the king of the dead. The language of the poem is monotonous and repetitive, which creates the impression of a "death knell."[37] The repetition of the sound "z" in "prozrachnom" ("transparent"), "vzdokhe" ("breath"), and "vozdukh" ("air") is linked with the Russian "z" in Prozerpina, who defeats the goddess Athena with her stone helmet, by extension also defeating the stony solidity and endurance of Petersburg.[38] Jane G. Harris notes the loss here of what she calls "the celebratory image of St. Petersburg."[39] The imperial city ceases to be, but Mandelstam refuses to perceive the metamorphosis of it into a seat of yet another empire. As the suffocating stench of death permeates the air, rule over the devastated city is entrusted to the queen of the Underworld. Solomon Volkov observes that "to suffer together with Petersburg became a ritual" for Russian poets.[40]

Another Mandelstam poem, written in 1918 immediately following the Revolution, reinforces the theme of suffering and inevitable despair expressed in the last line of the first stanza, which becomes the poem's refrain:

A light wandering terribly high,
But does a star glitter so?
O transparent star, wandering light,
Your brother, Petropolis, is dying.

In the last stanza Mandelstam offers a variation on the refrain with the emphatic repetition of "your," first with the "city," then with "brother," to draw attention to his personal, familial attachment to the city destined for demise.

But if you are a star, Petropolis,
your city, your brother, Petropolis, is dying. [41]

Unsurprisingly, this and many other poems Mandelstam wrote after the Revolution dwell on death and strip St. Petersburg of its status as the New Rome. Peter's dreamy, imperial city becomes a devastated, ravaged environment that is almost a stranger to the poet, eliciting fear, anxiety, and a premonition of his own destruction. His love for St. Petersburg becomes equivocal when Mandelstam positions himself as an exile within his own city. While it is possible to interpret these lines not as the death of the beloved city but as its metamorphosis, for Mandelstam the changes are harder to bear than destruction. Therefore he transforms his city into a dream, a myth.[42]

This "poetic reality" of St. Petersburg strikes close to Mandelstam's perception of Rome.[43] The city exists only in his poetic imagination. The world beyond the window is the city-vampire, its metamorphosis occurring in the poet's imagination. Mandelstam's imaginary city remains Petersburg, and Roman in its idealization, whereas the city of Petrograd and Leningrad is a physical entity and is associated with destruction and death. The "death of Petersburg" caused by war and revolution led Mandelstam to evoke in his poetry the elements of the "old" city. That nostalgia for the past (a nostalgia that clings to the city today, as the chapter by Stephen Norris emphasizes) finds expression in his poem written in 1931, at the start of Stalin's terror:

I was only childishly tied to the mighty world,
afraid of oysters, cautious with policemen,
and not a grain of my soul owes it a thing,
though I tormented myself; we all do.

I never stood under a bank's Egyptian portico,
in a beaver mitre, scowling with stupid
importance, and no gypsy danced for me over
the lemon Neva, never, to the crackle of hundred-ruble notes.
Sensing executions, I ran from rebellion's howl,
Ran to Black Sea Nereids—

And how much torment and grief I took
From Europe's tender women, from the beauties of those times.

And why has this city these ancient rights
over my thoughts, my feelings?
It's more insolent after fires than frosts,
Touchy, damned, empty, and young!

Maybe it's because, on a child's picture, I saw
Lady Godiva with her ginger mane let down,
maybe that's why I still say to myself, secretly,
goodbye, Lady Godiva . . . Godiva,
I don't remember, I don't . . . [44]

The poem presents two different views of the city: on the one hand, the mythic St. Petersburg of the glamorous past (the "derzhavnyi mir" of pre-revolutionary St. Petersburg), of which Mandelstam was unable to partake because he experienced it while still a child; on the other hand, the all too real Leningrad (the "cradle of the Revolution"), plundered, rebellious, and violated, yet a city from which he cannot separate himself. The poem conveys a mood of despair and irrevocable loss by the repetition of the word "nikogda." Mandelstam's nostalgia for the city that is lost to him starkly differs from Ovid's, for the Roman enjoyed all the luxurious and decadent aspects of Rome without ever witnessing the decline of the city. Mandelstam's flight from the city to the Black Sea (also the locus of Ovid's exile) is full of "torment and grief," and, as the last lines indicate, his city—not what it used to be, though still "young" and "touchy"—continues to hold sway over him. The idealization, however, is gone, for the city is also "damned" and "empty." The image of Lady Godiva, which brings the reader back to the poet's childhood memories, is eloquent: Like Godiva, vulnerable in her nakedness, partly hidden by her luxurious mane of hair, Mandelstam's beloved city is impressive only on the outside, but "naked" and unprotected under its deceptive glamour.

Yet Mandelstam's relationship with the city that simultaneously inspired and devastated him resembles Ovid's relationship with Rome in the nostalgia both experienced. Mandelstam's exile, unlike Ovid's, is not physical, but internal; his loss is not geographical, but spiritual. Faced now with the reality of the metamorphosis undergone by St. Petersburg, he feels alienated from it, exiled to the outskirts of his own memory, which yearns to preserve his earlier apperception of the city, a place where he had friends, loved, and suffered. One of his most famous poems, written in the winter of 1920–1921, begins with the lines that inscribe his painful familiarity with Piter:

> We shall meet again in Petersburg
> As if we had buried the sun there,
> And shall pronounce for the first time
> That blessed senseless word.[45]

While evoking nostalgia for that city that is lost forever,[46] Mandelstam introduces the image, extraordinary to anyone familiar with St. Petersburg's far from sunny climate, of Petersburg as a city where the sun "is buried." That startling image is explicated in his essay "Pushkin and Scriabin":

> Pushkin and Scriabin, two transformations of the same sun . . . served as an example of a collective Russian death. . . .
> Pushkin was buried at night . . . secretly. . . . The sun was placed in the coffin at night, and the sled runners scraped the frozen January ground as they bore the poet's remains away for the funeral.[47]

The buried sun, in short, is a metaphor for the source and the summit of the Russian poetic tradition—Pushkin. With the death of the supreme poet, the power of the poetic word as prophesy perished.

The theme of Petersburg in Russian poetry is closely connected with Pushkin, who exerted an incalculable influence on Mandelstam. As a Russian poet and especially as a poet of Petersburg, Mandelstam could not escape the powerful aura of Pushkin's poetry. He also nurtured a certain reverence toward Pushkin's name, which appears only twice in all of his poetry. That reverence—bordering on worship—also has a biographical basis: Mandelstam's childhood was spent in Kolomna, where Pushkin had his first apartment, and the Tenishev School, with its preference for the humanities, unusual teachers, and poetry evenings, was for young Mandelstam essentially what the Lyceum in Tsarskoe Selo was for Pushkin. In his formation as a poet Mandelstam felt a close affinity to Pushkin, and his contemporaries even observed similarities in the two poets' physical appearance.[48] Given the intertwining of Petersburg and Pushkin in Mandelstam's poetic imagination, the metaphor of the "buried sun" constitutes Mandelstam's homage to The Poet whose fate and fame are inseparable from Mandelstam's beloved city.

The reference to the "blessed, meaningless word," echoing another poem by Mandelstam, which opens with the phrase, "I have forgotten the word that I wanted to say," poses a riddle. In both works the poet tries to remember some mystical, unspeakable word, connected to a mysterious, elusive world. This word most likely is the all-embracing Greek *logos*, a word that for the Acmeists represented the ultimate "reality."[49] As Mandelstam contended, "The word, as conceived by Hellenism, is active flesh, ready to give birth to the event,"[50] and thus for him it is not a static utterance, but an enabling entity capable of changing the course of events in the world.

Harris interprets this cryptic line as a reference to Hades: "Another remarkable aspect of 'I have forgotten the word' is its vivid, almost tangible portrayal of the netherworld."[51] The shadows inhabiting the realm of Proserpina do not speak, and, more importantly, Pushkin, the embodiment of the poetic voice, is dead and silenced, imposing his muteness on other poets. The word uttered by a poetic genius becomes lost as the city that once brimmed with vitality, emotion, and passion becomes devastated and ruined. The only way to regain all these elements is to return to that city and reunite with friends, so that the word will be reanimated.

Whatever the moribund predictions prompted by the Revolution, Mandelstam acutely suffered from the loss of his beloved Petropolis. A poem of his from 1930 eloquently captures his ambivalence upon his internal return:

> I returned to my city, familiar to the point of tears,
> Like my veins, like children's half-swollen glands.
>
> You've returned here—then swallow at once
> The cod liver-oil of Leningrad's river lamps.[52]

Nothing idealized or grand marks his depiction of the city, which is a far cry from Rome, with its imperial flora and the perfect symbiosis between the human race and nature. "Children's half-swollen glands" result from the city's perpetual humidity; the cod liver-oil of the street lamps represents the city whose everyday life is too familiar to the poet, unlike the life of Rome, which remains in his imagination clad in marble and void of human flesh.

In his article on Mandelstam, A. I. Nemirovskii observes that he could never decide whether Mandelstam had really visited Rome or whether all his poems about the Eternal City simply sprang from his imagination.[53] For Mandelstam, such a question was irrelevant, for his poetry needed not a concrete, modern Rome, but a city equal to the task of symbolizing a grand idea. Not so with St. Petersburg, however: Its idealized image is circumscribed by the poet's everyday interaction with the city. Nostalgia for it is not sweet, but painful, and therefore devoid of Ovidian elements. The city is "familiar to the point of tears," shed not on account of a long anticipated reunion, but, as the rest of the poem makes clear, in expectation of imminent arrests and suffering:

> Petersburg! I am not ready to die yet:
> You've still got all my telephone numbers.
>
> Petersburg! I still have the addresses
> For finding the voices of the dead.
>
> I live on a black staircase, and the bell yanked
> Out with flesh hits me in the temple.
>
> And all night long I wait for my dear guests,
> Rattling like shackles the chains of my door.[54]

Though the poet returns to the city without which his life is unthinkable, the reunion is not a happy one—a stance clear to anyone who lived through the horrors of Stalin's persecutions. Nocturnal arrests as people sat in the darkness of their apartments listening for steps on the staircase and hoping that the terror of secret police ("dear guests") would bypass their doors was all too familiar to Mandelstam, whose "voices of the dead" refers to those friends and acquaintances of his who fell victim during this chilling epoch.

The sorrow of Ovid's nostalgia, as conceived in Mandelstam's imagination, was lucid and bright, even joyous. Mandelstam's return to his city, however, could not ignore brutal reality, as the city that had once served as symbol—as the embodiment of a historical idea—now proved lethal, with himself as the next victim. St. Petersburg as a city of death informs yet another of his poems written in 1931:

Lord, help me to live through this night.
I fear for my life—for Your servant I fear.
Living in Petersburg is like sleeping in a coffin.[55]

Whereas earlier poems about St. Petersburg contain some philosophical and psychological ambivalence toward the city undergoing drastic historical changes, by 1931, Mandelstam's city has metamorphosed into a threat, a hostile force familiar from the pages of works by Dostoevsky. Poems written in anticipation of his arrest and exile are utterly devoid of idealization and nostalgic, for the northern Palmyra had become as tortured and sorrowful as its inhabitants.

For many poets cities are the most important protagonists of their poetry. For Sophocles, Athens was a tragic hero; for Ovid, Rome was the cruel object of his unrequited love; for Mandelstam, St. Petersburg was both of the above. These cities entered the Western poetic imagination endowed with the power to mesmerize, intimidate, and devastate the poets who "sang" of them.

Cities, and especially ancient ones, are easy to idealize. Mandelstam sometimes depicted his poetic Petersburg in the same way he characterized Rome—as a detached, idealized, towering idea that simultaneously attracts and intimidates. The ancient Rome of his verses is the realm of Caesars, military triumphs, and perfect harmony between nature and humanity. While Rome's past may elicit reverence and awe as a great civilization, it nonetheless raises qualms when one considers the human cost of such national glory. As an Acmeist, Mandelstam perceived Rome as the embodied "acme" of human creativity and ceaseless inspiration for posterity. His poetic *Roma aeterna* had little to do with the rise and fall of ancient Rome as a historical city, verging, instead, on the mystical. His representation of it unites the visual image of the city with its cultural legacy, while the act of material observation reflects his changing emotional and poetic experience.

In his early poems dedicated to St. Petersburg Mandelstam views his beloved city as historical yet eternal, creating an homage to cultural continuity, in which he perceived St. Petersburg as another Rome. The myth of St. Petersburg is developed through later juxtaposition of "the cold, dark, northern capital and the world of sunlight" associated for Mandelstam with the Crimea, the Black Sea, and the entire Mediterranean world.[56]

The sources of that juxtaposition clearly lie in the myth of Rome, which for Mandelstam represented the perfect symbiosis between art and life.

The Crimea and the Black Sea, however, are precisely the region Ovid portrays as a bare northern wasteland in which barbarians drive their chariots across the frozen river. Thus there is at play in Mandelstam at least a double displacement. As Allen Miller observed, "Mandelstam's Rome is in exile from itself, yet Ovid's exile is depicted as if it were played out in Mandelstam's Rome, when in fact it is located on the very coast of the Black Sea that for the Russian poet stands as synecdoche for a myth of Mediterranean sunshine, culture and civilization, a lost Golden Age of the seamless marriage of nature and art."[57] That myth gives rise to the celebratory image of St. Petersburg, a city of dazzling magnificence and classical heritage.

In stark opposition to that ideal St. Petersburg emerges yet another Petropolis, neither Roman nor bathed in sunshine, in which glamour is transformed into intimidation, the monotonous, regal flow of the Neva River becomes a threat, and harmony and calmness yield to anxiety, loss, and death. That side of the Petersburg myth reflects Mandelstam's concern over Russia's cultural heritage, the continuity of civilization as a never-ceasing process of human creativity. Ambivalent and yearning, Mandelstam sees St. Petersburg as created in the seductive image of Italian classical form, which is irresistible to the poet. Yet with the years it became harder to idealize the city that turned inimical as the storms of history swept it off its classical foundations. The poet confronted the challenge of St. Petersburg's changes with the desire to soar over the abyss of time and history that he could never actualize. In his poetic vision ancient Rome meets that ideal of unchanging civilization, but St. Petersburg does not. Mandelstam's passionate attachment to St. Petersburg resulted in his depiction of the city's death as the death of a tragic protagonist—tortured, yet triumphant in its suffering. The city-protagonist succumbs to the all-devouring power of time and historical change, but remains invincible by the power of the poetic word it inspires.

Notes

1. Quoted in G. H. Hamilton, *Art and Architecture of Russia* (New Haven, 1983), 327. See also Bruce Lincoln, *Sunlight at Midnight: St. Petersburg and the Rise of Modern Russia* (New York, 2000), 112.

2. Solomon Volkov, *St. Petersburg: A Cultural History* (New York, 2000). See also Orlando Figes, *Natasha's Dance: A Cultural History of Russia* (New York, 2002), which points

out that Moscow was proclaimed the Third Rome especially after the fall of Constantinople to the Turks because the city was seen as the "last remaining seat of the Orthodox religion, with a messianic role to save the Christian world," 300.

3. See G. S. Knabe, *Russkaia antichnost'* (Moscow, 2000), 185.

4. Quoted in ibid., 185.

5. Volkov, *St. Petersburg*, 31. See also Figes, *Natasha's Dance*, who observes that "the idea of Moscow as a 'Russian' city developed from the notion of St. Petersburg as a foreign civilization," 157.

6. Ryszard Przybylski, *An Essay on the Poetry of Osip Mandelstam: God's Grateful Guest*, Madeline G. Levine, trans. (Ann Arbor, 1987), 137.

7. "Proslavim, brat'ia, sumerki svobody."

8. In *Complete Poetry of Osip Emilevich Mandelstam*, Burton Raffel and Alla Burago, trans. (Albany, NY, 1973):

> Net, nikogda, nichei ia ne byl
> Sovremennik.
> Mne ne s ruki pochet takoi.

9. Victor Terras "Classical Motives in the Poetry of Osip Mandelstam," *Slavic and East European Journal* 10/3 (1966), 255.

10. Tr. by B. Raffel and A. Burago: "Pust' imena tsvetushchikh gorodov, Laskaiut slukh znachitel'nost'iu brennoi. Ne gorod Rim zhivet sredi vekov, A mesto cheloveka vo vselennoi. Im ovladet' pytaiutsia tsari, Sviashchenniki opravdyvaiut voiny, I bez nego prezreniia dostoiny, Kak zhalkii sor, doma i altari."

11. There is also another level of interpretation in this poem, pointed out by Gleb Struve ("Ital'ianskie obrazy i motivy v poezii Osipa Mandelstama," *Studi in onore di Ettore Lo Gatto e Giovanni Maver* [Rome, 1962] 601–614, 606). The symbol of Rome in this poem is closely connected with Mandelstam's preoccupation during this time with Catholicism, and more specifically with Chaadaev. In 1915 Mandelstam publishes in *Apollon* (No. 6–7, pp. 57–63) an essay on Chaadaev. He writes:

> "Chaadaev's thought is national in its sources, national even when it flows into
> Rome. Only a Russian could discover this West, which is far denser and more
> concrete than the historical West itself." In J. G. Harris, ed., *Osip Mandelstam:
> The Collected Critical Prose and Letters*, J. G. Harris and C. Link, trans. (Ann
> Arbor, 1979; hereafter I refer to this edition as CPL). Here Mandelstam
> explicitly makes the connection between Rome and Russian tradition, although
> he has Catholic Rome in mind more than the ancient city.

12. Przybylski (*An Essay on the Poetry*, 15) points out that there are two extant versions of this poem. Their first stanzas are similar, but the theme emphasized in the first version expresses a dichotomy between ancient Rome and modern times and is more concerned with humankind's place within that dichotomy:

> Kogda derzhalsia Rim v soiuze s estestvom,
> Nosilis' obrazy ego grazhdanskoi moshchi
> V prozrachom vozdukhe, kak v tsirke golubom,

Na forume polei i v kollonade roshchi.
A nyne chelovek—ne rab, ne vlastelin,
Ne op'ianen soboi, a tol'ko otumanen;
Nevol'no govorish': vsemirnyi gorozhanin,
A khochetsia skazat': vsemirnyi grazhdanin.

When Rome maintained her union with nature
The images of her civic might were lofted
In the transparent air as in blue circus,
In the forum of fields and the colonnade of groves.
But now man is neither slave nor master,
Not intoxicated with himself, but only confused;
Involuntarily you say: universal city dweller,
But you meant to say: universal citizen.

13. My translation:

Priroda—tot zhe Rim i otrazilas' v nem.
My vidim obrazy ego grazhdanskoi moshchi,
V prozrachnom vozdukhe, kak v tsirke golubom,
Na forume polei i v kolonnade roshchi.

Priroda—tot zhe Rim, i, kazhetsia, opiat'
Nam nezachem bogov naprasno bespokoit'—
Est' vnutrennosti zhertv, chtob o voine gadat',
Raby, chtoby molchat', i kamni, chtoby stroit'.

14. See Ryszard Przybylski, "Rim Osipa Mandel'shtama," in *Mande'lshtam i antichnost'*, O. A. Lekmanov, ed. (Moscow, 1995), 33–65, esp. 37.

15. Friedrich Schiller suggests that all the evil created by culture can be remedied, paradoxically, only by culture. And in the struggle against evil, the human race needs cultural models to follow. In his search for those models Schiller turns not to pastoral Arcadia and the "age of innocence," but to Greek civilization, where, he feels, culture and nature achieved an unprecedented harmony. Mandelstam rejects the Greek utopia of Schiller, replacing it instead with his own Roman utopia. Here is the city, in Mandelstam's opinion, that is the solution to every philosophical problem.

16. See Przybylski, *An Essay on the Poetry*, 39.

17. O. Mandel'shtam, "O sobesednike," "O poezii: Sbornik statei" (1928), 25. Translation is mine.

18. On loss, nostalgia, and name changes, see the chapters in this volume by Buckler, Goscilo, Khazan, Simmons, and Norris.

19. At the peak of his poetic success, in AD 8 Ovid was unexpectedly relegated by Octavian Augustus to the Black Sea, at Tomi (today Constanța). The reasons for this relegation, which unlike exile did not include the loss of property and citizenship, have never been made fully clear (Ovid alludes to them in a veiled manner in Tristia 2.107). G. B. Conte suggests that "the suspicion is that behind the official accusations of the immorality of his poetry, especially the *Ars Amatoria*, the real intention was to punish his involvement in the

scandalous adultery of Julia Minor, Augustus' granddaughter, with Decimus Junius Silanus." Ovid never received a pardon. He died at Tomi in AD 17 or 18. See G. B. Conte, *Latin Literature: A History*, J. B. Solodow, trans. (Baltimore and London, 1994), 340.

20. Tr. by B. Raffel and A. Burago:

> Kogda s driakhleiuschei lubov'iu,
> Meshaia v pesniakh Rim i sneg,
> Ovidii pel arbu volov'iu
> V pokhodakh varvarskikh teleg.

21. For numerous layers of poetic allusions in this poem ranging from Ovid and Pushkin to Verlaine and Villon, see O. A. Lekmanov, "To chto verno ob odnom poete, verno obo vsekh (vokrug antichnykh stikhotvorenii Mandel'shtama)," in Lekmanov, ed., *Mandel'shtam i antichnost'*, 142–153. See also S. A. Osherov "'Tristia' Mandel'shtama i antichnaia kul'tura," ibid., 188–203.

22. Tr. by B. Raffel and A. Burago:

> S veselym rzhaniem pasutsia tabuny,
> rimskoi rzhavchinoi okrasilas' dolina;
> Sukhoe zoloto klassicheskoi vesny
> Unosit vremeni prozrachnaia stremnina.
>
> Topcha po oseni dubovye listy,
> Chto gusto stelutsia pustynnoiu tropinkoi.
> Ia vspomniu Tsezaria prekrasnye cherty—
> Sei profil' zhenstvennyi s kovarnoiu gorbinkoi.
>
> Zdes', Kapitoliia i Foruma vdali,
> Sred' uviadaniia spokoinogo prirody,
> Ia slyshu Avgusta i na kraiu zemli
> Derzhavnym iablokom katiaschiesia gody.
>
> Da budet v starosti pechal' moia svetla:
> Ia v Rime rodilsia, i on ko mne vernulsia;
> Mne osen' dobraia volchitseiu byla,
> I—mesiats tsezarey—mne avgust ulybnulsia.

23. See note 11 on Struve's interpretation of the Roman theme in Mandelstam.

24. Tr. Harris and Link (see note 11).

25. Terras, "Classical Motives," 257.

26. I want to thank Paul Allen Miller, who pointed this out to me in his response to my talk during the panel "Classical Tradition in Russian Poetry of the 20th Century" at the *American Association for the Advancement of Slavic Studies Convention* in Washington, DC, November 17, 2006.

27. "I returned to my city" and "We shall meet again in Petersburg."

28. Vladimir Khazan also discusses the idea of "internal" exile in this volume.

29. See Lincoln, *Sunlight at Midnight*, 222.

30. See Volkov, *St. Petersburg*, 222. See also Przybylski, *An Essay on the Poetry*, 136.

31. The poem is not cited in full. For the full versions see Raffel and Burago, *Complete Poetry*.

32. Tr. by B. Raffel and A. Burago:

> Nad zheltiznoi pravitel'stvennykh zdanii
> Kruzhilas' dolgo mutnaia metel'.
> I pravoved opiat' saditsia v sani,
> Shirokim zhestom zapakhnuv shinel'.
>
> Zimuiut parokhody. Na pripeke
> Zazhglos' kaiuty tolstoe steklo.
> Chudovischna,—kak bronenosets v doke,—
> Rossiia otdykhaet tiazhelo . . .
>
> Tiazhka obuza severnogo snoba
> Onegina starinnaia toska;
> Na ploschadi Senata—val sugroba,
> Dymok kostra i kholodok shtyka . . .
>
> Cherpali vodu ialiki, i chaiki
> Morskie poseshchali sklad pen'ki,
> Gde, prodavaia sbiten' ili saiki,
> Lish' opernye brodiat muzhiki.
>
> Letit v tuman motorov verenitsa,
> Samoliubivyi, skromnyi peshekhod,
> Chudak Evgenii, bednosti styditsia,
> Benzin vdykhaet i sud'bu klianet.

33. The importance of Pushkin for Mandelstam's poetic consciousness will be discussed later in the article.

34. *Osip Mandelstam: Selected Poems*, David McDuff, trans. (New York, 1975):

> Lad'ia vozdushnaia i machta-nedotroga,
> Sluzha lineikoiu preemnikam Petra,
> On uchit: krasota—ne prikhot' poluboga,
> A khishchnyi glazomer prostogo stoliara.

35. J. G. Harris, *Osip Mandelstam* (Boston, 1988), 24.

36. Tr. by David McDuff:

> V Petropole prozrachnom my umrem,
> Gde vlastvuet nad nami Prozerpina.
> My v kazhdom vzdokhe smertnyi vozdukh p'em,
> I kazhdyi chas nam smertnaia godina.

37. The comparison was made by John. M. Kopper in his talk "Multiple Sadnesses: Osip Mandelstam's *Tristia* and the Critic's Dilemma in Approaching a Literature of Disengagement," *17th Congress of the International Comparative Literature Association*, Hong

Kong, 2004. Available online at www.ln.edu.hk/eng/staff/eoyang/icla/Dissemination.htm (last visited on December 18, 2006).

38. The image of the stony solidity of St. Petersburg, as John Copper (2004) pointed out (see the note above), was "a central Acmeist mythologeme of the city—indeed 'stone' is the title of Mandelstam's first verse collection."

39. Harris, *Osip Mandelstam* (1988), 38.

40. Volkov, *St. Petersburg*, 223.

41. My translation:

> Na strashnoi vysote bluzhdaiusdchii ogon',
> No razve tak zvezda mertsaet?
> Prozrachnaia zvezda, bluzhdaiushchii ogon',
> Tvoi brat, Petropol', umiraet.
>
> O, esli ty zvezda,—Petropol', gorod tvoi,
> Tvoi brat, Petropol', umiraet.

42. Przybylski, *An Essay on the Poetry*, 144.

43. Ibid.

44. Tr. by B. Raffel and A. Brurago:

> S mirom derzhavnym ia byl lish' rebiacheski sviazan,
> Ustrits boialsia i na gvardeitsev gliadel ispodlob'ia
> I ni krupitsei dushi ia emu ne obiazan,
> Kak ia ni muchal sebia po chuzhomu podob'iu.
> S vazhnost'iu glupoi, nasupivshis' v mitre bobrovoi,
> Ia ne stoial pod egipetskim portikom banka,
> I nad limonnoi Nevoiu pod khrust storublevyi
> Mne nikogda, nikogda ne pliasala tsyganka.
>
> Chuia griadushchie kazni, ot reva sobytii miatezhnykh,
> Ia ubezhal k nereidam na Chernoe more,
> I ot krasavits togdashnikh, ot tekh evropeianok nezhnykh,
> Skol'ko ia prinial smushchen'ia, nadsady i goria!
>
> Tak otchego zh do sikh por etot gorod dovleet
> Mysliam i chuvstvam moim po starinnomu pravu?
> On ot pozharov eshche i morozov nagleet,
> Samoliubivyi, prokliatyi, pustoi, molozhavyi.
>
> Ne potomu l', chto ia videl na detskoi kartinke
> Ledi Godivu s raspushchennoi ryzheiu grivoi,
> Ia povtoriaiu eshche pro sebia, pod surdinku:
> Ledi Godiva, proshchai! Ia ne pomniu, Godiva . . .

45. My translation:

> V Peterburge my soidemsia snova,
> Slovno solntse my pokhoronili v nem,

I blazhennoe, bessmyslennoe slovo
V pervyi raz proiznesem.

46. Cynthia Simmons, in her article on the siege in this volume, notes that "to its inhabitants, 'Piter' was the most 'civilized' city in the nation." See also the chapter in this volume
by Steven Duke, who sees the attraction of St. Petersburg as "a focal point of 'polite society.'" The feeling of loss and longing for this "civilized" city that was no more echoes
through most of Mandelstam's poetry written after the Revolution.

47. CPL, 90.

48. A. Tsvetaeva, "Osip Mandelstam i ego brat Aleksandr," *Daugava* 7 (1980), 71.

49. See O. Mandelstam "On the Nature of the Word" (CPL 61–62): "Too often we fail
to see that the poet raises a phenomenon to its tenth power, and the modest exterior of a
work of art often deceives us with regard to the monstrously condensed reality contained
within. In poetry this reality is the word as such."

50. O. Mandelstam, "O Prirode Slova," *O Poezii*, 43. Quoted from Terras, "Classical
Motives," 252.

51. Harris, *Osip Mandelstam* (1988), 46.

52. My translation:

Ia vernulsia v moi gorod, znakomyi do slez,
Do prozhilok, do detskikh pripukhlykh zhelez.

Ty vernulsia siuda, tak glotai zhe skorei
Rybii zhir leningradskikh rechnykh fonarei.

53. A. I. Nemirovskii, "Pogovorim o Rime" in Lekmanov, ed., *Mandel'shtam i antichnost'*, 129–140, especially 138. Struve, "Ital'ianskie obrazy i motivy," 602, asks the same question and does not offer a definitive answer as to whether or not Mandelstam visited Italy
and whether his Italian motifs are purely a result of his poetic imagination.

54. My translation:

Peterburg, ia eshche ne khochu umirat':
U tebia telefonov moikh nomera.

Peterburg, u menia eshche est' adresa,
Po kotorym naidu mertvetsov golosa.

Ia na lestnitse chernoi zhivu, i v visok
Udariaet mne vyrvannyi s miasom zvonok.

I vsiu noch' naprolet zhdu gostei dorogikh,
Shevelia kandalami tsepochek dvernykh.

55. My translation:

Pomogi, Gospod', etu noch' prozhit':
Ia za zhizn' boius'—za Tvoiu rabu—
V Peterburge zhit'—slovno spat' v grobu.

56. Harris, *Osip Mandelstam* (1988), 37.

57. Paul Allen Miller, response to AAASS Panel "Classical Tradition in Russian Culture of the 20th Century." For a more detailed discussion of Mandelstam's treatment of Crimean and Hellensitic themes see Iu. I. Levin, "Zametki o 'krymsko-ellinskikh' stikhakh O. Mandel'shtama," in Lekmanov, ed., *Mandel'shtam i antichnost'*, 77–103.

Five

Petersburg in the Poetry of the Russian Emigration

Vladimir Khazan

Petersburg is one of the recurrent and most extensive themes in Russian émigré literature, including poetry. In the artistic consciousness of those who found themselves outside of their native country after the October 1917 Revolution, the former capital of the Russian empire represented an important artistic space. Understandably, sociopolitical and cultural factors played a primary role here: Petersburg was customarily associated with state power, military glory, the flourishing of sciences and the arts (including, of course, the city's unique characteristic of being itself a work of art), but there was also something else, less subject to rational logic and which, perhaps, can be conveyed only by the metaphysical language of poetry.[1]

This can be seen in an example that, at first glance, seems rather amusing, but is most graphic and significant. The Muscovite Ia. N. Gorbov, who after Moscow University studied in the Petersburg Nikolaev military academy, wrote the following in a review of the book of poetry *Blue World* (*Sinii mir*; New York, 1961) by an émigré poetess, N. Belavina, who not only had never lived in Petersburg but also, apparently, had never even been there (at age five she was taken from the Crimea to Constantinople, then to Yugoslavia and from there to the West):

In St. Petersburg, whether on Ekaterininskii or Morskaia, on Kamennoostrovskii or on Nevsky or on the Moika, or someplace else, on some evenings, one could see from the window, or from the depths of the room, some kind of blue light, amazing but not strange, lightly glimmering, come right up to the glass, of a kind that one wanted to ask it some unspoken question and receive an unspoken answer, or exchange glances or a smile . . . St. Petersburg was a unique city. The blue evening light, probably, even now remains there as something unique . . . The title *Blue World*, written in blue letters on Nonna Belavina's poetry collection, reminds those who saw the St. Petersburg blue light of its magic. Or perhaps an eternal promise of a better future, the elusive Bluebird?[2]

It is curious that in the review, Belavina, who never saw Petersburg with her own eyes, is almost transformed into the inveterate Petersburg author. The closeness between the title of her collection and the luminous effects of the Petersburg air are based on the reviewer's sensory "aberrations" and are deeply associative in their origin. The last sentence about Maeterlinck's *Blue Bird* somewhat clarifies the nature of these associations but it does not entirely dispel the sensation that Belavina's verse is permeated with the Petersburg atmosphere with which she was not familiar!

Nostalgia, Exile, and the Petersburg Syndrome

At the heart of this curiosity, however, lies a very important and serious problem. The "Petersburg syndrome" does not necessarily testify to the fact that a poet was born in the city on the Neva. Rather, it is a matter of the profound intentions of Russian poetic culture in general, gravitating in its moral and spiritual insights toward the Pushkinian artistic heritage and therefore inseparably linked to the "Petersburg period" of Russian literature understood in the broad historical perspective.

Indisputably, the former residents of Petersburg were the ones who felt the greatest nostalgia for Petersburg. "You have to be a 'Peterburzhets' [resident of Petersburg] in order to understand the longing for Petersburg," someone wrote under the pseudonym Petronius in the sketch "Petersburg." "You have to be thoroughly soaked by the miasmas of the Marquisan Meadow, smoked by the Petersburg fogs, in order to dream of Petersburg amid the glitter and comfort of European centers. Berlin and Paris are now seething with such dreamers; and we dream about our foggy swamp as ardently as mountaineers thrust into the valleys dream about their azure heights."[3]

In emigration, however, even those who had never been there and knew the city only from books or oral tales also wrote poems about Petersburg (or about the adjacent cultural-geographical areas). One example is A. Shteiger, who wrote the two-part cycle *Tsarskoe Selo*, whose interest in Petersburg was purely literary in origin. Georgii Adamovich, who knew Shteiger well, re-called that he "was capable of asking endlessly about Petersburg, about the Poets' Guild (Tsekh poetov), about the evenings in the Stray Dog [café], even about the Petersburg ballet. For him this was some kind of paradise lost, incidentally, not even lost but unfamiliar because he had never been in Petersburg."[4] It is worth comparing this with the remark of Iurii Terapiano about the kind of "Petersburg syndrome" that developed among the émigré intelligentsia dreaming about the city "which they had not seen in their life-time."[5] This syndrome, in which not only Petersburg residents but even people who had never been in the Russian capital found themselves "cap-tives of its magnificent granite" (an image from the poetry of O. Annen-kova, who never left Russia but remained there as an "internal émigré"), was so widespread among the emigrant community that it cannot but attract attention to itself.

Petersburg was a symbol of paradise lost, exile from which became a turn-ing point in Russian history. The most potent symbol—the horseman on the rearing steed—receded into historical oblivion and gave way to new idols.[6] The fall of one state order and its replacement by another was accompanied, as is usual and happens in times of stormy revolutionary cataclysms, by ac-tive myth creation in society. On one side of the border, in the USSR, Pe-tersburg, which became Leningrad, in Soviet mythology was turned into the "cradle of three revolutions." This version presented the legendary location sanctified by semi-official Soviet historiography and linked it with the name of "the leader of the worldwide proletariat." It is quite clear that Petersburg/ Leningrad images in Russian literature of the Soviet age did not reproduce in the automatic form these ideological clichés (it should be sufficient to recall such texts as "Satyr Chorus" (*Kozlinaia pesn'*) by K. Vaginov, "Crazy Ship" (*Sumasshedshii korabl'*) by O. Forsh, "Poem without a Hero" (*Poema bez geroia*) by A. Akhmatova, etc.). But in the official Soviet history, Lenin-grad had been highlighted as the revolutionary myth. This did not, however, hinder the city's provincialization, economic decline, and gradual loss of its former greatness. On the other side of the border, in emigration, Petersburg personified the lost state power, the utopian dream of rebuilding the collapsed state.[7] Forced to live in a phantom sociopolitical reality, the emigrants naturally dreamed of their own state, capable of uniting them not virtually or metaphysically but as full-fledged citizens with equal rights.[8] This is the source for the émigré longing for Petersburg as a city that once played the role of a unifying center for a Russia of diverse peoples.

The Petersburg Image

This characteristic leads us to a very essential point for an understanding of the "Petersburg myth" in general and its frequent occurrence in emigration in particular. It boils down to the fact that the image of Petersburg, the center of the national-cultural cosmos, more so than any other Russian city, is inseparable from Russian literature. It is in equal measure the creation of Peter and Pushkin, as can be seen, for example, in the lines from the poem of Ivan Bunin, "The Day in Peter's Memory" (*Den' pamiati Petra*): "Great and sacred City, / Created by Peter and Pushkin." The Russian émigré poet A. Topol'skii, who lived in Warsaw, went even further in his notion of the true founder of Petersburg: "You were created / Not by Peter but by Dostoevsky." In this context, it is worth mentioning the mocking epistle of the satirical poet Don-Aminado (A. P. Shpolianskii) to Igor' Severianin. While striving for a parody, at the same time the poet established a certain truth that was difficult to refute when he wrote in one of his verse feuilletons called "The Reason of all Reasons" (*Prichina vsekh prichin*):

Well, is this Petersburg fruit
A peach or a pear?!
How we lived! How we ate!
What did we read, what did we listen to
Near the Neva's granite waters?!

[. . .] And at times I think with sadness,
Keeping an eye on gloomy fate,
That it is the result of sins
And that everything was the sum
Chiefly of verse! . . .[9]

This very pointed idea is not without its metaphysical depth about the "responsibility" of poetry for everything that happened to Russia and its capital. It once again emphasizes the dense, mystical, literary (and artistic in general) aura enveloping Petersburg that was perceived in emigration as the most genuine and real life. Even the name of the city, Petrograd, was used by Pushkin in *The Bronze Horseman* (1833) long before August 18, 1914, when Russia entered World War I and the seemingly "German" name "Sankt Peterburg" was cast off. "O'er darkened Petrograd there rolled / November's breath of autumn cold." It may be somewhat of an exaggeration, but without distorting on the whole the true scale of the significance of Pushkin's genius for the life of the Russian emigration, one could say that the entire emigration, like Fedor Godunov-Cherdyntsev, the hero of V. Nabokov's novel *The Gift*, linked its life "to the purest sound from Pushkin's tuning fork."[10]

The following fragment from Antonin Ladinskii's sketch "St. Petersburg" is not just the usual allusion to Russian literature's treasured names and texts: "Liza wrung her hands at the Winter Ditch (Zimnei Kanavkoi), the white plumage of Herman's hat was visible, the Hussar pelisse of Lermontov gleamed in the dark window, and someone's hands tossed a silvery fur onto the sloping shoulders of Nataliia Pushkin."[11] The role of such citations and allusions went beyond the framework of a usual literary device in the tragic situation of exile and separation from one's roots and sources, when it was necessary as if anew to show that they were an inseparable part of oneself. The inseparability of the city on the Neva and Russian literature is a fact that cannot be removed from the spiritual biographies of either one.

In his poem "Kamnegrad," cursing the allegorical Beast that destroyed the Russian capital, the famous Russian poet Konstantin Bal'mont, who found himself in exile, wrote:

> The capital is a thought, where the pivot is the Nevsky [Prospect],
> Where the Neva was married with Pushkin,
> Where Dostoevsky, the spirit of Copernicus,
> And the slayer of matter,
> Said the most elevated words.[12]

The ghosts of Russian literature therefore appear momentarily on the streets and in the alleys of Petersburg in the emigrants' poetry even when the city was least inclined toward literary play as, for instance, in the second poem from V. Bulich's cycle *A Medal for the Defense of Leningrad* (*Medal' za oborony Leningrada*), in which the heroes of Pushkin's *Queen of Spades* and

The Bronze Horseman appear in the city that has been besieged by the Nazis. Who would think to reproach the poetess for inappropriate literary associations?![13]

For the exile, alluding to Petersburg literary motifs (not necessarily mentioning them directly but rather in the form of a hidden, implicit dialogue with Russian literary tradition as such) became a demonstrative form of affirming native rights to the appellation of a Russian writer, even if the rights of Russian citizenship had been repudiated. Nekrasov's famous formulation about "the poet and citizen" ("A poet you might not be, but to be citizen you are obliged"—"*Poetom mozhesh' ty ne byt', no grazhdaninom byt' obiazan*") in this case appeared to be turned inside out. For the refugee poets, Petersburg (to paraphrase Dostoevsky's well-known saying about "the most premeditated city"), the most literary polis in Russian history, became more than a memory about its former beauty and power, or a search for a glorious but vanished past, or a sorrowful lamentation about disrupted human and creative fates. All these elements indisputably are present in some form or another in the emigrant interpretation of the Petersburg theme, but they are only its component parts. The integrative factor is the consciousness that through Pushkin's Petersburg or the Petersburg of Dostoevsky in its infinitely varied forms, the writer is united with the mother lode of his native culture. In this sense one can speak without irony [*aieroni*] about the "therapeutic" functions of the "Petersburg text" of Russian literature for the émigré writer or poet, especially about the elimination of the psychological burden of cultural rejection. Marc Raeff, who has studied the history of the Russian emigration, was undoubtedly correct in writing that "a veritable Pushkin cult developed in Russia abroad . . . In emigration . . . the educated Russians rediscovered Pushkin as someone truly their own, the poet closest to them not only by language and form, but also by his stress on individual creative freedom, a freedom utterly destroyed in Bolshevik Russia.[14]

We shall touch on only one theme that was persistently developed in émigré poetry, the theme linked to Pushkin's *Queen of Spades*. The story is represented frequently and diversely in the "Petersburg text" of the emigration; it literally grips the poets' imagination with its haunting magic and its unresolved puzzle. Those who alluded to it include N. Agnivtsev ("Sankt-Peterburg"); V. Dukel'skii ("Epistle to S. L. Bertenson"); Kal'ma ("Queen of Spades"); V. Popper ("To My Friend"); S. Pregel' ("Queen of Spades"); M. Vega ("Petersburg"); V. Zlobin ("To Obliging Maidens without

Malice")—the list is probably incomplete.[15] Poets preferred this theme, of course, primarily but not exclusively because of its connection to Pushkin's work. It is worth noting that in almost all of the poems mentioned above, the focus is on the operatic version of *The Queen of Spades* or, as in the case of Dukel'skii, its theatrical metaphysics. See also the poem of Igor' Severianin, "Play the Whole Evening" (*Igrai tselyi vecher*): "Play for me from *The Queen of Spades* / Almost the most painful of operas, / So touching in this most / Rational, hardhearted Europe."[16]

The memory of Petersburg as a scenic, theatrical spectacle was seemingly revived through this mystical card game theme, through which the secret of fate itself could be glimpsed. (Incidentally, this was characteristic not only of émigré but also of "continental" poetry, as for example the poem of V. Zorgenfrei, "German," or "Windblown and Suntanned Like a Sailor" by N. Pavlovich.[17]) In other words, it blends together the Pushkinian theme of a card game puzzle as a metonym of fate (which possesses a unique and dense Petersburg coloration) and personal memories about the imperial capital that are inconceivable outside of a theatrical perspective. Thus occurs the artistically rewarding transformation of cultural archetypes and traditions into personal creative emotions.

Petersburg as a Cultural Text

The vast theme of preserving the spiritual precepts of the Silver Age in emigration belongs to this same line of historical-cultural and historical-literary reminiscences and allusions of the "Petersburg text." The émigrés, who had been subject to persecution and denunciation in the Soviet period, found themselves in an exile of long duration. Many of them perceived the past epoch as their own real life in art; for them, the names of Alexander Blok, Nikolai Gumilev, Mikhail Kuz'min, Anna Akhmatova, and Osip Mandelstam were not some kind of abstract textbook signifiers but stood for familiar Petersburg poets. In this sense, the "Petersburg text" expressed some kind of cultural space densely populated with artistic associations that in the émigrés' consciousness went back to the exclusively concrete, memorable, and sensorily recognizable past. An example is Gumilev's "lost streetcar" that rumbled loudly in émigré poetry and directly linked the exiles' nostalgia with the Petersburg themes. See, for example, the poem by Argus, "In Petrograd" or I. Chinnov's "Poets Just Up and Died" or the image of the "lost streetcar" in the poem of Iurii Ivask, "Portuguese Proletariat."[18]

Undoubtedly, the specificity and recognizability of the Petersburg past only intensified the metaphysical overtones of the theme of the capital on the Neva, joining together distant and recent times in a unified literary image as, for example, in Vladimir Nabokov's three-line requiem "In Gumilev's Memory" (1923):

> Proudly and clearly you died, you died as the muse taught you.
> Now, in the quiet of the Elysian Fields, Pushkin speaks with you
> About the flying bronze Peter and about the savage African winds.[19]

The above discussion in no way denigrates the literary school that used the popular Pushkinian term of the "dowager in purple" as the other center of the Russian cultural cosmos. The division of poetry (and literature in general) into "Muscovite" and "Petersburgian" was applicable to Russian literature abroad throughout its entire history, beginning with the early days of the Changing Landmarks (*smenavekhovtsy*) movement and including both the prewar and postwar periods.[20]

The basic line is the apotheosis of a poetic vision of the world from distant exile—the uniqueness, exclusivity of "resplendent St. Petersburg" (the pithy term of the poet N. Agnivtsev).[21] The coloration of all the details of everyday life is determined by the fact that they once were part of the "Petersburg cosmos," or were connected to it in some way, and bear some mark. One symptomatic but entertaining example utilizes puns. In a rather experimental "quatrain about snow" (the collection *Sannoderzhavie* [Paris, 1939]) by a former Petersburg resident, B. Bozhnev, that nevertheless maintains the necessary serious tone, the coloration takes on not only an external linguistic form but also, an inner intonation, which is particularly important. The verse entails word play on the first part of the name Saint (Sankt in Russian) Petersburg:

> A saint-puff of smoke (*sankt-dymok*) rises from saint-smokestacks (*sankt-truby*)
> Saint-doves (*sankt-golubi*) stroll along the saint-roofs (*sankt-kryshe*) . . .
> The snow fell like a milky epilogue,
> But I already hear a prologue of [future] shining.[22]

For the Russian emigrants, it was an incontrovertible fact that Petersburg was the most beautiful city on earth; the local population in the countries of exile, which regarded Petersburg as the end of the world, however, reacted to such views with disbelief.[23]

The sacred nature of Petersburg was reinforced by the tragic bloody spectacle that was played out on the stage of Russian history in the revolutionary period. In the eyes of the Russian intelligentsia, the first victims of the prophesies about the "collapse of humanism" and the decline into cultural savagery were the Petersburg poets Alexander Blok and Nikolai Gumilev. With their death, as Nina Berberova wrote, "a historical period was closing . . . a cycle of Russian destinies was being completed, . . . an epoch was stopping to turn and rush off to other predicaments."[24] A scant century after the fatal shot on the Black River, "the death of the poet" recurred in Petersburg. The Pushkinian halo that illuminated the Poet with a prophetic gift was transformed in the new historical circumstances into a symbol of martyrdom and violent death.

In émigré literature the sadness about Petersburg of the "days of yore" was inexhaustible. Sometimes it acquired the tone of a lightly ironic burlesque as, for example, in the poem of P. Iakobi, "About Thirty-Five Years Ago," that was printed in the Riga weekly *Dlia vas:*

About 35 years ago,
The splendid Neva glittered with lights
And Karabchevskii flew from the Senate
In beaver fur to a masquerade
About 35 years ago.

. . . . .

About 35 years ago
Maestro Galkin drew us to Pavlovsk,
Captivating with "Medved'" or "Palkin" caviar.
Ah! There was balylk [dried sturgeon]! A row of hors d'oeuvres . . .
About 35 years ago![25]

The Petersburg theme in emigration is characterized, however, on the whole, by tragic visions and "specters on the Petersburg ice" (as in the 1923 poem of G. Ivanov, "A January Day. On the Neva's Bank").[26] It was a subject that was often treated in the tone of a requiem. In the literature of exile, Petersburg embodies its most true image of a spectral city, a phantom city (cf.: "Petersburg is not stucco, not stones. Petersburg is an apparition"). Seemingly, the prophecy of the Empress Avdot'ia, who cursed Peter I's insane undertaking, was fulfilled: "May this place be empty!"

Dead Petersburg

The motif of the historic mistake of Petersburg's founder and of the fatal prophecy first resounded in the verse of the future émigrés before, in fact, they had emigrated. Thus, for example, in the poem "Petrograd," written in 1918, when he had not yet left Russia, P. Bulygin rhetorically questioned the "wonder-working builder":

Threatening with a mighty arm,
He gleams in the wind in the yellow fog.
Will freedom pay back Peter in some way?
He didn't expect such a denouement . . .

It would have been better to remain as it had been in the olden days,
But here He carved out a window . . . [27]
Your Son was wise, Sovereign!
Why did You destroy Him?[28]

The lament for the "dead city" became one of the recurrent themes of poetry in emigration.[29] The variations are the most diverse, but the set of topics and their repetition are rather constant and stable. Thus the comparison of Petersburg with Rome in the period of its decline was invariable: "I compared your fate / With the bitter glory of Rome."[30] In another poem by the same author, "Our climate—the Muses and the Elements" (*Nash klimat—muzy i stikhii*), the fall of Rome and the Russian revolutionary storm are mixed together.[31] Similarly, parallels were drawn between the fate of the Russian capital and the destroyed Pompeii. In this case, the destruction refers to an inner, spiritual break that cannot be repaired by any external physical efforts. Only the emigrants from Petersburg (or those like Anna Akhmatova, who "plugged their ears" but remained faithful to the precepts of the pre-Soviet period) were able fully to evaluate the monstrous damage to the city that was generated by the revolutionary Vesuvius.

A little less than a half century later, A. Borman (the son of the well-known political and social figure, writer, and publicist, A. V. Tyrkova-Vil'iams), one of those who had to leave his native Petersburg, wrote in his memoir:

Yes, if I were now to walk along the forgotten but still familiar streets of the city
in which I grew up, then all these dark thoughts and memories would probably

grip me and I would see all around only restored (sometimes perhaps even not badly) dead buildings from which the former Petersburg life had flown, that once had bubbled . . . It probably would seem to me that I was walking in restored Pompeii, in the rebuilt ruins in which life had begun to stir.[32]

The death of Petersburg, smothered by the "whirlwind of rebellion," as the poet I. Voinov expressed it, was one of the central motifs of the great mass of texts written, in particular, in the early period of the development of refugee poetry although it also echoes in one form or another in later works.[33]

The following are a sample of the numerous poems in which the poets mourn the death of Petersburg. I. Tkhorzhevskii, in "On the New Year," (1920) wrote:

The fireplace is enveloped by the flame of losses:
The pain hovers over the heap of consumed years;
And in scarlet wounds, dead Petrograd
Looks out from the ashes, a city of lepers![34]

In the poem "Petersburg" ("Here he is, the former charmer") (1921), V. Nabokov wrote about the city as tormented by hunger, a "fallen sovereign," who had "died, grief-stricken and alone."[35]

The image of Petersburg drowning like Atlantis is engraved in the poem by M. Vega, "Atlantis":[36]

And in the slow circling of white snowstorms,
Where the striking of chimes is discerned through the wind,
That shadow, that spirit, whose name is Petersburg,
Cannot help recognizing its Atlases.[37]

In the poem "Oceanic Depth, Oceanic Breadth" by A. Golovina, if Petersburg is not yet dead, then it is bleeding in agony.

Pitersburgh, Petersburg, Petrograd, Leningrad . . .
This, Krylov's shining Summer Garden.[38]

Why is it eternally in blood and snow?

The memory of those who were expelled from the "Petersburg paradise," in preserving the past, thus purposely or unwittingly idealized this past, elevating it above the unenviable present. This idealization was naturally mixed with a feeling of resentment, hatred, and vengeful malice toward the new masters of the city at whose hands, as Ivan Bunin wrote, "her beauty, her stronghold / And altars were destroyed" ("The Day in Peter's Memory").

Petersburg as World Capital

The Russian emigration was able to cultivate energetically the "Petersburg myth" on this soil that was so vigorously fertilized by irreconcilable sociopolitical conflicts. At the basis of this myth was a nostalgic perception of Petersburg as the incomparable "capital of the world": "There was only one capital on earth, / All the others were simply cities."[39] In the context of the refugees' unstable life, loss of foundations, and painful sensations of a phantom existence, attributing the features of a "super-city" or "the best city on earth" to the "Northern Palmyra" was equal to an assertion of the proud recognition of one's own past—origin, memory, and tradition—as the highest cultural value despite all the social upheavals. At the strictly poetic level, this emotional effect of "patriotic condescension" was manifested by the fact that the Petersburg setting totally suppressed any other settings that were alien to the émigré, no matter how enchantingly beautiful they actually were.

One thing remained invariable in the varied projections of Petersburg onto the exile's surrounding world: Petersburg was the "universal city" (Blok), the center of the world. There are innumerable examples in Russian émigré poetry in which the capital on the Neva is described as beyond comparison to any other city on earth; there does not seem to be any example of the opposite viewpoint. Despite the individual creative preferences, political or other priorities, worshipping of different, sometimes opposite, ideals and idols, the poets were completely unanimous on this point. The following are some examples of what could be termed "Petersburg-centrism" or even "pan-Petersburgism."

A Petersburg mirage pursues V. D. von Ditrichshtein in the Sea of Marmara in the poem "White Steed":

This prickly night the Bronze Horseman
Flies above the smooth surface of the black waters,
And Peter is wrathful, on the victorious way,
Calling his people to glory![40]

N. Svetlov (whose real name was Svin'in), left Petersburg in his youth and lived in China. He corrects and evens out the crooked urban space in the poem "Overseas":[41]

> The crooked street in front of me
> Takes on a Petersburg look.

As if embodying the words of A. Perfil'ev in his poem "Point" ("*Tochka*") that "The distance between Petersburg and Paris / is a few steps," the Paris landscape borders on the Petersburg one in the poem of G. Adamovich, "You Are Here Again . . . Unfaithful, What Do You Want?":[42]

> Obedient words fly as in days of yore
> With some kind of Neva-like breeze from the Seine.
>
> The day comes, almost supernaturally bright.
> The predawn fog is dispersed,
> The eternal spire of the Admiralty
> Soars above the arch on the Champs-Elysées.

The same approach is characteristic of the poem by G. Raevskii, "The Frost is Getting Harder and Cracking":

> Suddenly I see when awake
> Not the frozen Seine,—
> The ice, snowy wind, and the Neva,
> Unique in the universe.[43]

Similarly, N. Otsup wrote in his postwar cycle "Emigrant":

> The Place de la Concorde and Champs-Elysées,
> But the Sadovaia [Street] and Nevsky [Prospect] in memory,
> The Petersburg land above Blok,
> Tolstoy and Dostoevsky above all countries.[44]

V. Korvin-Piotrovskii dreams in Berlin of the "Winter Capital" in the poem "I Fell in Love with Ponderous Berlin" ("*Ia poliubil Berlin tiazhelyi*"). Boston looks like Peterhof to V. Dukel'skii in "Athens of the North":

> Boston seemed to me like
> A window to the past; my mother assured me:
> "Here is Peterhof—no more and no less!"[45]

Z. Trotskaia, who experienced two emigrations, living first in Paris and then in New York, could not figure out in which city she was:

I am not in the same city as an hour ago.
I wandered, I remember, earlier in Paris—
Now New York . . . no, it's like Petrograd.[46]

In K. Pomerantsev's poem "Florence," Petersburg blends together with the Italian city:

Outside the window is the Florentine sky
And the Petersburg dawn in it.[47]

The "illusions," "aberrations," "displacements" of memory, "confusing" an alien expanse with one's native one, overlaying one on another were often motivated by the peculiar emotional state of the author himself (in poetry) or of his hero (in prose).

Often the play on Petersburg and emigrant locations is connected to the Neva and the "rivers of Babylon." The Neva is the initial location for comparison (cf. the kind of mirror-like complementary images of Odoevtseva's two books of memoirs, *On the Banks of the Neva* and *On the Banks of the Seine* [*Na beregakh Nevy* and *Na beregakh Seny*]). In the emigrant consciousness (in particular of former Petersburg residents), the Neva is not only an invariable structural element of the "Petersburg text," but also serves as a customary trope, the basis for related emotional and spiritual states as, for example, in the poem by V. Lur'e, "Rotation":

But now you again became more dear to me
And my head spins as before.
May you be colder and sterner tomorrow,
Than the Neva covered by thick ice.[48]

As a result of the above-mentioned play on spaces, the Neva can appear in Paris[49] or in London,[50] New York[51] or Rome,[52] or even in China.[53] Presumably, this spatial confusion in which one geographical location can be moved freely to another, no matter what real physical distance separates them, is a specific feature precisely of émigré literature, unwittingly adapting the ancient genre of the journey to the nomadic world view imposed on it. See, for example, the lines in the poem by O. Il'inskii, "Triumphal Arches": "Where are we? In New York? But the barriers have been washed away: / We have been pushed into the framework of another stratum; / Through the slit in the cast iron fences of Petrograd / Ice floes dive into the spans of the bridge."[54] This brings to the spatial "play" inversions and "strange rapprochements" built on whimsical cultural-historical associations. The time and space of history are based on mirror reflections—either they are parallels of urban architectural ensembles or a polite national mutual exchange of "services": at one time life mobilizes French tutors for the upbringing of Russian Onegins and Larins, at another, the descendants of the latter are mustered to provide the taxi service of the French capital. See, for example in "Diary in Verse" by N. Otsup:

> The embankment, the expanses of the Neva,
> The Seine with the second-hand booksellers on the Quai,
> The Russian chauffeurs at Montmarte,
> And Monsieur Triquet at the Larins.[55]

Leningrad: What's in the Name?

The emigrants were particularly upset by what they regarded as an oppressive act of violence against Petersburg—the changing of its "beautiful-terrible" name (Zinaida Gippius) to Leningrad, even though in the émigré milieu the city had many parodic names, in particular Hamburg (city of Ham; in Russian "Ham" means a boor): "An alien, evil name 'Leningrad'! / In that city where giants lived" (M. Kolosova); "What did they do to you, my city? / They renamed you . . ." (Iu. Trubetskoi). The attitude of Russian outcasts to their former capital closed a circle of the historic transformations in its appearance. In the postwar displaced persons camps, a joke made the rounds: "Where were you born?" "In Petersburg." "Where did you go to school?" "In Petrograd." "And where did you live after that?" "In Leningrad." "And where would you like to return to?" "To Petersburg."[56]

The changing names of the city—Petersburg-Petrograd-Leningrad (just like Tsarskoe Selo—Detskoe Selo—Pushkin)—provide a pattern for a corresponding cyclical depiction of various stages of its history. This pattern is maintained in the lyrical as well as the novelistic genres, as, for example, in the poetic cycle of A. Ugriumov, *Saint-Petersburg-Petrograd-Leningrad*[57] or the trilogy of novels by D. Vonliar-Liarskii, *Cain's Smoke (Kainov dym)* with the first part—*Sin at the Door (Grekh u dveri) (Petersburg)*;[58] the second part—*Petrograd*; and the third—*Leningrad*. See also the story by Lada Niko-laenko, "Petersburg in Leningrad,"[59] or the punning poem by V. Nabokov, "Leningrad" (1924):

> Sometimes, there are
> Great changes . . .
> But, ardent men,
> What does this dream mean?
> There was Petrograd, it is worse
> than Petersburg, I won't hide it,
> but no matter how you look at it,
> it isn't like Troy:
> why then did you give it a nickname—
> so affectionately, moreover,
> in honor of Helen?[60]

The renaming affected not only the city as a whole but also separate parts and elements such as streets and squares. The city's new qualities en-gender the amusing term "the Soviet Neva" in *Diary in Verse* by N. Otsup (part 1, chapter 14) and the joke of the above-mentioned poet-satirist Argus: "Now, in view of the stormy development of Soviet industry, the Liteinyi [Boulevard] is being renamed Staleliteinyi [Steel Liteinyi]."

The renaming of Petersburg was accompanied by an incongruous re-dressing of the city in Soviet clothing. The emigrants, however, contin-ued to believe that despite the funeral rites for "the old Petersburg," the spirit of the city was indomitable and neither red Petrograd nor Soviet Leningrad was capable of destroying it. The tradition of calling the city Petersburg or even St. Petersburg, not only in everyday speech but also in poetry, was a constant in émigré poetry in both the pre- and postwar years.

> Like the child of the Emperors,
>   city of glory and victories,
> a trace of the past in you,
>   despised by the innovator.
> But you served as the capital
>   with the tsars for hundreds of years
> And you live as their right hand
>   although already without the name,—

Thus wrote N. P. Solodkov in the poem "City of the Past," published in the Brussels émigré journal *Chasovoi*.[61]

"In Petersburg we shall meet again"

The return to Petersburg or its revival is a major theme in emigrant poetry although, in the words of Nabokov from the poem "Petersburg" ("Here he is, the former charmer," 1921), nothing of the "former or kindred" can be found in it.

An expression of the hidden desire to spy on the life in one's native city can be found not only in the familiar "free" lyrical fantasies but also in the epic tales. The hero of V. Krymov's novel *Fugue*,[62] in the last part of the trilogy, *For Money*, sets out for Petersburg to recover hidden jewels. On the whole, the novel was not well received by the critics; for example, in a review, Iu. Mandel'shtam wrote of "the awkward and severe boredom emanating from every page of the novel."[63] Another reviewer, N. Reznikova, however, wrote sympathetically: "Here the author reflected the desire of all emigrants to at least peek out of the corner of their eyes into Russia, to have the opportunity to breathe its air, to see with their own eyes what was happening there, in the motherland, which became so distant."[64]

Osip Mandelstam's famous wish—"In Petersburg we shall meet again, / As if we had buried the sun in it / And for the first time we shall pronounce / The blessed, senseless word . . ."—inspired a number of responses in refugee literature. For example, G. Ivanov was referring to these lines in his poem, "A Quarter of a Century Passed Abroad" (1951): "And the prophecy of a distant friend / Surely must be fulfilled." Ivanov cites them also in his sketch "Sunset over Petersburg" (1953): "And sometimes the words of poets contain a magical force. And what if, suddenly, Mandelstam's prophecy will come true all the same and

> In Petersburg we shall meet again?
> But who will meet? Ghosts? After all,—
> All those who shone in 1913,
> Are only phantoms on the Petersburg ice . . .[65]

In a letter to Iu. Ivask of January 2, 1945, Iu. Gal' cites the Mandelstamian return to the "sun buried in Petersburg" and A. El'kan alludes to this image indirectly at the beginning of his memoirs about Petersburg: "The cold, snowy, hungry winter of 1919. Petersburg. We had not yet buried the sun then, our strange northern sun, raspberry red in the frost and pale gold in the long spring days without nights."[66]

However, the very idea of returning to Petersburg as a reincarnation of the past life was illusory because of the impossibility of implementing it. Indeed, V. Nabokov (in the poem "For Nocturnal Wandering I Don't Need," 1929) related how his "passportless shadow . . . jumps with customary silence . . . onto the Russian shore of the border river" and "secretly, easily, effortlessly," having overcome the obstacles, makes its way through to his native city, but all this is either a metaphysical exaggeration or the fruit of a nocturnal imagination. And if one even supposes the improbable, as Nabokov did in another poem, "Refugees" (*Bezhentsy*, 1921)—that "the exile, after all, can dip in the same water twice and return to his native Petersburg, once he is there, he will, all the same, feel like a stranger."[67] Directly addressing the already deceased Mandelstam, N. Otsup wrote in *Diary in Verse*:

> "In Petersburg we shall meet again . . ."
> There is no one to meet, my dear
> Osip . . . Neither you nor Gumilev are alive
> And Akhmatova became gray-haired,
> And like me, Ivanov and Adamovich
> Are not young, brothers in springtime,
> In fate: neither falsity nor fogs,
> Nor hope . . .[68]

Apparently, Joseph Brodsky closes this circle. In the poem "December in Florence" (1976), he also (and, evidently, primarily) had Petersburg in mind when he wrote, "there are cities to which there is no return."[69]

The poet's return may be a virtual one, but the return of poetry cannot be. The émigré poet I. Chinnov, who during the period of perestroika managed to visit Petersburg, the city of his birth, completed his poetry collection *Autograph* (*Avtograf*) with the poem "The Solemn Façade Was Illuminated." The poem ended with the following lines:

> And it is a vain labor to dream
> That our corpses will travel to Petrograd [. . .]
> But [our] poems will make it. The poems will make it.[70]

Notes

1. The metaphysics and mythology of the historic parallels connected to the Petersburg theme represent an extensive cultural stratum in émigré literature as well. Without dealing with it in this work, I shall refer only to one amusing example. In the middle of the eighteenth century, the English traveler Robert Wood published *The Ruins of Palmyra*, known in Hebrew and Arabic as Tadmor. (This ancient desert city, located in northeast Syria, was destroyed by the Romans in the third century during the reign of the Empress Zinovia.) This book was given as a gift to Catherine II with the inscription: "To Catherine II, the Zinovia of the northern Palmyra." After the October Revolution, the former northern Palmyra fell into the hands of a person with the name Zinov'ev (the pseudonym of Grigorii Evseevich Radomysl'skii, 1883–1936), who did everything possible to destroy it.

2. Ia. N. Gorbov, *Vozrozhdenie* (Paris, 1962), 126.

3. Petronius, "Petersburg," *Golos Rossii* (Berlin), March 16, 1921, 3.

4. Georgii Adamovich, "O Shteigere, o stikhakh, o poezii i prochem (Zametki)" *Opyty* (New York) 1956, 7.

5. Iu. Terapiano, *Vstrechi, 1926–1971* (Moscow, 2002), 185.

6. In one of the cartoons published in the émigré newspaper *Golos Rossii*, published in Berlin, the Bronze Horseman was depicted in the following way: against the background of people falling off their feet from hunger, Trotsky sat on the playful horse with a laurel wreath and five-pointed star on his head; see *Golos Rossii* 27, February 1, 1920, 3.

7. At the same time, in the consciousness of the emigrants, the "former Petersburg" invariably embodied the idea of the imperial, powerful city. See in the article by the above-mentioned Petronius: "About half the entire population of Denmark lives in Copenhagen. About a sixth of the population in London. A tenth of the population in Paris. In Petersburg (pre-Bolshevik) a total of one hundredth. Yet in no other world capital was the power (*derzhavnost'*) of the state felt as much as in this center, thrust to the very edge of the unbounded Empire, by its periphery. The illogicality of Petersburg seemingly left its imprint on its autocracy. The dream of the poet and the logic of the historian yielded in the face of this illogicality" (*Golos Rossii* 610, March 15, 1921, 3).

8. The image of the so-called "émigré state" can be found frequently in verse by refugees. See the figurative expression of the dilemma of the state duality of émigrés, the feeling of those who lived in France of non-allegiance to either of the "flags"—the Soviet or French—in the poem of Georgii Ivanov, "My Passport Burned Sometime" (*Pasport moi sgorel kogda-to*), 1955 (G. V. Ivanov, *Sobranie sochinenii v. 3-kh tomakh* Vol. I (Moscow, 1994), 537): "The red flag or the tricolor? / Divine will or fate? / The mild predawn / breeze does not answer." Cf. Adamovich's poem, "When We Shall Return to Russia" (*Kogda my v Rossiiu vernemsia . . .*), 1936: "The miserable flag fluttered above us like a tricolored disgrace." G. V. Adamovich, *Sobranie sochinenii: Stikhi, proza, perevody* (St. Petersburg, 1999), 94. With regard to the "émigré state" motif, see the poem of V. Pereleshin, "We" (*My*) (1934): "In all republics and kingdoms, / Having intruded into alien cities, / We are a state in states, / Having united forever." Valerii Pereleshin, *Russkii poet v gostiakh u Kitaia, 1920–1952: Sbornik stikihotvorenii*, Russian Émigré Literature in the Twentieth Century Studies and Texts Vol. 4, Jan Paul Hinrichs, ed. (The Hague, 1989), 7.

9. Don-Aminado, "Prichina vsekh prichin," *Poslednie novosti* (Paris) October 3, 1920, 3.
The Russian:

> Nu ne persik, nu ne grusha li
> Peterburgskii etot plod?!
> Kak my zhili! Chto my kushali!
> Chto chitali, chto my slushali
> U granitnykh nevskikh vod?!
>
> [...] I poroi ia s grust'iu dumaiu,
> Za sud'boi sledia ugriumoiu,
> Chto ona—itog grekhov
> I chto vse iavilos' summoiu
> Glavnym obrazom stikhov!..\

10. Vladimir Nabokov, *The Gift* (London, 1963), 97.
11. Ant. Ladinskii, "Sankt-Peterburg," *Poslednie novosti* (Paris) June 3, 1928, 4.

12. Stolitsa—mysl', gde sterzhen'—Nevskii,
> Venchalas' s Pushkinym Neva,
> Gde vysochaishie slova
> Skazal srazitel' veshchestva,
> Kopernik dukha Dostoevskii.

13. Pushkin's two works, *The Bronze Horseman* and *The Queen of Spades*, which fulfill a special role in Russian culture as prototexts that created a long tradition, became some of the most popular sources of references in émigré poetry. Without delving into this question here (for greater detail see Vladimir Khazan, "O nekotorykh osobennostiakh emigrantskikh toposov (k postanovke voprosa)," *Humanitāro zinātņu vēstnesis* no. 3 (Daugavpils, 2003), 37–49. I shall refer only to an example from the musical rather than the literary sphere—the cantata "The Bronze Horseman," written in 1953—the year of the 250th anniversary of the founding of St. Petersburg—by a graduate of the Imperial Aleksandrovskii Lyceum, A. S. Il'iashenko, a composer of symphonic music who had worked in the editorial division of the office of the State Duma (1884–1954).

14. Marc Raeff, *Russia Abroad: A Cultural History of the Russian Emigration, 1919–1939* (New York, 1990), 96.

15. N. Agnitsev, "Sankt-Peterburg" (1923), 15; V. Dukel'skii, "Poslanie k S. L. Bertensonu," in *Poslaniia* (Munich, 1962), 24–29; Kal'ma, "Pikovaia dama," *Otkliki* 2 (23 March 1921), 8; V. Popper, *Gora favor* (Helsinki, 1987); S. Pregel', *Berega* (Paris, 1953), 24–25; M. Vega, *Lilit* (Paris, 1955), 35–48; V. Zlobin, "Liubeznym devam ne na zlo," *Sovremennye zapiski* (Paris) 24 (1925), 172–173.

16. I. Severianin, "Igrai tselyi vecher," *Segodnia* (Riga) 100 (May 6, 1927), 2.

17. N. Pavlovich, "Obvetrennyi i zagorelyi, kak matros," in *Bereg* (Petersburg, 1922), 26.

18. Argus, "V Petrograde" in *Polushutia-poluser'ezno: Satira, iumor, lirika* (New York, 1959), 261; I. Chinnov, "A poety vzali da i vymerli," in *Sobranie sochinenii* Vol. II (Moscow, 2002), 18; Iurii Ivask, "Portugal'skii proletarii," in *Zolushka* (New York, 1970), 46.

19. Vladimir Nabokov, "Pamiati Gumileva," in *Stikhotvoreniia* (St. Petersburg, 2002), 261:

> Gordo i iasno ty umer, umer, kak Muza uchila.
> Nyne, v tishi Eliseiskoi, s toboi govorit o letiashchem
> Mednom Petre i o dikikh vetrakh afrikanskikh—Pushkin.

20. For the first period see the articles by Em. Mindlin, "Unrealized Petersburg" (*Neosushchestvlennyi Peterburg*), *Nakanune* (Berlin) 425 (September 14, 1923), 2–3; the article by N. Otsup, "About Poetry and Poets" (*O poezii i poetakh*) in connection with the response to the collection by Berlin poets, *Grove* (*Roshcha*), in the journal *Chisla* 6, (1931), 142; or his review of the Fifth Collection of the Union of Young Poets and Writers in Paris (1931), *Chisla* 5 (1931), 230. For the postwar period, see, in particular, P. Sergienko's review of the poetry collection of the former Petersburg resident Z. Trotska (her real name was Zil'berkveit), "Under One's Breath" (*Vpolgolosa*): "From the technical point of view, Zinaida Trotska's poems are constructed in the spirit of the pre-revolutionary 'Petersburg school'; they are put together well and they are harmonic," *Sovremennik* (Toronto) 5 (1962), 75. Such examples are numerous.

21. This term had been repeated after him by many émigré poets and writers. See, for example, the opening of the sketch by G. Ivanov, "Sunset over Petersburg" (*Zakat nad Peterburgom*) (1953): "Resplendent St. Petersburg was at the time of its flourishing indeed a splendid capital" (Ivanov, *Sobranie sochinenii*, III: 456), or Iu. Trubetskoi's prose description of Petersburg's desolation in the period of revolutionary apocalypse: "Resplendent St. Petersburg faded. The works of Monferrant, Gvarengi, Rossi, Cameron, and Voronikhin faded" (Trubetskoi, 1950, 32).

22. Iz sankt-truby voskhodit sankt-dymok,
    Sankt-golubi guliaiut po sankt-kryshe . . .
    Sneg vypal, kak molochnyi epilog,
    No ia uzhe prolog sverkan'ia slyshu.

23. See, for example I. Surguchev's story "Fourteen Old Men" (*Chetyrnadtsat' starikov*) in which the narrator-hero describes to a French family the unique beauty of Petersburg and encounters a naive lack of comprehension:

> I said that in Europe you wouldn't find many quays like the Petersburg ones, streets like Nevsky Prospect or squares like the Palace or Senate Squares.
> Then Koko himself began to speak, slightly ruddy after having eaten:
> "Is there steam heating in Russia?"
> I said that there was no steam heat in Russia.
> "Then how do you manage with your cold?" the host inquired.
> I replied, "When it is cold, they light fires in the streets. People come out of all the houses and warm themselves. Having warmed up, they go back and go to sleep."
> Looking around, they smiled approvingly and believed it.

(from Iu. Surguchev, *Emigrantskie rasskazy* [Paris, 1927], 143–144).

24. Nina Berberova, *The Italics Are Mine* (New York, 1969), 128; Iurii Trubetskoi, "Zhizn' moego priiatelia," *Sovremennik* (Toronto) 1, 1960, 32.

25. P. Iakobi, "Let 35 tomu nazad" *Dlia vas* (Riga) 20 (May 13, 1934), 14. In Russian:

Let 35 tomu nazad
Blistal ogniami pyshnyi Nevskii
I iz Senata Karabchevskii
V bobrakh letel na maskarad
Let 35 tomu nazad.

. . . . . .

Let 35 tomu nazad
Nas v Pavlovsk vlek maestro Galkin,
Plenial ikroi "Medved'" il' "Palkin."
Ah! Byl balyk! Zakusok riad . . .
Let 35 tomu nazad!

26. G. Ivanov, "Ianvarskii den'. Na beregu Nevy," in *Sobranie sochinenii*, III: 287.

27. An allusion to the prologue of Pushkin's poem *The Bronze Horseman*.

28. P. Bulygin, *Stikhotvoreniia* (Berlin, 1922), 67; reprinted in *Petersburg v stikhotvoreni-iakh* (1923), 96. He later developed this theme in his long poem "Newly Fallen Snow" (*Porosha*).

V zheltom tumane blestit na vetru
Groziashchii moguchei rukoi.
Chem-to otplatit svoboda Petru?
Ne zdal On razviazki takoi . . .

Luchshe b ostalos', kak bylo vstar',—
A On zdes' okno prorubil . . .
Mudryi byl Syn y Tebia, Gosudar'!
Zachem Ty Ego pogubil?

29. The depiction of Petersburg as the new capital of European Christian civilization, created by the "miracle-making builder" with an anti-Roman purpose, takes a turn in the direction of a necropolis theme. See Gleb Lebedev, "Rim i Peterburg: Arkheologiia urbanizma i substantsiia vechnogo goroda," in *Metafizika Peterburga* (St. Petersburg, 1993), 47–62.

30. Ant. Ladinskii, "Elegiia," in his collections of poems *Stikhi o Evrope* (Paris, 1937), 11.

31. The poem was published in *Russkie zapiski* (Paris-Shanghai) I (1937), 132.

32. Arkadii Borman, "Moi Peterburg" *Novoe russkoe slovo* (New York) 20501 (April 26, 1969), 3.

33. I. Voinov, "The City Depopulated by Crimson Banners [*Gorod, obezliuzhennyi alymi znamenami*]," *Novaia russkaia zhizn'* (Helsingfors) 150 (July 6, 1921), 3. For more, see, for example, the poem of R. Blokh, "You Are Sad Again, My Friend, My Dear One" (*Ty snova grusten, moi drug, moi milyi* [1919]): "Look, the huge city has died / The crosses are burning from the cathedrals' summits" [Blokh, *Moi gorod* (Berlin, 1928), 12]; or the later story by I. Lukash, "The End of Petersburg": "The entire former life has already withered away. Even earlier than the people, things and stones surrendered to the cold silence and desolation. Petersburg, with its frozen colonnades, embankments, and empty palaces stood in the snow like a majestic sepulcher, and the striking of the chimes in Petropavlosk Fortress

sounded like a penetrating funeral tolling in the frozen silence" [Lukash, "Konets Peterburga," *Vozrozhdenie* (Paris) 3273 (May 20, 1934), 3].

34. I. Tkhorzhevskii "Na novyi god," *Novaia russkaia zhizn'* (Helsingfors) 1 (1920).

> Kamin okhvachen plamenem utrat:
> Vitaet bol' nad grudoi let sozhzhennykh;
> I, v alykh ranakh, mertvyi Petrograd
> Gliadit iz pepla, gorod prokazhennykh!

35. Nabokov, *Stikhotvoreniia*, 240.

36. On the motif of the sunken Atlantis in Russian émigré poetry, see Vladimir Khazan, "'Moia Atlantida—Rossiia' (K nekotorym chertam 'morskogo' mifa v poezii russkoi emigratsii)," *From the Other Shore* (Toronto) 2, 2002, 1–20.

37. M. Vega, "Atlantida," in *Lilit*, 138.

> I v medlennom kruzhen'e belykh purg,
> Gde chuditsia skvoz' veter boi kurantov,
> Ta ten', tot dukh, ch'e imia—Peterburg,
> Ne mozhet ne uznat' svoikh atlantov.

38. A. Golovina "Okeanskaia glub', okeanskaia shir'," in *Gorodskoi angel* (Brussels, 1989), 107.

> Piterburg, Peterburg, Petrograd, Leningrad...
> Eto Letnii krylovskii siiaiushchii sad.
>
> Pochemu zhe on vechno v krovi i v snegu?

39. G. V. Adamovich, *Sobranie sochinenii*, 95.

40. Vl. Diterikhs fon Ditrikhshtein, "Belyi zhrebii," in *Sobranie stikhov (1912–1964)* (Brussels, 1965), 122.

> Sei noch'iu mglistoi Vsadnik Mednyi
> Letit nad glad'iu chernykh vod,
> I gneven Petr, stezei pobednoi
> Vozvavshii k slave svoi narod!

41. N. Svetlov, "Za rubezhom," in *Russkaia poeziia Kitaia* (Moscow, 2001), 476S.

> Predo mnoiu ulitsa krivaia
> Prinimaet peterburgskii vid.

Gollerbakh, in designing *Three Homelands* (Tri rodiny), the poetry collection of V. Pereleshin, who had lived in China, depicted on the cover the figure of the Bronze Horseman and a Chinese dragon behind him.

42. A. Perfil'ev, *Stikhi* (Munich, 1976), 123; G. Adamovich, "Ty snova zdes'... Nevernaia, chto nado," *Novyi zhurnal* 58 (1960), 93–94.

> S kakim-to nevskim veterkom ot Seny
> Letiat kak vstar' poslushnye slova,

Den' nastaet pochti nezdeshne iarkii.
Raskhoditsia predutrenniaia mgla,
Vzvivaetsia nad Eliseiskoi arkoi
Admiralteistva vechnaia igla . . .

In the story "Lutetia," by N. Gorodetskaia, the heroine, a Russian emigrant living in Paris, loses her topographical orientation and, not knowing exactly "where she was living, . . . she went along the embankment of the Seine and thought about the blue Neva, and, like a victory march, recited *The Bronze Horseman*" (N. Gorodetskaia, "Lutetia," *Vozrozhdenie* (Paris) 3335, July 21, 1934, 3). Like her, the hallucinating hero of G. Gazdanov's story, "Queen Mary" (*Kniazhna Meri*), 1953, is infatuated with the lines from Blok's poem, "Night, Street, Lantern, Pharmacy," applying them to his own Parisian "terrible world," although "it could have been anywhere—in London or Amsterdam— this perspective of a winter street, lanterns, the dim light of the windows, the silent movement through the snow and the cold, the uncertainty of what happened yesterday, the uncertainty of what would happen tomorrow, the slipping consciousness of one's own existence . . ." Gaito Gazdanov, *Sobranie sochinenii v 3-kh tomakh*, Vol. III (Moscow, 1996), 554.

Incidentally, a similar contiguity was possible also in Soviet poetry, but in that case, it was invariably ideological: a comparison of revolutionary Petrograd with Paris of the period of the great French Revolution, when "gloomy Petrograd / became gay Paris for an hour." Emmanuil German, *Rastoplennyi polius* (Moscow, 1929), 17.

43. G. Raevsky, "Krepchaet i treshchit moroz," *Vozrozhdenie* (Paris) 1367 (February 28, 1928), 3.

> Vnezapno vizhu naiavu
> Ne zamerzaiushchuiu Senu,—
> Led, snezhnyi veter i Nevu,
> Edinstvennuiu vo vselennoi.

44. N. Otsup, *Okean Vremeni* (St. Petersburg, 1993), 160.

> Konkord i Eliseiskie polia,
> A v pamiati Sadovaia i Nevskii,
> Nad Blokom peterburgskaia zemlia,
> Nad vsemi stranami Tolstoi i Dostoevsky.

45. Vladimir Dukel'skii, "Afiny Severa," in *Kartinnaiia galeriia* (Munich, 1965), 28.

> Mne Boston v proshloe okontsem
> Kazalsia; uveriala mat':
> "Zdes' Petergof—ni dat', ni vziat'!"

46. Zinaida Trotskaia, "Mne chasto snitsia svet kakoi-to smutnyi," in *Vpolgolosa* (Paris, 1961), 9.

> Ne v tom ia gorode, chto chas nazad.
> Brodila, pomniu, ran'she po Parizhu—
> Teper' New-York . . . net, slovno Petrograd.

47. Konstantin Pomerantsev, *Sodruzhestvo* (Washington, DC, 1966), 372.

> Za oknom florentiiskoe nebo
> i na nem peterburgskii rassvet.

48. V. Lur'e, "Krugovorot," in *Stikhotvoreniia* (Berlin, 1987), 100.

> No ty mne stal teper' opiat' dorozhe
> I kruzhitsia kak prezhde golova.
> Pust' zavtra budesh' kholodnei i strozhe,
> Chem l'dom gustym pokrytaia Neva.

49. See, for example, in the poem by G. Struve, "The February Day Is Painfully Uneasy" (*Fevral'skii den' tomitel'no-trevozhen*): "The February day is painfully uneasy / The clouds are lilac above the Seine / I recall—more agitated and stern—/ Another ice-bound river." (*Mednyi vsadnik*, 1923, 215–216). On a parodic-comic level, creating a flavor of emigrant folklore, see in the story by N. A. Teffi "Town" (*Gorodok*): "A river flowed through the town. In olden days they called the river Sekvana, then the Seine, and when a little city was founded on it, the inhabitants began to call it 'their Neva'" (Teffi, *Sobranie sochinenii* Vol. III [Moscow, 1998], 146).

50. L. Strakhovskii compares the Neva to the Thames in the poem "Over the Thames" (*Nad Temzoi*); Strakhovskii, 1953, 13; first published in *Russkaia Mysl'* (Sofia), nos. 10–12 (1921), 177. Similarly, N. Nadezhdin, who wound up in London during his wanderings as an emigrant, wrote in the long poem *Razuveren'e* (*Dissuasion*): "Longing arises for my former life. / What am I longing for? For my homeland. / I look at the Thames, and the Neva / is what I see again as if in reality." Nikolai Nadezhdin, *Razuveren'e* (Prague, 1925), 114.

51. In the poem of B. Nartsissov, "Morning on Broadway," the Neva "flows" in the center of New York. Boris Nartsissov, *Stikhi* (New York, 1958), 42.

52. In the poem of V. Sumbatov, the waves of the Neva mix with the currents of the Tiber: "In the currents of the Tiber, I see the waves of the Neva, / The reflections of Petersburg palaces . . ." Vasilii Sumbatov, *Prozrachnaia t'ma: Stikhi raznykh let* (Livorno, 1969), 6.

53. A. Parkau, living in Harbin, in the poem "Recollection" (*Vospominanie*) described the Sungari as indistinguishably reminiscent of the Neva.

54. Oleg Il'inskii, "Triumfal'nye arki" in *Stikhi* (Munich, 1966), 68. (Gde my? V N'iu-Iork'e? No smyty pregrady: / My vdvinuty v ramki inogo plasta; / Skvoz' prorez' chugunnykh ograd Petrograda / L'diny nyriaiut v prolety mosta.)

55. Nikolai Otsup, *Stikhotvoreniia: Dnevnik v stikhakh: Stat'i i vospominaniia* (St. Petersburg—Dusseldorf, 1993), 449.

> Naberezhnaia, Nevy prostory,
> Sena s bukinistami na Quai,
> Na Monmartre russkie shofery,
> A u Larinykh Monsieur Trike.

56. G. Stosius, "Sankt-Peterburg," *Novoe russkoe slovo* (New York) 21992 (August 30, 1970), 4.

57. This is the name of the cycle in the manuscript (preserved in the Russian archive in Leeds. MS 1396/1041. My thanks to Dr. R. Davies for the opportunity to see the manuscript.) In the book by A. Ugriumov, *My Past and Thoughts: A Notebook of Verse* (*Perezhitoe i peredumannoe: Tetrad' stikhov*), (Cambridge, 1958), 84–87, these poems are not formally united into a cycle.

58. The book was published initially in English and only later in Russian.

59. Lada Nikolaenko, "Petersburg in Leningrad," an excerpt from "A Story about Losses," *Grani* 1 (1969). In emigration the expression "Leningrad's Petersburg" (*Leningradskii Peterburg*) was common; see the article by that name by Georgii Petrov (*Grani* 18 [1953], 39–50) or the series of sketches by B. Fillipov, "Leningrad's Petersburg in Russian Poetry" (*Leningradskii Peterburg v russkoi poezii*).

60. V. Nabokov, *Stikhotvoreniia*, 281. The play on words here concerns the renaming of Petrograd into Leningrad, which in Russian sounds close to Elena's City or Elenagrad (Elena is the Russian name for Helen).

> Velikie, poroiu,
> byvaiut peremeny . . .
> No, plamennye muzhi,
> chto znachit etot son?
> Byl Petrograd—on khuzhe,
> chem Peterburg,—ne skroiu,—
> no ne pokhodit on,—
> kak ni verti,—na Troiu:
> zachem zhe v chest' Eleny—
> tak laskovo k tomu zhe
> on vami okreshchen?

61. N. P. Solodkov, "Gorod proshlogo," *Chasovoi* (Brussels) 338 (1954), 22.

> Kak ditia Imperatorov,
>   —gorod slavy, pobed,—
> Nenavidim novatorom
>   v tebe proshlogo sled.
> No s Tsariami stolitseiu
>   prosluzhil sotni let
> I zhivesh' Ikh desnitseiu,
>   khot' nazvan'ia uzh net,—

62. V. Krymov, *Fuga* (Paris, 1935).

63. Quoted in *Vozrozhdenie* 3515 (17 January 1935), 4.

64. *Rubezh* (Harbin) 7 (1935), 24.

65. G. Ivanov, "Chetvert' veka proshlo za granitsei," in *Sobranie sochinenii* I: 395; "Zakat nad Peterburgom," in ibid. III: 469–470.

66. Iu. Gal', "Pis'ma," *Opyty* IV (1955), 99; Anna El'kan, "Dom iskusstv," *Mosty* 5 (1960), 287.

67. Nabokov, *Stikhotvoreniia*, 346–347, 236.

68. N. Otsup, *Stikhotvoreniia*, 420.

"V Peterburge my soidemsia snova..."
Nekomu skhoditsia, dorogoi
Osip... Net tebia, net Gumileva...
Stala i Akhmatova sedoi,
I, kak ia,—ne molody Ivanov,
Adamovich, brat'ia po vesne,
Po sud'bam: ni fal'shi, ni tumanov,
Ni nadezhdy...

69. I. Brodskii, "Dekabr' vo Florentsii," in *Sochineniia Iosefa Brodskogo* Vol. III (St. Petersburg, 1998–2000), 113.

70. I. Chinnov, "Byl osveshchen torzhestvennyi fasad," in *Sobraniie sochinenii* (Moscow, 2002), 535.

I mechtat' naprasnyi trud,
Chto nashi trupy v'edut v Petrograd [...]
A vot stikhi—doidut. Stikhi—doidut.

Six

Multiethnic St. Petersburg: The Late Imperial Period

Steven Duke

In May 2003 the city of St. Petersburg celebrated the 300th anniversary of its founding. Peter the Great's famous "Window onto Europe" has seen significant changes over the last three centuries. The city that began as a rough settlement in a marshy river delta was transformed into an imperial capital before seeing revolution, civil war, Nazi siege, postwar reconstruction, and the proliferation of centrally planned apartment blocks. Now it is changing again, as Western shops and market-driven values compete with Soviet-era remnants. Although St. Petersburg's glamorous days as the capital city of a major world empire are long over, visitors to this "Venice of the North" can still catch a glimpse of Russia's imperial tradition in the city's architecture, museums, and monuments (see William Brumfield's chapter in the present volume). Yet something that is often overlooked and that went missing from most of St. Petersburg's official tercentenary celebrations was recognition of its multiethnic, multi-confessional character and history. The contributions of ethnic and religious minorities to St. Petersburg's construction and development were largely ignored, relegated to the dustbins of history.[1] In fact, the most recent book on multinational St. Petersburg opens with a reminder of the city's multiethnic character, asserting that many residents of St. Petersburg think it a city composed only of Russians, and all non-Russians there—merely visitors.[2]

Popular ignorance in Russia about St. Petersburg's multiethnic and multiconfessional heritage is not surprising in light of Soviet policies, which emphasized the "friendship of nations" and the development of *Homo sovieticus* while minimizing national, ethnic, linguistic, and religious communities and identities. The extensive Russian-language historiography on the imperial capital[3] almost completely ignores the city's diverse national and religious minorities, despite efforts by N. V. Iukhneva[4] and a handful of other Russian ethnographers and historians to create a more inclusive and complete picture of the city's inhabitants.[5] For a variety of reasons, Western scholarship on St. Petersburg has also tended to ignore the city's minorities, creating the impression that the city was almost exclusively inhabited by Orthodox Russians and a handful of prominent foreigners. Yet, given the ethnic diversity of late Imperial Russia and the population's increasing mobility, St. Petersburg's ethnic and religious diversity should come as no surprise,[6] though few studies have concentrated specifically on the city's ethnic and religious minorities.[7]

This chapter briefly surveys overall demographic changes in the ethnic and religious makeup of St. Petersburg during the tsarist period, with particular attention to the city's decennial censuses to assess changes in the post-reform era. It then analyzes some of the reasons that ethnic and religious minorities (including foreigners) were attracted to St. Petersburg and examines the ways in which they contributed to the city's economic, political, social, and cultural development. Finally, a more detailed discussion of St. Petersburg's Finnish-speaking community as a case study provides insight into how St. Petersburg changed over time and how those changes affected individual minority communities and identities.[8]

Demographic Overview

To understand fully why St. Petersburg was a multiethnic and multiconfessional urban space, it is important to know the city's "pre-history"—the history of the surrounding region prior to the founding of Peter I's fortress in 1703. The territory that later became St. Petersburg (and St. Petersburg Province) has been a multiethnic region throughout history. During early medieval times, the region was largely influenced by Scandinavian culture.

Scandinavian (Varangian) and Slavic merchants used the Neva River and other waterways to trade with the region's inhabitants; they also traded as far south as the Black Sea. By the eleventh century, with the rise of Kievan Rus' and other Slavic states, the region came under the influence of Lord Novgorod the Great. As part of Novgorod's zone of influence, the Neva River delta and the rest of "Vodskaia Piatina" (the term "Izhorskaia Zemlia" was used in some contexts) provided access to trading partners on the Baltic Sea. Slavic speakers inhabited the region alongside people speaking Karelian, Izhorian, Vepsian, and Votic, four Balto-Finnic languages related to modern Finnish. Orthodoxy gradually replaced pagan traditions.[9]

In the late sixteenth and early seventeenth centuries the region became a military battleground, as the Kingdom of Sweden (which at the time included the area of present-day Finland) attempted to capture the area. At the conclusion of one series of battles, the Peace of Stolbova of 1617 transferred control of the territory to Sweden. The fighting, disease, and destruction associated with waves of war (both before and after 1617) devastated the population. In addition, Sweden's active efforts to introduce Lutheranism into the area induced thousands to move eastward into Russian territory. To repopulate the region, Sweden invited thousands of free Finnish-speaking peasants to move to the region. The city of Nyen (its fortress was called Nyenschantz) was established on the Neva River, in the Malaia Okhta section of present-day St. Petersburg. By the late seventeenth century many locales in the area, which the Swedes called Ingermanland, had been transformed, and in many areas Finnish and Balto-Finnic speakers came to predominate. Religion (Lutheranism and Orthodoxy) and language helped to shape community and individual identities.[10]

While the immediate history of St. Petersburg rightly begins in 1703 with Peter I's acquisition of the region in the Great Northern War, one must not forget that this rapidly growing city relied on local labor and affected the local population directly. The city's founding and development contributed to significant changes for local inhabitants (Russian, Finnish, and Balto-Finnic alike), not only because the region's peasant population lost land and freedom when Peter I captured the region and enserfed the peasants, but also because thousands lost their lives in the dramatic construction activities of Peter's reign. Many areas, including Nyen and its fortress, were destroyed in the fighting. The local economy changed markedly as the construction of St. Petersburg intensified and the population grew.[11]

Thousands of non-Russians moved to the city under Peter I and his successors. During the eighteenth century, most foreigners and many non-Russian imperial subjects lived in various *"slobody"* or special neighborhoods built apart from the areas reserved for "Russian" inhabitants. In the eighteenth century, St. Petersburg was not the contiguous urban space visible today; rather, it comprised numerous neighborhoods or groups of buildings separated by small farms, orchards, fields, rivers, and canals and connected by roads or bridges. Finnish speakers, who had remained on their farms even after the city's founding, inhabited many of the farming areas inside or near the city. Many decades passed before farms were replaced by buildings and neighborhoods grew together. The slobody constructed for the city's German, French, English, Dutch, and Tatar speakers were fairly distinct at first and separate from the city's Russian neighborhoods. Each sloboda had its own character, including non-Orthodox confessional buildings. Non-Orthodox churches built during the eighteenth century tended to be located in or near these slobody, whereas confessional buildings constructed in nineteenth and twentieth centuries tended to be farther from the center, in neighborhoods where a certain ethnic group was concentrated (the Estonian and Latvian Lutheran churches, for example). The Tatar mosque built in the early 1900s bucked the latter trend, as it was close to the former Tatar sloboda on the Petersburg side.[12] Although St. Petersburg grew rapidly and Russian neighborhoods gradually merged with foreign slobody, various districts retained their own character into the early twentieth century. The socioeconomic character of the city's districts affected the number and type of ethnic minorities that settled in those districts over time.[13]

It is hard to determine precisely how many non-Russians (including foreigners) lived in St. Petersburg before 1869, when the first citywide census was conducted.[14] Various earlier statistical surveys and estimates of the ethnic and foreign population in St. Petersburg provide only "ballpark" figures. For example, a statistical survey of 1750 reported 68,721 "Russians" and 5,562 foreigners. Scholars analyzing this survey believe that the data exclude children, and estimate the population at the time as 25–30 percent greater. Foreigners (i.e., citizens of foreign countries) reportedly comprised 6–8 percent of the city's population in 1750. It is difficult to establish how many non-Russian speakers the category of "Russians" included, since the category itself likely meant subjects of the Russian Empire and therefore probably included Baltic Germans as well as local Finnish and Swedish speakers, among others.[15]

A much clearer picture of the ethnic, social, and religious composition of St. Petersburg's population emerges in the first citywide census of 1869. Additional city censuses were conducted every ten years: in 1881, 1890, 1900, and 1910.[16] These decennial censuses, like the 1897 imperial census, suffered from the imprecision unavoidably shared by all censuses: they depended on the truthfulness of the respondents and on finding the city's residents where they could be counted on census day (typically, December 15). In addition, the nature of census questions in late Imperial Russia—which focused on political, social, religious, and linguistic categories, not on self-selected identity—makes the modern historian's job of assessing identity and community formation difficult. In short, census data should not be taken at face value but must be interpreted carefully.[17]

Analyzing raw data from St. Petersburg's decennial censuses provides the following general picture of the city's inhabitants. Of the nearly 620,000 people counted by name in 1869, just over 515,000 gave Orthodoxy as their confession.[18] In 1869, virtually all (99 percent) Orthodox believers were Russian speakers, accounting for nearly 83 percent of the city's population. While social and cultural variations certainly existed even among the Russian Orthodox population, it is the other 17 percent of the population, more than 106,000 strong in 1869, that requires our attention here. Overall, the 1869 census counted nearly 74,000 Protestants, nearly 19,000 Catholics, and more than 1,600 Muslims in the city, the majority of whom claimed a language other than Russian as their native tongue. The largest non-Russian group, German speakers, comprised more than 7 percent of the city's population in 1869; some 42,000 German speakers were Lutheran, 2,600 were Catholic, and a few hundred were Jewish. An additional 32,000 Protestants spoke a variety of languages, including Finnish, Swedish, Russian, Estonian, Latvian, English, French, and Dutch. Catholic believers were nearly as diverse as Protestants, including speakers of Polish, Russian, German, French, Lithuanian, and Italian. Jews, Raskol'niki, Muslims, Armeno-Gregorian Christians, and a few idol-worshipers were also counted.[19]

Over the following decades, the city's population grew rapidly, swelling from 667,000 in 1869 to 860,000 in 1881 and 954,000 in 1890. While the proportion of Russian speakers increased slightly, to 84.39 percent in 1890, the percentage of other speakers changed over time: the percentage of German speakers declined despite some numerical growth, while Polish-speaking Catholics and Yiddish-speaking Jews jumped noticeably, both in overall numbers as well as in proportion to the total population.

By 1900 St. Petersburg's population (not counting those in four substantial suburbs) had grown to nearly 1,250,000. Ten years later, the population had risen to nearly 1,600,000 (nearly doubling the population of 1881). According to the raw census data, the percentage of "Russian" speakers in the city continued to rise, from 82.88 percent in 1869 to 86.10 percent in 1910. Yet raw data from St. Petersburg's decennial censuses minimized the number of certain ethnic minorities while overcounting the number of "Russian" speakers, according to Iukhneva, a Russian historical ethnographer who has spent the last three decades studying St. Petersburg's population. Having carefully analyzed and reconstructed St. Petersburg's census data, Iukhneva believes that the number of Russian speakers in the city was actually lower than the raw census figures suggest. Census takers overcounted the number of Russian speakers and undercounted ethnic minorities for several reasons, most notably because questions about native language use were imprecise and some individuals reported their native language as Russian because they feared reprisal. According to her reconstructions, the percentage of Russian speakers actually declined from 1869 onward, from 83.2 percent in 1869 to 82.9 percent in 1890 and 82.3 percent in 1910. The biggest difference between the raw data and her reconstructed data concerns the city's Ukrainian and Belorussian inhabitants, who, Iukhneva believes, were substantially undercounted by census takers. Iukhneva's reconstructed data for these and other ethnic groups (by analyzing data on the province of origin) also raise the number of other minorities in the city, including Lithuanian, French, English, and Finnish speakers.[20]

Although decennial censuses counted non-Russian speakers who were also Orthodox believers (a small Estonian Orthodox community grew steadily), the vast majority of non-Russians professed the same religious traditions as their ethnic counterparts elsewhere in the empire: Roman Catholicism, Evangelical Lutheranism, Judaism, Islam, Armeno-Gregorian Christianity, and so forth. For example, Finnish, Estonian, and Latvian speakers were predominantly Lutheran, Polish and Lithuanian speakers were mostly Catholic (as were some Latvian speakers from Letgallia), and Tatar speakers were overwhelmingly Muslim. As a result, confessional congregations were organized largely by language.[21] The city's Jewish population was unique, for steady immigration was accompanied by a rapid shift in language usage from Yiddish to Russian. St. Petersburg's Jews faced substantial legal hurdles in living in the city, including limits on the number of Jews permitted to enroll in different types of educational institutions. Despite these challenges and widespread discrimination, the Jewish community in St. Petersburg grew steadily, as many Jews fled the Pale of Settlement and sought new opportunity in the imperial capital.[22] On the whole, it is therefore surprising that although the city's ethnic and religious communities increased in size and diversity prior to World War I, many aspects of those communities' experience remain unstudied or forgotten.

The Attraction of St. Petersburg

These basic demographic data urge the question: What was it about St. Petersburg that attracted ethnic and religious minorities, including foreigners, to the city? Why would non-Russian and non-Orthodox minorities leave their home areas and travel to this bustling metropolis? One might expect that nobles, merchants, and peasants alike first entered the city with a mixture of trepidation and excitement, regardless of their economic, linguistic, and religious backgrounds. The thrill of traveling or moving to this rapidly growing imperial capital probably jostled with feelings of being overwhelmed by the city's sheer size and the daunting task of maneuvering in a predominantly Russian-language urban space. Certainly there were many reasons that people, including ethnic and religious minorities, moved to St. Petersburg. While recognizing other motivations, here I focus on three reasons for ethnic minorities' attraction to the city: it served concurrently as the seat of power and as a focal point of "high society"; it offered a wide range of economic opportunities; and it provided opportunities for higher education.

St. Petersburg's role as the imperial capital and as a focal point of "polite society" attracted thousands of ethnic minorities over the course of the tsarist regime. I begin with this general attraction partly to recognize the important position of foreigners in both polite society and positions of power. I anticipate that most Russians today, if asked about the contributions of non-Russians to the city's development, would point immediately to the work of foreign architects and artists such as Bartolomeo Rastrelli, Carlo Rossi, and others. As Julie Buckler and William Brumfield note in their chapters in this volume, Rastrelli and other foreign architects and artists left an indelible imprint on the appearance, palaces, and monuments of the city. Yet artists and architects were only one segment of the foreign population who exerted their influence; nobles, wealthy merchants, ambassadors and their staff, and those who served in the bureaucracy or helped create the Academy of Sciences also participated in polite society and influenced government decision making. Examples include Burkhard Christoph von Munnich (in Russian, Minikh) from Denmark, who served as Governor-General of St. Petersburg from 1728 and as President of the War College from 1732, and K. V. Nessel'rode, who served as Minister of Foreign Affairs under Nicholas I. Germans and other foreigners dominated the Academy of Sciences throughout the eighteenth century, the period when foreigners also participated actively in the growing military complex, especially the Admiralty.[23]

The wide range of economic and social opportunities in St. Petersburg also attracted ethnic minorities. At the upper end of the economic scale were positions and opportunities for nobles, merchants of higher guilds, and individuals from prominent families. Baltic German nobles played a substantial role in St. Petersburg's development through their service in the bureaucracy, the military, education and science, and the economy. Many Baltic German families owned homes in St. Petersburg, where they could interact with other nobles and prominent individuals, attend balls and parties, visit salons, and promote their own careers and those of others. According to one estimate, Baltic Germans accounted for 20 percent of governors and 18 percent of the Governing Senate under Nicholas I. Prince K. A. Liven, for example, served as Minister of Education from 1828 to 1833. Although Baltic Germans comprised a diminishing percentage of those in government service from the mid-nineteenth century, they maintained a strong presence in the imperial capital. Polish nobles (Prince Adam Czartoryski, whom Alexander I included in his "secret committee," is but one example) also had access to prominent government positions.[24]

Another important sector of St. Petersburg's economy that attracted minorities involved architecture, art, and skilled trades. In trying to make St. Petersburg an imperial capital that could compete with its European counterparts, Russia's tsars and tsarinas actively recruited foreign specialists of all kinds to the city. Rastrelli, Rossi, Giacomo Quarenghi, and J.-B. Vallin de la Mothe famously number among the many foreign-born architects who contributed to the city's development. Other skilled trades that attracted non-Russians were those of clockmakers, jewelers, silversmiths, and goldsmiths. Finnish and Swedish speakers played an important role among such skilled craftsmen, including the employees of the Fabergé and Bolin companies. Twenty-three of the twenty-six jewelers active in Helsingfors/ Helsinki in the second half of the nineteenth century received their training in St. Petersburg. The artisanal sector was a key part of St. Petersburg's diverse economy, providing a much larger number of jobs than many industrially focused studies would lead us to believe.[25]

Merchants, industrialists, and bankers were also attracted to St. Petersburg, for the city was not only the site of important government offices (including tax, passport, and customs offices), but also an increasingly active port. Large foreign merchant firms played a pivotal role in St. Petersburg's (and Russia's) international trade throughout the tsarist period. Foreign-owned firms often employed German speakers, including subjects of various German states as well as Baltic German and Russian German families. Swedish, Polish, Jewish, and other domestic merchants and bankers likewise played a vital part in the city's economy. Prominent industrialists included the Swedes Ludvig and Immanuel Nobel, whose factory in the Vyborg District employed numerous Finnish workers, and the Scots David and James Maxwell, who ran the Petrovskaia and Spasskaia cotton mills. Foreign bankers gained even more influence after 1908, as France and other countries invested millions of rubles in Russia's industrial sector.[26]

Ethnic minorities similarly worked in the city's white-collar sector, serving as accountants and bookkeepers, low-level government servants, lawyers, insurance representatives, teachers, and in a host of other positions. A few non-Russians employed in these sectors played pivotal roles in nationalist movements of nineteenth century, such as the civil servants Karl Robert Jakobson, who later published the radical Estonian newspaper *Sakala*, and Krisjan Valdemars, who published the Latvian *Peterburgas avises* (*Petersburg Newspaper*, 1862–1865). Other non-Russians made their own contributions. The Estonian August Janson, for example, served as inspector and later director of a commercial school, operated a mutual credit association for many years, and was elected to the St. Petersburg City Council in 1912.[27]

Many non-Russians were also drawn to St. Petersburg's industrial sector, where they worked as skilled and unskilled workers. Given the dynamic nature of many factories, it is impossible to verify precisely how many ethnic minorities they employed. To my knowledge, few factories kept detailed records about the ethnic heritage of their employees, making it difficult to assess how employment in this sector changed over time. However, given the growing number of skilled industrial workers in predominantly non-Russian parts of the empire (for example, in the Baltic region), it should not be surprising that many ethnic minorities sought economic opportunity in St. Petersburg's factories. Ludvig Nobel's factory in the Vyborg district employed numerous Finnish industrial workers, as did the Finland Train Station, Veiss's shoe factory, and the Suominen and Lyytikainen sewing shops, for example. In addition, around two-thirds of the city's chimney sweeps in 1869 were reportedly Finnish.[28]

Another area of opportunity for ethnic minorities was confessional service, which drew pastors, priests, rabbis, imams, and so forth. Some in this group interacted with government officials from the Department of Spiritual Affairs of Foreign Confessions, which reported to the Minister of Education and Spiritual Affairs from 1817 to 1832 and to the Minister of Internal Affairs from February 1832. This department had responsibility for coordinating with non-Orthodox confessional leaders, who themselves worked actively to promote and defend the rights conferred upon them by Peter I, Catherine II, and other rulers. Baltic Germans, for example, staffed the Lutheran General Consistory in St. Petersburg, which oversaw Lutheran congregations throughout the empire while also advocating Lutheran religious autonomy and native-language education. Poles and Tatars played predominant roles in representing the city's (and, by extension, the empire's) Catholics and Muslims, respectively.[29]

Finally, an additional important employment sector for ethnic minorities was household service, particularly in the homes of non-Russian families (German and Polish nobles, foreign ambassadors and their staff, Jewish merchants, and so on). Household servants comprised the city's largest employment sector in 1910 (34.6 percent of jobs reported),[30] with women constituting the majority. Yet non-Russian leaders in the city did not view this employment sector as free of problems. Jakob Hurt, a prominent Estonian nationalist who for decades also served as the Pastor of St. John's Lutheran church, published a personal warning that unethical persons, usually females, often recruited young Estonian women (and presumably women from other ethnic groups as well) to work in St. Petersburg. These recruiters reportedly flattered girls by promising wonderful working conditions, high salaries, and nice clothes, plus pocket money. Many girls ended up in St. Petersburg by taking the bait, Hurt reported, only to become trapped in poor working conditions. There was no lack of servants in St. Petersburg, as people streamed from all parts of the empire to the capital in search of employment. Hurt asserted that those seeking work in St. Petersburg should do so through trusted individuals, arrange residence with relatives if at all possible, and bring enough money to live on for several weeks.[31]

Not only employment, but also access to higher education attracted to St. Petersburg numerous ethnic minorities who attended a variety of advanced educational institutions in the imperial capital, ranging from St. Petersburg University to the advanced courses for women and the Conservatory of the Imperial Music Society. While some of these individuals remained in the city, many others returned to their home region, where they used the knowledge and connections gained in St. Petersburg to benefit themselves and, in many cases, various nationalist movements. Still others, including the Ukrainian poet and painter Taras Shevchenko, participated in the city's many cultural areas or used it as inspiration for their work.[32]

Finnish Speakers as a Microcosm of an Ethnic Community

Turning to St. Petersburg's Finnish-speaking minority, one notes that this community, under-studied by Anglophone specialists, underwent most of the basic changes experienced by the city's major ethnic communities and therefore serves as a valuable case study for tracking changes in the city's ethnic population. As indicated above, Finnish and Balto-Finnic speakers had inhabited the region around St. Petersburg long before Peter I's forces captured the area in 1703. Finnish-speaking peasants and craftsmen were recruited alongside other peasants and workers (Russian and non-Russian alike) to participate in building Peter's Venice of the North. In practical terms, this meant hauling stone, wood, sand, and other building materials into the burgeoning city; working to drain the marshy soil of the Neva River delta; and constructing the roads, bridges, canals, and buildings that constituted St. Petersburg's growing infrastructure. Yet this work represented only part of St. Petersburg's development, for the city's population also required food, clothing, tools, household goods, and much more.

Given its proximity to St. Petersburg, Ingria (the territory Sweden had controlled and named "Ingermanland") played a crucial role in these wide-ranging activities. Ingrian Finns and Izhorians not only hauled vegetables, grains, foodstuffs, and construction materials into St. Petersburg from Ingria, but also served as middlemen who received these goods from both Karelia and the Grand Duchy of Finland, then transported them to the city for sale. As a result, the number of Finnish speakers in St. Petersburg constantly fluctuated. By necessity, those involved in cartage (*izvoz*) interacted daily with Russian merchants and traders.

In addition to those individuals who traveled to and from St. Petersburg, thousands of Finnish speakers lived in the city on a continuous basis. At first most of them were unskilled or poorly skilled, since most Finns were peasants. Over many decades, however, a group of highly skilled Finnish craftsmen began to emerge in professional trades such as gold and silver smithing, metalworking, clock making, textiles, and carpentry. Moreover, a small number of Finnish speakers came to own private businesses in St. Petersburg (including bookstores and food markets) or served as doctors, lawyers, engineers and merchants, and chimney sweeps, and the Grand Duchy's government offices in St. Petersburg employed another group. Though few in number, individuals in these sectors gradually formed the vital core of a small professional middle class, which by the 1840s began to demand increased opportunities for Finnish children, particularly increased primary education in their native language.[33]

The core institution of the Finnish-speaking community in St. Petersburg was the Lutheran church, and the Lutheran congregation of St. Catherine was founded soon after St. Petersburg came into being. St. Catherine's church was located on Bol'shaia Konniushennaia after 1733, across from the German Lutheran church of St. Peter. Until 1745, both Swedish and Finnish speakers attended this congregation together. Disagreements between the two language groups, however, led to the creation in 1745 of the congregation of St. Mary, which thereafter most Finnish speakers in St. Petersburg attended. Some Finnish speakers from Kronstadt and the region outside St. Petersburg also attended St. Mary's, as did Estonian speakers until 1787. By the early 1800s the congregation boasted nearly 5,000 members, and congregation records show that number increased to 16,000 during the 1880s.[34]

The Lutheran Church played a key role in Finnish community activities and the formation of national and personal identities, in Finland proper, in

Ingria, and in St. Petersburg. The church figured significantly not only in events marking rites of passage (birth, confirmation, marriage, death), but also in activities associated with calendar rituals (Christmas and Easter celebrations, for example). In addition, in multiethnic St. Petersburg and Ingria (from where most Finnish speakers traveled to the city), the church and its clergy played a central role in several endeavors intent on preserving ethnic identity: teaching children to read and write (particularly in "confirmation schools"); perpetuating Finnish language and culture; and defending confessional separation and native-language privileges in the moral upbringing of youth. The church and its clergy likewise were vital to the development of formalized schooling, which began with the founding of St. Mary's church-school in 1844. Although St. Mary's importance in coordinating community activities diminished somewhat in the late tsarist era, when social organizations were established (see below), it nonetheless remained critical to Finnish social life and community activities in the city.[35]

Not only religious, but also purely secular institutions shaped St. Petersburg's Finnish-speaking community, and these included the government offices of the neighboring Grand Duchy of Finland. Russia invaded Finland (then part of Sweden) in 1808 and acquired the Grand Duchy by treaty the following year. Because the Grand Duchy had a separate government structure and came under the direct (albeit nominal) rule of the Russian Tsar, it never became fully integrated into the Russian empire. Alexander I's experiment with constitutional government resulted in the creation of Finnish government offices on Ekateringofskii Prospekt,[36] near St. Nicholas Cathedral, in St. Petersburg, which also housed the Finnish Affairs Committee, tax, passport, and customs offices. Though most of the staff at first consisted of Swedish speakers (the Grand Duchy government itself operated in Swedish until the second half of the nineteenth century, and in both Swedish and Finnish thereafter), the number of employed Finnish speakers steadily grew.[37] One should add that more than 3,300 Swedish-Finnish noblemen served as officers in the Russian army between 1809 and 1917, including Aleksandr Rediger, War Minister in 1905–1909, and Karl Mannerheim, who later led White Finnish forces in Finland's war for independence in 1918.[38]

The Grand Duchy's attachment to Russia's ruler had benefits for St. Petersburg's Finnish speakers, especially in the form of government assistance to St. Mary's—the strongest supporter of Finnish-language schooling in the city during the tsarist era. Built on Bol'shaia Konniushennaia in downtown

St. Petersburg, the church complex included offices and a school building; its first primary school for boys opened in 1844, and it admitted girls after 1849. By the late 1880s, the congregation was operating seven church-schools in various parts of the city, plus four more in small settlements outside the city limits. Courses were taught in both Finnish and Russian under the direction of a special church-school council and a Finnish church-school inspector, who collaborated with a Russian school inspector. Together, these educational institutions enrolled more than 900 pupils in fall 1892, and more than 1,000 in 1897; most pupils were native Finnish speakers born in St. Petersburg, supplemented by other ethnic groups.[39] By the late nineteenth century, St. Mary's original primary school had been transformed into an advanced primary school, and in 1905 it became a secondary school (lycée) with seven classes. Students who completed the seventh class could transfer to another lycée in the Grand Duchy, complete their eighth year, and then enter the University of Helsinki.[40]

Lutheranism and native-language education were central to a growing sense of Finnish national identity, in both the homeland and St. Petersburg. The constant movement of people between the Grand Duchy and Russia's capital early ensured the palpable awareness of the Finnish national movement in St. Petersburg. A major driving force behind the Finns' national awakening, the study of folklore and folk poetry, began in the 1810s and contributed to the publication in 1835 of the Finnish national epic, *Kalevala*, compiled by Elias Lönnrot, who collected poetry and oral tales in eastern Finland and Karelia, then wove them into composite poetic works. Other ethnographers and poetry collectors who both preceded and followed Lönnrot traveled widely throughout Karelia and Ingria to study what they considered age-old Finnish traditions, and to document local traditions as well as study Finnish dialects. Many of these national activists visited St. Petersburg or used it as their home base during their forays in data collection, including August Ahlqvist, D. E. D. Europeaus, H. A. Reinholm, Fredrik Saxbäck, and Anders Johan Sjögren. This attention to local customs stimulated feelings of national identity, which carried over into the social sphere. Consequently, by the turn of the century, rural Finnish-speaking residents increasingly thought of themselves in national terms—as Ingrians.[41]

Finnish-language newspapers published in St. Petersburg similarly contributed to a growing sense of Finnish national identity. After a series of newspapers published between 1870 and 1883 closed owing to financial problems and personality conflicts, the Finnish newspaper *Ingria* (Inkeri) debuted in 1884, to fill the void. During the following two decades, *Ingria* actively supported a sense of Finnishness in St. Petersburg and Ingria. While not overtly espousing Finnish independence or a radical political agenda, it adopted a pro–Grand Duchy stance in the increasingly bitter war of words about Finland's separate political status and promoted feelings of community among the Finnish-speaking population.[42]

One of the main editors of *Ingria* was Mooses Putro, an 1872 graduate of the Lutheran (and Finnish-language) Teacher Training Seminary in Maloe Kolpino (Kolppana in Finnish), south of St. Petersburg, near Gatchina. A teacher at one of St. Mary's church-schools in St. Petersburg for over three decades and an 1878 graduate of the St. Petersburg Conservatory of the Imperial Music Society, Putro combined his love of music with an equally strong love of Finnish Ingria. He promoted Ingrian Finnish nationalism through music: he wrote the hymn "Arise, Ingria" (first performed in 1888), encouraged choral activity in St. Petersburg and throughout Ingria, and organized song festivals in Ingria. His efforts paid off, for the six song festivals held between 1899 and 1913 involved thousands of participants, including schoolchildren. Putro's work from his home base in St. Petersburg reveals how directly the imperial capital was connected to the surrounding rural areas, both economically and metaphorically. Undeniably, St. Petersburg was the unofficial capital of Ingria, for it provided jobs and opportunities, resources and leadership, educational models and newspapers.[43]

In socioeconomic terms, the Finnish community in St. Petersburg improved steadily throughout the imperial period. Although many Finnish working-class families still continued to live in crowded, poorly appointed dwellings (the term "Finnish slums" stems from an 1849 Finnish-language novel, *The Finnish Way of Life in St. Petersburg*), the financial situation of a small but increasing number slowly but steadily improved. The regular participation of many Finns in the city's Finnish cultural and voluntary organizations, which arranged a variety of social events, indicates that they had sufficient funds to attend such activities at least once a month. For their "entertainment," Finns could choose among events sponsored by the temperance societies Alku and Inkeri, Putro's choral groups, two Finnish women's organizations, sports clubs, a "Finnish society," a Christian organization for young men and women, and an organization for railroad workers. Three Finnish bookstores and numerous Finnish stalls at fish and food markets enabled Finnish speakers to interact regularly among themselves, though intercourse with Russians and people from other ethnic communities was also part of daily life.[44]

Yet, in both relative and absolute terms, St. Petersburg's Finnish-speaking community actually shrank in the last few decades of the tsarist regime, declining from approximately 18,000 in 1881 to around 15,000 in 1910. This demographic decline of the Finnish-speaking community, which had been St. Petersburg's third largest in 1869, matched that of the German community, which had predominated in the city for decades but decreased gradually in absolute terms. Finnish historians attribute this loss to two factors: the move of highly skilled craftsmen (goldsmiths, silversmiths, clockmakers, and their like) to Helsinki, and the changing economic and social status of Finland, which attracted workers from St. Petersburg.

The outbreak of World War I in 1914 initially had little impact on St. Petersburg's Finnish community. The remoteness of the frontline initially ensured the safety of the city's ethnic and religious minorities. Yet the war did affect the city's population directly, as tens of thousands of people fleeing the fighting sought refuge in St. Petersburg and many other large cities. Peter Gattrell's claim that the whole empire "was walking" is no exaggeration: Thousands of ethnic minorities as well as Russians became refugees, seeking food and shelter away from the battlefront.[45] Although authorities tried to transfer many of the refugees to rural areas, thousands of these temporary residents remained in St. Petersburg when the revolutions of 1917 broke out. Most refugees left the city at war's end in late 1918 and returned to their homes and farms, but many others stayed. Soviet authorities, eager to enlist ethnic and religious minorities in support of the new regime, briefly legislated ethnic and religious tolerance. Finnish schools in Petrograd (on the bewildering changes in the city's name over the years, see Helena Goscilo's chapter in this volume), as well as many other non-Russian schools, were able to function autonomously even after 1918, though ethnic tolerance diminished steadily in the 1920s.[46]

Conclusion

Analysis of pre-revolutionary St. Petersburg's ethnic and religious minority communities reveals a wide variety of ways in which they contributed to the ever-changing fabric of the city's economic life and cultural development. Although many of the city's ethnic and religious communities were small and therefore attracted little notice or attention from Western and Soviet writers, luckily enough documentary evidence remains to allow the patient researcher to discover a rich and diverse history of minority communities in the imperial capital. Though under-studied, the city's minority communities contributed directly not only to the city's physical landscape (through their architectural, artistic, and construction efforts), but also to its culture (the Academy of Science, institutions of higher learning, music, and so forth) and governing functions (government officials, military officers, and servants of the Grand Duchy of Finland). Unsurprisingly, ethnic minorities flocked in large numbers to the imperial capital, which served as a focal point for polite society and offered economic opportunity, higher education, and religious diversity. Once settled, they made distinctive contributions in virtually every sphere of the northern capital's life. Hopefully, more of the chapters in St. Petersburg's forgotten multiethnic history will be discovered and written.

Notes

1. St. Petersburg's official website for the 300th anniversary jubilee, http://www.300 .spb.ru/jubilee/index_en.htm [accessed multiple times in 2002 and 2003], made no mention of specific plans to commemorate the participation of ethnic minorities in the city's development and history.

2. *Mnogonatsional'nyi Peterburg: Istoriia, Religii, Narody* (St. Petersburg, 2002), 3. On the lack of understanding among Russians about the city's and region's multiethnic history, see K. V. Chistov, ed., *My zhivem na odnoi zemle: Naselenie Peterburga i Leningradskoi oblasti* (St. Petersburg, 1992), 4–7.

3. See, for example, V. G. Avseenko, *Istoriia goroda S.-Peterburga v litsakh i kartinkakh, 1703–1903: Istoricheskii ocherk* (St. Petersburg, 1993); *Sankt Peterburg—Petrograd—Leningrad* (St. Petersburg, 1992); Regina V. V. Mavrodin, *Osnovanie Peterburga* (Leningrad, 1978).

4. N. V. Iukhneva has edited the following volumes: *Etnograficheskie issledovaniia Severo-Zapada SSSR: Traditsii i kul'tura sel'skogo naseleniia: Etnografiia Peterburga* (Leningrad, 1977); *Staryi Peterburg: Istoriko-etnograficheskie issledovaniia* (Leningrad, 1982); *Peterburg i guberniia: Istoriko-etnograficheskie issledovaniia* (Leningrad, 1989); *Etnografiia Peterburga-Leningrada* (3 vols. Leningrad/St. Petersburg, 1987–1994). She also authored numerous articles in those volumes, as well as *Etnicheskii sostav i etnosotsial'naia struktura naseleniia Peterburga: Vtoraia polovina XIX–nachalo XX veka* (Leningrad, 1984).

5. Chistov, ed., *My zhivem na odnoi zemle;* O. M. Fishman, ed., *Naselenie Leningradskoi oblasti: Materialy i issledovaniia po istorii i traditsionnoi kul'ture* (St. Petersburg, 1992); P. M. Ianson, *Natsional'nye men'shinstva Leningradskoi oblasti* (Leningrad, 1929); Galina Vasil'evna Starovoitova, *Etnicheskaia gruppa v sovremennom sovetskom gorode: Sotsiologicheskie ocherki* (Leningrad, 1987). Interestingly, the most in-depth work on the history of ethnic minorities in the area has been done in the last decade on the German speakers of St. Petersburg. See T. G. Bitkova, ed., *Nemtsy v Rossii: Istoriko-kul'turnye aspekty* (Moscow, 1994); T. V. Gromova, ed., *Deutsche in Russland, Russen in Deutschland: Zeitalter der Aufklärung: Ausstellungskatalog, Moskau, März–April 1994* (2 vols. Moscow, 1994); N. V. Kolpakova and G. I. Smagina, eds., *Nemtsy i razvitie obrazovaniia v Rossii.* (St. Petersburg, 1998); L. V. Slavgorodskaia, ed., *Nemtsy v Rossii: Liudi i sud'by* (St. Petersburg, 1998); L. V. Slavgorodskaia, ed., *Nemtsy v Rossii: Problemy kul'turnogo vzaimodeistviia* (St. Petersburg, 1998).

6. Important recent works on Russia as a multiethnic empire include Daniel R. Brower and Edward J. Lazzerini, eds., *Russia's Orient: Imperial Borderlands and People, 1700–1917* (Bloomington, IN, 1997); Wayne Dowler, *Classroom and Empire: The Politics of Schooling Russia's Eastern Nationalities, 1860–1917* (Montreal, 2001); Robert P. Geraci, *Window on the East: National and Imperial Identities in Late Tsarist Russia* (Ithaca, 2001); Theodore R. Weeks, *Nation and State in Late Imperial Russia: Nationalism and Russification on the Western Frontier, 1863–1914* (DeKalb, 1996); Paul W. Werth, *At the Margins of Orthodoxy: Mission, Governance, and Confessional Politics in Russia's Volga-Kama region, 1827–1905* (Ithaca, 2002).

7. Benjamin Nathans, *Beyond the Pale: The Jewish Encounter with Late Imperial Russia* (Berkeley, 2002); Anders Henriksson, "Nationalism, Assimilation and Identity in Late Imperial Russia: The St. Petersburg Germans, 1906–1914," *Russian Review* 52:3 (July 1993): 341–353; Anders Henriksson, "The St. Petersburger Zeitung: Tribune of Baltic German Conservatism in Late Nineteenth-Century Russia," *Journal of Baltic Studies* 20:4 (Winter 1989): 365–378; Mikhail Beizer, *The Jews of St. Petersburg: Excursions Through a Noble Past,* Michael Sherbourne, trans. (New York and Philadelphia, 1989); Alexander Orbach, *The Pogroms of 1881–1882: The Response from St. Petersburg Jewry* (Pittsburgh, n.d.); Erich Franz Sommer, "Die Deutschen in Moskau und St. Petersburg," in Boris Meissner, Helmut Neubauer, and Alfred Aisfeld, eds., *Die Russlanddeutschen: Gestern und heute* (Cologne, 1992), 127–141.

8. Clearly, more comparative analysis and in-depth research in St. Petersburg's local archives must be done for a more complete understanding of the city's multiethnic and multiconfessional history to emerge.

9. Dmitrii Machinskii, "Russko-shvedskii pra-Peterburg," in Aleksandr Kobak et al., eds., *Shvedy na beregakh Nevy: Sbornik statei* (Stockholm, 1998), 11–16; David Kirby, *Northern Europe in the Early Modern Period: The Baltic World 1492–1772* (London, 1990), 118–123; *Mnogonatsional'nyi Peterburg,* 73–75.

10. Jill Lisk, *The Struggle for Supremacy in the Baltic 1600–1725* (New York, 1968), 62; Machinskii, "Russko-shvedskii pra-Peterburg," 12–16; *Spisok naselennykh mest po svedeniiam 1862 goda: Vol 37: Sanktpeterburgskaia Guberniia* (St. Petersburg, 1864), XXVII—XXXVII; L. V. Suni, "Ingermanlandskie finny: Istoricheskii ocherk," in E. S. Kiuru, ed., *Finny v Rossii: Istoriia, kul'tura, sud'ba* (Petrozavodsk, 1998), 4–10; Veijo Saloheimo, "Inkerinmaan asutus ja väestö 1618–1700," in Pekka Nevalainen and Hannes Sihvo, eds., *Inkeri:*

Historia, kansa, kulttuuri (Helsinki, 1992), 67–81; "Ingermanlandiia," *Entsiklopedicheskii slovar'* (82 vols. St. Petersburg, 1890–1904), vol. 25, 53–54; V. I. Musaev, *Ingermanlandskii vopros v XX veke* (St. Petersburg, 1999), 5–8; *Mnogonatsional'nyi Peterburg*, 14–17; Saulo Kepsu, *Pietari ennen Pietaria: Nevansuun vaiheita ennen Pietarin kaupungin perustamista* (Helsinki, 1995).

11. Iukhneva, *Etnicheskii sostav*, 18–19; Georgii Priamurskii, "Sankt-Peterburg i sud'ba Nienshantsa," in Kobak et al., eds., *Shvedy na beregakh Nevy*, 44–47.

12. *Mnogonatsional'nyi Peterburg*, 54–57; Andreas Kappeler, *The Russian Empire*, Alfred Clayton, trans. (London, 2001), 50.

13. *Ves' Peterburg na 1900 god: Adresnaia i spravochnaia kniga g. S.-Peterburga* (St. Petersburg, 1900), 31; *Mnogonatsional'nyi Peterburg*, 60–70.

14. Russian scholars also complain about the lack of statistics for the city as a whole. See *Ocherki istorii Leningrada* (7 vols. Moscow and Leningrad, 1955–1957), Vol. I, 102.

15. *Ocherki istorii Leningrada* I: 103; *Mnogonatsional'nyi Peterburg*, 18–22.

16. *Sanktpeterburg po perepisi 10 dekabria 1869 g.* (3 vols. St. Petersburg; 1872); *S.-Peterburg po perepisi 15 dekabria 1881 g.* (St. Petersburg; 1883); *S.-Peterburg po perepisi 15 dekabria 1890 g.* (St. Petersburg; 1891); *S.-Peterburg po perepisi 15 dekabria 1900 g.* (St. Petersburg; 1903); *Petrograd po perepisi naseleniia 15 dekabria 1910 goda* (2 vols. Petrograd; 1910).

17. On censuses conducted in Russia and the Soviet Union, see Ralph S. Clem, ed., *Research Guide to the Russian and Soviet Censuses* (Ithaca, 1986). On the difficulties of using St. Petersburg's censuses, see Iukhneva, *Etnicheskii sostav*, 8–11; *Mnogonatsional'nyi Peterburg*, 22–23.

18. The 1869 census counted a total of 667,963 individuals, only 619,696 of which were counted individually; an additional 48,267 persons were identified through other means, although data by categories for the latter group were not provided. See *Sanktpeterburg po perepisi 10 dekabria 1869 g.*, I–IV, 2.

19. *Sanktpeterburg po perepisi 10 dekabria 1869 goda* (St. Petersburg, 1872), 22–65.

20. Iukhneva's original reconstructions were published in N. V. Iukhneva, *Etnicheskii sostav i etnosotsial'naia struktura naseleniia Peterburga: Vtoraia polovina XIX—nachalo XX veka* (Leningrad, 1984). In the subsequent two decades her reconstructed data have been modified slightly and published in various pieces, most recently in *Mnogonatsional'nyi Peterburg*, 26. I have used her latest data in the present analysis. Note: Iukhneva's data for 1900 and 1910 include the city's four suburbs.

21. Anthony Cross, *By the Banks of the Neva: Chapters from the Lives and Careers of the British in Eighteenth-Century Russia* (Cambridge, 1997).

22. Valuable works on St. Petersburg's Jewish population include Nathans, *Beyond the Pale*; Benjamin Nathans, "Conflict, Community, and the Jews of Late Nineteenth-Century St. Petersburg," *Jahrbücher für Geschichte Osteuropas* 44:2 (1996): 178–216; Mikhail Beizer, *The Jews of St. Petersburg*; S. Grinberg, *Jewish Life in St. Petersburg* (Cambridge, 1914); John Klier, *Imperial Russia's Jewish Question, 1855–1881* (Cambridge, 1995).

23. *Ocherki istorii Leningrada* I: 103; *Mnogonatsional'nyi Peterburg*, 18–21, 89.

24. *Mnogonatsional'nyi Peterburg*, 89. The literature on German speakers in St. Petersburg is extensive. The following sources represent a small portion of this rich literature. *Nordost-Archiv*, vol. 3, no. 1 (special volume entitled "Deutsche in St. Petersburg und

Moskau vom 18. Jahrhundert bis zum Ausbruch des Ersten Weltkrieges," edited by Dittmar Dahlmann and Karl-Heinz Ruffmann (Luneburg, 1994); *Russko-nemetskie kontakty v biografii Peterburga*, Vypusk 2 (St. Petersburg, 1993); Erik Amburger, *Deutsche in Staat, Wirtschaft und Gesellschaft Russlands: Die Familie Amburger in St. Petersburg, 1770–1920* (Wiesbaden, 1986); John Armstrong, "Mobilized Diaspora in Tsarist Russia: The Case of the Baltic Germans," in Jeremy Azrael, ed., *Soviet Nationality Policies and Practices* (New York; 1978), 63–104; Anders Henriksson, "Nationalism, Assimilation and Identity in Late Imperial Russia, 341–353.

25. *Mnogonatsional'nyi Peterburg*, 79–81; Ul'f Abel', "Shvedskie khudozhniki v Sankt-Peterburge," in Kobak et al., eds., *Shvedy na beregakh Nevy*, 191–197; Susani Sil'verstol'pe, "Shvedskie zolotykh i serebrianykh del mastera v Sankt-Peterburge," ibid., 198–207; Viktor Antonov, "Karl Estedt—Shvedskii iuvelir XVIII veka v Peterburge," ibid., 208–213; Valentin Skurlov, "Pridvornye iuveliry Bolin," ibid., 214–223; Robert McKean, *St. Petersburg Between the Revolutions: Workers and Revolutionaries, June 1907–February 1917*, (New Haven, 1990), xii, 2–5.

26. Herbert Kaplan, *Russian Overseas Commerce with Great Britain during the Reign of Catherine II* (Independence Square, 1995); *Mnogonatsional'nyi Peterburg*, 65–68; Martin Fritts, "Shvedskie promyshlenniki v Peterburge na rubezhe XX veka," in Kobak et al., eds., *Shvedy na beregakh*, 267–276; Vladimir Meshkunov, "Blagotvoritel'naia deiatel'nost' sem'i Nobel," ibid., 277–282; McKean, *St. Petersburg Between the Revolutions*, 6.

27. *Postimees* #167 (31 July 1897), 1; #45 (24 Feb. 1899), 2; *Peterburi Teataja* #8 (14 November 1908), 3; #9 (21 January 1912), 1; *Ves' Peterburg na 1914 goda: Adresnaia i spravochnaia kniga* (St. Petersburg, 1914), 321–323; *Mnogonatsional'nyi Peterburg*, 117–119.

28. Martin Fritts, "Shvedskie promyshlenniki," 267–270; *Mnogonatsional'nyi Peterburg*, 79–82.

29. Rossiiskii Gosudarstvennyi Istoricheskii Arkhiv (RGIA), fond 821, opis 5, "Inventarnaia Opis'," III. See also the guide to RGIA fond 821, which is the department's main archival unit. Much remains to be learned about the department and its day-to-day functioning and interaction with the confessions it was assigned to oversee.

30. McKean, *St. Petersburg Between the Revolutions*, 3.

31. *Postimees* #31 (7 February 1897), 1–2.

32. A. D. Dridzo, "K istoriografii estonskogo naseleniia Peterburga (60–80-e gody XIX v.)," in Iukhneva, ed., *Staryi Peterburg*, 77–79; *Mnogonatsional'nyi Peterburg*, 117–119; *Leningrad and its Environs* (Leningrad), 101.

33. Max Engman, "Migration from Finland to Russia During the Nineteenth Century," *Scandinavian Journal of History* 3 (1978): 155–160, 164–177; Max Engman and Sune Iungar [Jungar], "Pereselencheskoe dvizhenie iz Finliandii v Rossiiu v 1908–1917 gg.," *Materialy VI sovetsko-finskogo simpoziuma istorikov: Rossiia i Finliandiia, 1700–1917* (Leningrad, 1980), 115–125, 129–130; Max Engman, "Pietarin suomalaiset ruokatavarakaupat," in Pekka Laaksonen and Virtaranta, eds., *Ulkosuomalaisia*, (Helsinki, 1982), 246–252, 257–258; Kaarina Kaurinkoski, *Pietarin Kaupunki* (Helsinki, 1988), 212–215; E. S. Kiuru and L. V. Suni, "Ocherk kul'tury rossiiskikh finnov," in Kiuru, ed., *Finny v Rossii*, 46–47; *Mnogonatsional'nyi Peterburg*, 79–81.

34. Varpu Myllyniemi, "Pyhän Marian suomalainen seurakunta Pietarissa 1890–1917" (Church History Thesis, University of Helsinki, 1990), 4–8.

35. The quote is from Pekka Nevalainen, "Silmäys Inkerin kirkollisiin oloihin, 1704–1917," in Nevalainen and Sihvo, eds., *Inkeri*, 162. See also Ibid, 162–163; Engman and Jungar, "Pereselencheskoe dvizhenie," 133; Myllyniemi, "Pyhän Marian suomalainen seurakunta Pietarissa," 4–13, 96–99.

36. According to S. V. Alekseeva, A. G. Vladimorovich, and A. D. Erofeev, comps., *Gorodskie imena segodnia i vchera: Peterburgksaia toponimika: Polnyi Svod Nazvanii za tri veka*, 2nd ed. (St. Petersburg, 1997), 187, the section of late nineteenth-century Ekateringofskii Prospekt on which this office was located is now known as Prospekt Rimskogo-Korsakogo.

37. Eino Jutikkala and Kauko Pirinen, *A History of Finland*, rev. ed., Paul Sjöblom, trans. (New York, 1988), 162–163; Osmo Jussila, "The Presentation of Baltic and Finnish Affairs Within the Tsarist Government in the 18th and 19th Centuries," *Journal of Baltic Studies* 16:4 (Winter 1985): 373–382; Kappeler, *The Russian Empire*, 94–98; Toivo Flink, *Maaorjuuden ja vallankumouksen puristuksessa: Inkerin ja Pietarin suomalaisten sivistys-, kulttuuri-ja itsetunto-pyrkimyskiä vuosina 1861–1917* (Turku, 2000), 55–56; *Ves' Petrograd na 1915 god: Adresnaia i spravochnaia kniga g. Petrograda* (Petrograd, 1915), 357–360.

38. J. E. O. Screen, "The Entry of Finnish Officers into Russian Military Service 1809–1917" (Ph.D. thesis, University of London, 1976), 287–288; Engman, "Migration," 155–160, 164–177; Engman and Jungar, "Pereselencheskoe dvizhenie," 115–125, 129–130. Grand Duchy subjects were not drafted into Russia's regular armed forces, so these noblemen served voluntarily.

39. Tsentral'nyi Gosudarstvennyi Istoricheskii Arkhiv S.-Peterburga (TsGIA SPb), f. 165, op. 1, d. 2, ll. 1–40; Kalevi Kajava, "Pietarin suomalaisen kirkkokoulun vaiheista," *Koulu ja Meneisyys* (1963): 51–54; Antti Inkinen, "Suomalainen koululaitos Pietarissa," *Koulu ja Meneisyys* (1939), 93–101, 113–116; Alpo Juntunen, "Suomalaista kulttuuria Nevan rannoilla": Piirteitä Pietarin suomalaisen siirtokunnan kulttuurielämästä 1900-luvun alussa (Turku, 1970), 18–21; Flink, *Maaorjuuden ja vallankumouksen puristuksessa*, 239.

40. Antti Inkinen, "Suomalainen koululaitos Pietarissa," 89–103; Kalevi Kajava, "Pietarin suomalaisesta yhteiskoulusta," *Koulu ja Meneisyys* (1965), 13–21; Kalevi Kajava, "Pietarin suomalaisen kirkkokoulun vaiheista," 44–47, 65–66; Flink, *Maaorjuuden ja vallankumouksen puristuksessa*, 64–66, 71–72, 260; Myllyniemi, "Pyhän Marian suomalainen seurakunta Pietarissa," 96; Juuso Mustonen, "Inkerin kansanopetuksen alkuvaiheita," *Koulu ja Meneisyys* (1935), 84–85; Juntunen, *Suomalaista kulttuuria Nevan rannoilla*, 19, 24–29; *Pietarin Suomalainen Yhteiskoulu: Kertomus lukuvuodelta 1909–1910* (St. Petersburg, n.d.), 3; *Pietarin Suomalainen Yhteiskoulu lukuvuonna 1912–1913* (Viipuri, 1913), 3.

41. Flink, *Maaorjuuden ja vallankumouksen puristuksessa*, 81–99; William A. Wilson, *Folklore and Nationalism in Modern Finland* (Bloomington, IN, 1976), 27–44.

42. Kalervo Huttunen, *Pietarin suomenkielisen sanomalehdistön alkuvaiheet vuosina 1870–1883* (Helsinki, 1981); Flink, *Maaorjuuden ja vallankumouksen puristuksessa*, 191–213, 310–320; Juntunen, *Suomalaista kulttuuria Nevan rannoilla*, 58–66, 89–95, 104–106.

43. Hannes Sihvo, "Inkerin maa—Kullervon kansa kirjalisuuden heijastamana," in Hannes Sihvo, ed., *Inkerinmaalla: Muistoja Inkerin maasta ja kansasta sanoin ja kuvin* (Hämeenlinna, 1989), 16; J. Raski, "Kertomus Kolppanan seminaarin vaiheista," in *Kolppanan seminaari 1863–1913: Juhlajulkaisu Kolppanan seminaarin viisikymmenvuotisen toiminnan muistoksi* (Viipuri, 1913), 116–127. *Kolppanan seminaari 1863–1913*, 117; *Kansalais-kalenteri*

Inkerinmaalla ja Pietarissa 1914 (St. Petersburg, 1914), 80–86; Juntunen, *Suomalaista kulttuuria Nevan rannoilla*, 40–50.

44. *Kansalais-kalenteri Inkerinmaalla ja Pietarissa 1914*, 52–53; *Kansalais-kalenteri Inkerinmaalla ja Pietarissa* (Helsinki, 1909), 29–30; Max Engman, "Pietarin suomalaiset ruokatavarakaupat," in Laaksonen and Virtaranta, eds., *Ulkosuomalaisia*, 246–259.

45. Peter Gatrell, *A Whole Empire Walking: Refugees in Russia during World War I* (Bloomington, IN, 1999); N. V. Iukhneva, "Sovremennyi Leningrad—Peterburg," in Chistov, ed., *My zhivem na odnoi zemle*, 51–53.

46. K. V. Chistov, "Vvedenie," in Chistov, ed., *My zhivem na odnoi zemle*, 12–13; Iukhneva, "Sovremennyi Leningrad—Peterburg," 51–55; Kiuru and Suni, "Ocherk kul'tury," 51–52, 57–59; Tsentral'nyi Gosudarstvennyi Istoricheskii Arkhiv Sankt-Peterburga (TsGIA-SPb), f 165, op 1, d. 2.

Seven

Leningrad Culture under Siege (1941–1944)

Cynthia Simmons

The legacy of the Siege of Leningrad includes remarkable documents chronicling both unimaginable suffering and seemingly superhuman resilience. Among those who memorialized this catastrophe were some of the most astute minds and gifted writers of the Leningrad intellectual elite. Many of them pondered the new culture of the Siege in relation to previous siege warfare and the psychological ramifications of life under siege. Others analyzed the Siege in the context of Russian and Soviet history and, in particular, the history of the city itself. In some instances the more general and the more specific perspectives dovetailed in significant ways.

Of the most respected chroniclers of the Siege, perhaps no one wrote more perceptively about the experience than the literary scholar Lydia Ginzburg. Her *Blockade Diary*, first published in the journal *Neva* in 1984 (*Chelovek za pis'mennym stolom*; English translation, 1995), served as an emblem of the burgeoning revisionist reconsideration of the Siege.[1] The diary is replete with trenchant observations, which, taken individually, suggest themes that can characterize the culture of Leningrad transformed by bombardment and starvation.

Piter

An observation Ginzburg makes early on in her diary reveals the distinction between Soviet culture before the war and the culture of Leningrad under siege. For those who felt threatened in the Soviet Union under Stalin, attitudes and behavior differed greatly between official/public life and private life. As an intellectual, Ginzburg, who in the Stalinist era lived under the continual threat of extinction, had to harbor animosity toward what was officially Soviet. She reveals her attitude, if ambiguously, when she describes her first emotions upon hearing of the declaration of war: "There was as yet no suffering, no mortal anguish, no terror; on the contrary, there was an excitement—and a feeling bordering on elation that this life was coming to an end."[2] Ginzburg was referring also to an end to the tension of waiting for the war. This attitude of almost welcoming war as a means to destroy the status quo we also find expressed in Ol'ga Freidenberg's diary, when she describes the first day of the war (June 22, 1941): "It was a pleasant summer day . . . I was taken unawares. History was advancing from some dark hinterland. One felt: Oh, it's not that bad yet, things will shape up; we must trust life; real trouble is still far away; much will happen before events overtake us and cut into our days. And indeed, was it not high time for something to happen: 'Let it be worse so long as it's different.'"[3] Nonetheless, Ginzburg implies in the following pages that during the Siege, Leningraders on the whole came to acknowledge a growing connection with the war effort and the survival of the city as an entity. All Leningraders, of whatever political persuasion, embraced the Soviet campaign for survival. The web of communal connection, which had shrunk in the Soviet period to include, for some, only the most private sphere of family and friends, began to expand into the public arena, and to resemble there, as well, that elusive spiritual connectedness of Russian souls—*sobornost'*.[4] Ginzburg makes much of the newly and nearly universal feeling of solidarity in Leningrad. People would say, "We are surrounding Kharkov," "We have taken Orel."[5] She contrasts this attitude of collective endeavor with the "individualistic pacifism" of Erich Maria Remarque's famous World War I novel, *All Quiet on the Western Front*. Ginzburg claims that people of the post–World War I era, and especially in the West, did not want to understand that social life is a social contract. She

insists that the smallest acts that contributed to human survival constituted "courage" and supported the unspoken social contract that was the
nation's response to war: ". . . [W]ith an effort they wrenched their lives
away from malnutrition, and many of them, consciously or not, did their
bit for the common purpose" (*obshchee delo*).[6] Thus, from this broad perspective, Leningraders under siege might be said to have identified with
the nation and Soviet culture to a greater extent than was their custom
during peacetime.[7]

The citizens of St. Petersburg/Leningrad have always demonstrated a
particular pride in their city. Both Moscow and Petersburg may claim to be
the cultural center of the country, but Petersburg has the advantage of its
imperial glory days, when it vied, in terms of high culture, with the major
European capitals. At times the avowed greater connection between Petersburg and progressive trends in the West, and not only in high culture, has
rendered the city suspect from the vantage point of Moscow. The culminat-
ing historical event in this regard was the infamous Leningrad Affair of
1948–1950, when Stalin's representatives directed the wholesale purging of
Leningrad's political elite. Although the various impetuses to the purge and
exact chain of events await a consensual analysis of archival materials, resulting putative measures, like the closing of the commemorative museum
of the Siege of Leningrad, only exacerbated antagonism between the two
cities.

Since being replaced as the capital of the nation, St. Petersburg twice has
fostered an image, in the popular imagination, of a city-state. Such was certainly the case during the Siege of Leningrad (1941–1944). In fact, the city's
virtual autonomy during the Siege contributed to the impression in Moscow that Leningrad's leaders threatened Moscow's supremacy. More recently, and in the spirit of the post-Soviet surge in the interest in one's own
region (*kraevedenie*), historians of St. Petersburg have set out to revise perceived inaccuracies in the Soviet history of the city. In their textbook for the
study of history and regional studies, *The History of St. Petersburg in the 20th
Century* (*Istoriia Sankt-Peterburga XX vek*, 1997), A. V. Darinskii and V. I
Startsev provide copious statistics on the premier position of St. Petersburg
among Russian cities at the turn of the twentieth century and its then equal
footing with the major European capitals.[8] The tone remains laudatory as
St. Petersburg's contributions range from developments in the arts and industry to the city's role in the Bolshevik Revolution. Most noteworthy with

respect to revisionist history, however, is the chapter on the Siege. The authors write without reservation about Stalin's and the government's disregard for the fate of the city's inhabitants (e.g., the failure to store an adequate supply of provisions in preparation for war, inadequate protection for the Badaev warehouses, which burned to the ground in the first attack of September 8, 1941, and inept plans for evacuating the city), which anticipated the current interest in kraevedenie. Darinskii and Startsev imply and occasionally openly state that Leningrad was betrayed. They counter official failings with the incredible heroism and endurance of simple Leningraders. Their efforts contribute to the perception that St. Petersburg and its inhabitants hold a distinct and privileged position in the nation.

In the current St. Petersburg "text," the city is identified predominantly with its imperial cultural heritage. In her study of post-Soviet St. Petersburg, Elena Hellberg-Hirn analyzes both official and unofficial conceptions of the city: "As I write it, Soviet stories of the Revolution and the Siege have been largely devalued in favour of old Imperial stories with Peter the Great as the prime paragon of national and local pride."[9] Hellberg-Hirn recognizes in the privileging of imperial St. Petersburg during the city's tercentenary celebrations of 2003 a financial incentive as well: "In the official discourse, the Tercentenary's main strategy was to turn St. Petersburg into a tourist product. The key document, the *Concept for the Preparation of the Celebration of St. Petersburg's 300th Anniversary* (2000) . . . saw the city's potential as being generated by its imperial past."[10] Although their reasons vary, the city's leaders as well as the public prefer to identify with St. Petersburg's imperial past. In its first two centuries, the city represented the seat of high culture, a fount of "civilization," and a bulwark against barbarism. This was the Petersburg that Leningraders during the Siege fought so valiantly to preserve.

The Serbian architect Bogdan Bogdanović has written on the widespread false etymology of "city" and "civilization." In response to the outrage against attacks on Dubrovnik and Sarajevo during the Yugoslav wars of the 1990s, he wrote: "The horror felt by the West is understandable: for centuries it has linked the concepts 'city' and 'civilization', associating them even on an etymological level. It therefore has no choice but to view the destruction of cities as flagrant, wanton opposition to the highest values of civilization."[11] Accordingly, it is unsurprising that the citizens of Leningrad rushed to defend the city and its cultural monuments.

The emblematic story of preservation during the Siege is the effort to preserve the holdings of the Hermitage, the world-renowned repository created by Catherine the Great for Western European art. The museum remains, for many, the symbolic heart of the city. Aleksandr Sokurov, the director of the acclaimed film dedicated to the Russian imperial past and filmed in the Winter Palace/Hermitage, *Russian Ark* (*Russkii kovcheg*, 2002), echoed this sentiment in an interview chronicling the making of the film: "Without the Hermitage there would be no life in St. Petersburg. Who would care about this city without the Hermitage?"[12] Sokurov locates the seat of Russian high culture in the Hermitage in St. Petersburg. To the city's inhabitants, and in the spirit of Bogdanović's formulation, "Piter" was and remains the most "civilized" city in the nation.

Soviet Province?

By defending Leningrad, citizens became ever more identified with the general war effort. Although the basic social unit during the siege was the family, the concentric circles of connection, radiating out from the little wood stove that kept people warm (*burzhuika*), proved not a barrier, but a buttress. Family members cared for each other and, surviving, they kept the city alive. The battle for Leningrad, at and behind the frontlines, in turn kept the Germans "occupied," if not at bay, and thus defenders of the city contributed to the defense of the nation and to the Allied campaign on the Western front. The culture of Leningrad under siege in this way coalesced with Soviet culture to a greater extent than perhaps at any other time during the Soviet period.

With all that said, we must recognize the surprising degree to which many chroniclers of the Siege wrote from a perspective neither strictly nor predominantly "Soviet." It is as if the cataclysmic destruction of the nation led to a similar fragmentation of self and a reassessment of identities and loyalties. Siege survivors, at least those not writing officially, rarely defined themselves *first* as Soviet citizens or members of the Communist Party. Rather, they expressed their views as representatives of a specific ethnicity, gender, profession, and class: a woman, a Jew, an ethnic German, an artist, or a person of a particular cultural background. Steven Duke's chapter on multiethnic St. Petersburg describes the city's long history as workplace and home to various ethnic and religious minorities. In crisis, non-ethnic Russians often privileged these and other more strictly personal allegiances. Ginzburg's *Blockade Diary*, for example, recounts the Siege experience from the perspective of "N," a Leningrad intellectual (the "blockade man" of the translation is actually the genderless *blokadnyi chelovek*). Thus, paradoxically, in a country founded on the principles of communist internationalism, unofficial chroniclers of the Siege continually highlighted individual differences. Equally paradoxically, amid catastrophe, most of these besieged citizens discovered that they belonged, indeed, to the "world of nations."

In her diary, the well-known artist Anna Ostroumova-Lebedeva ponders the emotions of *all* soldiers and the goodness and villainy she perceived *everywhere*:

> And just think: among the nations of the entire world, especially among soldiers engaged in combat, how often have we seen manifested the ennobled feelings of heroism, self-sacrifice, courage and resourcefulness. What tremendous mental anguish soldiers must experience when they are commanded to kill the enemy—people just like themselves. We might assume, and I think without error, that three-quarters of the combatants do not thirst for the blood of their enemies.
>
> But simultaneously along with the valorous actions of our warriors and of people in general, how often have they demonstrated brutality, cruelty, often completely unnecessary and senseless. And how much deception and baseness![13]

While maintaining their legendary pride in their city, Leningraders engaged the broader Soviet culture of the war effort and commiserated more broadly with the suffering of all those who were touched by war. Yet, they did not identify themselves primarily as "Soviet" and, in fact, became more sensitive to membership in narrower subcultures (ethnic, religious, professional, gender-based).

Immured

Testimonies from the Siege of Leningrad will take their place among other accounts of physical imprisonment, whether in the Peter-Paul Fortress, the Gulag, or a concentration camp. Each prison has its specific traits, of course. As for Leningrad, it bears remembering that Stalinist repression continued despite the war. Dmitrii Likhachev characterizes the situation thus: "We were doubly besieged: by a double ring—internally and externally."[14] However, in accounts of existence radically cut off in this way, victims at some point testify to unexpected forms of liberation from the constraints of life as they knew it.

Many philosophical musings on the freedoms of physical isolation—in prison, the sickbed, and the madhouse—preceded the published diaries and memoirs of the Siege. This "canon" includes the Gulag memoir of Andrei Sinyavsky (Abram Tertz), *Golos iz khora* (*A Voice from the Chorus*, 1973), where he admits: "It was the most difficult time of my life, both physically and psychologically (the end, the loss of books, of my wife, of my son, who was eight months old when I was arrested), and at the same time, it was aesthetically the happiest."[15] Sinyavsky conveyed this revelation to his wife in many ways and on numerous occasions, in such observations as the following: "Here people think and philosophize more intensely than in the world of scholarship and science. Ideas are not culled from books, but grow out of a man's very bones. Nowhere is the life of the spirit lived at such a pitch, with such zest, as here, at the edge of the world. Heady stuff."[16]

Ginzburg likewise describes various newly found freedoms afforded by a radically circumscribed life: "Getting up was easy, easier than in the former life, when fried eggs were waiting and didn't need thinking about. The transition was simpler now as well. People slept almost without undressing; it was enough just to stick your legs quickly into the boots which stood by the bed."[17] Ginzburg notes that during the worst winter of the Siege (1941–1942), Leningraders ceased to feel pressed for time. Although there were tasks to accomplish (queuing for bread, fetching water, obtaining firewood), they were few in comparison to the demands of prewar existence. When conditions began to improve in the spring of 1942, Ginzburg could sense the start of recovery when "it seemed to be too long to wait forty minutes in a queue for a cup of wishy-washy coffee with saccharine."[18]

In addition to the freedom from daily chores and the clock, the besieged experienced other social and even political freedoms. In desperate times certain conventions lost meaning. In her memoir, the former oboist at the Leningrad Philharmonic Kseniia Matus recounts an intimate relationship with a young soldier that would have been unacceptable during peacetime.[19]

This experience might be likened to the "camp marriages" that occurred in the Gulag, or the general loss of social restraint in the crucible of war.

That some chroniclers dared to commit their political views to paper attests to their sense that they could write freely—there was nothing left to lose. Among other freedoms, the freedom to "speak," despite suffering under inhumane conditions, has characterized other liminal locales in the Russian history of immurement, written as both fact and fiction. Evgeniia Ginzburg, in her *Into the Whirlwind* and *Within the Whirlwind* (*Krutoi marshrut I* and *II*, first published in English in 1967 and 1981 respectively), as well as Solzhenitsyn in his fictional *One Day in the Life of Ivan Denisovich* (*Odin den' Ivana Denisovicha*, 1962) identified this freedom in the Gulag, while Sasha Sokolov found it in the madhouse and depicted it in his novel *School for Fools* (*Shkola dlia durakov*, 1976). Evgeniia Ginzburg in her memoir, and zeks (prisoners) in Solzhenitsyn's portrayal of one day in the life of Ivan Denisovich Sukhov, dare to criticize the system that has incarcerated them. Sokolov's adolescent schizophrenic narrator in *Schools for Fools*, as a "special" student in a "special" school, speaks and acts with impunity. He serves as an artistic metaphor for the freedom of spiritual and political exile that immurement can offer, as it did during the Siege. Among the open expressions of rage directed at Stalin and the government, the views of the artist Lidiia Shaporina and the classicist Ol'ga Freidenberg deserve particular attention.

In her diary, Shaporina describes the government's view of the common Russian as a "*quantité négligeable*," whom Stalin had been "grinding to a pulp for the past twenty years."[20] Yet she holds her own class, the intelligentsia, partly responsible and includes them in her scathing indictment:

> Yesterday I was thinking—Russia deserves punishment, and the heavy hammer (*tiazhkii mlat*) must forge in her a true love for her nation, for her land. For a hundred years, and maybe more, the intelligentsia have reviled their country, their government, received as tsar Manducus, and have begun basely and hyperbolically to bow down, to offer up incense, thinking only of their own skins.[21]

Shaporina writes within a tradition of questioning the intelligentsia's responsibility in determining Russia's fate. Like Shaporina, Andrei Sinyavsky represented his class well, but he still accepted responsibility for the intelligentsia's

complacency at historical turning points. Writing about the period of perestroika, he observed:

> When the first serious test of intellectual integrity and independence of
> thought came, that is, the implementation of the Gaidar market reforms, which
> marked the start of a drastic split in the social stratification of the country and
> led to a situation in which more than 30 percent of the population now lives
> below the poverty level, the intelligentsia closed its eyes. This reminded me of
> the beginning of the 1930s when the intelligentsia closed its eyes to the horren-
> dous famines and disasters in the villages and maintained its silence.
>
> I hold this against the intelligentsia and against myself. I had thought too
> much about the sufferings of the intelligentsia caused by official oppression
> and almost forgot how the intelligentsia had sold out.[22]

Shaporina writes with comparable self-reproach when she implicates her
starving peers in the nightmare of besieged Leningrad.

Freidenberg likewise exercised the relative freedom that the Siege afforded.
A person of unwavering principles, Freidenberg likely would have dared to
write so openly under any circumstances. Still, her recriminations reveal an
anger that was given voice during the Siege. She rails against Stalin:

> And the wheel rolled on. Under the pretense of the public's urging, Stalin
> bestowed upon himself the rank of Marshal.[23] My God! How powerful the
> magic of words and titles! A man who possesses everything in the world—
> endless land, endless power, money, adulation, all sorts of ranks and honors,
> all the epithets of a deity—he still needed the title, the simple combination of
> sounds, the word "marshal," an innocent acoustical window-dressing! In honor
> of the occasion, public enthusiasm was appropriately feigned. The fact that
> Stalin has become a marshal, figure-heads said at political rallies, spurs us to
> on to new achievements! Someone else's rank was to inspire servicemen
> without this rank to achieve new feats![24]

Freidenberg also decried the military strategists and their disregard for
human life:

> It was impossible to calculate the human sacrifice. All our young people had
> already been killed. All my students of all grades were decaying in the ground.
> Now there was no idiot who wouldn't know that we had been sending select
> young men to a bloodbath in Tallinn and Kingisepp, that they went unarmed
> and unprepared, that our weapons were defective, that we fought with the help
> of braggadocio and political indoctrination, that the entire cream of our

Leningrad youth suffered especially, forced to enlist as volunteers and in civilian battalions, driven to slaughter—our best youth, the seeds of our culture and of all our industrial specialties. All the college students had been slain, all the technicians, all the craftsmen and the best workers. Not a professional specialist remained in the city. All had been murdered, all lay dead. There was not a family that did not have a young man killed. I knew no one at the university, in my building, among friends and strangers, who had not lost sons, husbands, or brothers at Kingisepp or Tallinn, at the Finnish or Leningrad fronts. Millions fell outside Stalingrad and Moscow. It was worse when the victims served as pawns.[25]

Amid the traumatizing conditions of the Siege, both Shaporina and Freidenberg wrote more openly, perhaps, than they otherwise would have done. The sense of liminality served to embolden their inherent desire for justice. The Siege did not have such an effect on everyone. In his memoir "How We Remained Alive" (*Kak my ostalis' zhivy*), Dmitrii Likhachev observed that life lived in the extreme of starvation (and the freedom of the liminal) brought out the extremes of personality—for better *or* worse: "In starvation people showed themselves, revealed themselves, freed themselves from any kind of trumpery: some turned out to be wonderful, unparalleled heroes; others—villains, scoundrels, murderers, cannibals. There was no middle ground."[26] Likhachev himself stood as an example of the "unparalleled heroes." In his collection of essays in commemoration of the tercentenary of St. Petersburg in 2003, the writer Daniil Granin (author, with Ales' Adamovich, of *Book of the Blockade*), paid homage to Likhachev as a cultural icon:

> At one time the Leningrad authorities fiercely persecuted him, attempted to destroy him both morally and physically. They set his apartment on fire. They beat him. But he didn't look for any compromise. Nevertheless he doesn't talk about this, not in his memoirs, not in his public appearances. And in his stories about Solovki, where he was imprisoned, there is no description of his own suffering. What does he describe? The interesting people he was imprisoned with; he talks about how he kept busy. The vulgarity and filth of life did not make him embittered and, more likely, made him softer and more sensitive.[27]

We can recognize in words such as these the courage of Shaporina, Freidenberg, and Likhachev, but the horrific accounts of base actions speak to the freedom to do evil that others experienced.

On the subject of freedom, Ginzburg notes another of the numerous paradoxes of Siege culture. The unfreedom of immurement freed Leningraders from daily tasks, but it also denied some ("cultured" people/the intelligentsia) the work that separated them from what Ginzburg characterizes as the primitive, the barbarian. They became like the rest—egoists and savages:

> The egoist is a savage. The primitive mind is filled with terror at the hostility of the world. It is vanquished by culture—a hierarchical chain of values—by creativity, which makes what is one's own other, and by love, which makes what is other one's own.
>
> As a system of values breaks down, the cultured man undergoes a second primitivization. As his existence crumbles, he takes on caveman ways, a caveman's attitude to fire, to food, to clothes.[28]

The focus on quotidian needs and habits was requisite for survival. Ginzburg reminds us that Tolstoy, in his consideration of war, also realized the truth that the "stability of selfish interests and inveterate custom was objectively necessary. It was an indication that the whole existed."[29] However, this "second primitivization," while denying the cultured person a perceived intellectual freedom, resulted, paradoxically, in the greatest freedom of all, the egotism of the slave. Ginzburg observes: "Who is more egoistical than a rower permanently chained to the hull of a galley? Every objective element of life is taken from him; all that is left to him is his suffering body. The egoism of slaves is overshadowed by the intensity of their suffering and the paltriness of their desires and goals, but it is, essentially, limitless."[30]

In the vast philosophical literature on the meaning of freedom, we might recall the distinction drawn by the great social and political theorist and Russian émigré, Isaiah Berlin, between negative and positive freedoms. Negative freedom is the freedom from interference: "No man or body of men interferes with my activity."[31] We could expand this definition, with the Siege in mind, to include the imposition of responsibilities and the mundane tasks of life upon one's daily activities. In the circumscribed life of the Siege person, Ginzburg found new "negative" freedoms. Leningraders could not wash, so they did not need to devote their time to washing and changing clothes. They had little to eat, so they "wasted" no time cooking elaborate breakfasts. Time not "wasted" on personal hygiene is an odd sort of freedom, indeed. The instinct for survival no doubt prompted the characterization of starvation and the most abject living conditions as freedom "from." Yet, in their general distance and isolation, in the chaos of war, from official Stalinist arms of government, Leningraders experienced a significant increase in personal liberty. They could speak and write with less fear of reprisal.

Berlin defines "positive freedom" as the freedom "to"—the freedom to be one's own master/mistress. Negative freedom relates more to private life, while positive freedom is associated with participating in one's society and even government. In the chapter titled "The retreat to the inner citadel," Berlin comments on (and cautions against) the ability to derive positive freedom (freedom *to*) from a situation of unfreedom:

> This is the traditional self-emancipation of ascetics and quietists, of stoics or Buddhist sages, men of various religions or of none, who have fled the world, and escaped the yoke of society or public opinion, by some process of deliberate self-transformation that enables them to care no longer for any of its values, to remain, isolated and independent, on its edges, no longer vulnerable to its weapons.[32]

Ginzburg's description of the siege mentality and the ability to experience freedom in the assault on the body that was starvation is an exquisite example of the "retreat to the inner citadel" that Berlin attributes to the ascetic. By negating the body, victims of the Siege "triumphed" over starvation. We might decry such a rejection of material life in normal times as a shirking of one's responsibility to political life and human rights. However, a Leningrader's ability to recognize freedom ("from" or "to") in the merciless attack on human integrity during the Siege could prove salutary. For some, it was an effective defense mechanism.

In the most basic terms, immurement meant physical unfreedom. But in exclusion from the greater world, Leningraders experienced various "freedoms": the "simplicity" of a severely circumscribed life, a daring that resulted from being beyond punishment, and ultimately, the "freedom" of egoism and slavery. Yet, and as we know, there is no way that any human can escape or be excluded from reality—we are ultimately all inscribed in the world-text. Thus, Ginzburg recognizes yet another paradox. In the ultimate freedom of utter isolation and absolute egotism, the primitive Siege person survives. And by surviving, that one human being contributes, if unconsciously or unwillingly, to the communal purpose beyond the Siege:

> But man [the intellectual 'N' of Ginzburg's diary], aware of the pointless nature of egoistic suffering, is not yet conscious of the meaning of his behavior, the fact that everything he does has a second significance—that while he is preserving and saving the dimming flame of life within himself, on that other,

historical scale, his will to self-preservation is serving the vast complex whole of a country at war.[33]

The Front

Just as the Siege elicited contradictory perceptions of enclosure and liberation, it transformed the traditional notions of the frontline of battle. The military frontline, although in constant flux, lay, technically, beyond the boundaries of the city proper. Yet, inhabitants of Leningrad felt themselves to be direct defenders of the city—either officially as members of the People's Militia (*Narodnoe opolchenie*), as air-raid defense (MPVO) against air and artillery bombardment, or as private individuals, simply doing their work and keeping their families and themselves alive (Ginzburg's *obshchee delo*). Though besieged and cut off, Leningraders experienced the Siege's line of demarcation on more fronts than the battlefield narrowly defined.

Laying siege as a military strategy blurs the boundary between the homefront and the battlefront. Likewise, the starvation that may result broadens the conception of what constitutes a military arsenal. Some of the more intriguing, and poignant, observations by victims of the Siege concern their realization that the battlefront had encroached upon their own bodies. Ginzburg in her *Blockade Diary* recognizes this phenomenon, which, paradoxically, estranges the individual from her or his own body:

> The hostile world, approaching, advances outposts. Its closest outpost suddenly turned out to be one's own body . . . in the winter it had an eternal potential for suffering—with its ever new corners and ribs . . . while people discovered in themselves bone after bone, there occurred an alienation from the body, a splintering of conscious will from the body as a phenomenon of the hostile external world.[34]

Ginzburg's assessment is intentionally generic, but for many women victims of the Siege the assault on the body resulted in a loss of the sense of gender, of the inherently feminine (curvaceousness and desirability, menstruation and fertility), which disappeared with the loss of body fat. Matus, the oboist with the Leningrad Symphony referred to above, recalls looking out over the audience during the first concert organized during the Siege, and not being able to distinguish men from women.[35] Elena Martilla, a

gifted young artist of eighteen when the war began, was distressed that during the Siege people called her "Grandma." Her saving grace was her art:

> At one point in February I understood that I wouldn't make it until morning;
> were I to lie down, I would no longer be able to get up (I had already been
> having fainting spells two to four times a day). I didn't dare lie down and that
> was that. And how bitter I became: I'm a young woman and I'm forced to be
> snuffed out in my bed as if my life were worth nothing . . . Bah! Says who?
> That Fascist Hitler! And not in battle, but in my bed. . . . I'll die, but at least it
> will be like an artist with a brush in my hands . . . [36]

Martilla rails against the assaults on her young body, which threatens to be-
tray her and spell her demise. Her counterattack occurs also and inevitably
within her body. She fights back, paintbrush in hand, with mind and spirit.

Likhachev makes the observation that the last stronghold remained the
human brain:

> The human brain died last. When the hands and legs stopped working, the
> fingers couldn't button buttons, there was no strength to close the mouth, the
> skin darkened and covered the teeth, and on the face the skull clearly showed
> through, revealing laughing teeth—the brain continued to work. People wrote
> diaries, philosophical compositions, scientific works, thought sincerely "from
> their heart," and displayed unusual firmness, not yielding to the pressure of
> the wind, not giving in to vanity [*ne poddavaias' suete i tshcheslaviiu*].[37]

Thus Leningraders had the sense of fighting on numerous fronts—at the
actual front not far from the city; on the homefront, which was assaulted as
well and needed to be defended; and within their own bodies, which fought
against starvation and crippling despair. Technically cut off, the inhabitants
of the city engaged the enemy on multiple fronts. The chronicles of various
survivors detail this reality of the Siege and offer surprising insights into
this strategy of waging war.

"Treasure-Trove"

The extreme conditions of the Siege revealed much that had previously
gone unrecognized; for instance, personal failings (such as the selfishness
and egotism of Matus's young lover) that might have been tolerable in more
forgiving times, or the opposite—bravery that otherwise might not have

been tested. One came to appreciate inherent values of various kinds—the taste of food and the warmth of fire and clothing. Ginzburg describes warming one's hands at the stove as a "measureless enjoyment."[38] She also observes that when objects became distorted or lost their purpose during the worst days of the Siege—books were burnt for fuel or boots were never taken off—once conditions improved, people experienced "a discovered opportunity to return their original meaning to objects."[39] Books once again were for reading, and boots could be removed—they were no longer "an essential attribute of a human being."[40] Not everything was discovered or defamiliarized, however. Some values of their former life fortified Leningraders in excruciating times. Their legendary appreciation of high culture, for instance, proved salutary—it was not a revelation, but a confirmation of their way of life.

Even as Leningraders were selling their libraries to buy food or burning their books for fuel, they received nourishment from "the literary word," often simply memorized and remembered. Although an attachment to classic Russian literature characterized all educated Russians of the Siege era, Leningraders took ownership of Russian poets and the psychological realists of nineteenth-century literature. Ginzburg notes, for instance, that Leningraders read Tolstoy's *War and Peace* to determine whether they were reacting "properly" to the exigencies of war. And Likhachev twice recalls in his memoir how he and his wife attempted to retain some sense of normalcy and the wonder of life by teaching poetry to their children: "With the children we studied poetry. They learned by heart Tat'iana's dream, the ball at the Larins, they learned Pleshcheev's poetry: 'The children returned home from school, all flushed from the frost.' They learned Akhmatova's poetry: 'From my Tatar grandmother' and others. The children were four; they already knew a lot."[41] Leningraders discovered a treasure-trove in their national literature among the works of authors they considered their city's own.

The phenomenon of taking solace at such times in the transcendent power of the aesthetic was not unique to the Siege. Other victims of catastrophe have avoided despair through the salutary effect of art. In *Survival in Auschwitz* (1958), Primo Levi recounts that he survived his ordeal in great part because of his ability to withdraw emotionally and to live spiritually within the sphere of aesthetics. Levi's attempt to recall the verses of Dante's *Inferno* constituted an affirmation of his humanity. Even in our postmodern era, literature can proffer salvation. Azar Nafisi, author of *Reading "Lolita" in Tehran*, has written that during the Iran–Iraq

War, she (and her students) risked their lives for literature, for "it is precisely during such times, when our lives are transformed by violence, that we need works of imagination to confirm our faith in humanity."[42] She continues:

> My Tehran classroom at times overflowed with students who ignored the warnings about Iraq's chemical bombs so they could reckon with Tolstoy's ability to defamiliarize (a term coined by the Russian Formalist critics) everyday reality and offer it to us through new eyes. The excitement that came from discovering a hidden truth about "Anna Karenina" [sic] told me that Iraqi missiles had not succeeded in their mission. Indeed, the more Saddam Hussein wanted us to be defined by terror, the more we craved beauty.[43]

The conservators of high culture (writers, artists, professors . . .) have long acknowledged the transcendent power of art. In their traditional love of high culture, even "average" Leningraders came to appreciate Russian high culture as a defense against barbarism.

A Culture of the Siege?

The culture of Leningrad/St. Petersburg underwent significant and predictable changes during the Siege of 1941–1944. Inhabitants experienced the realities of immurement, bombardment, and starvation. Others have chronicled in different places and times the effects of the wartime strategy of blockading the perceived enemy, and the history of this phenomenon in Leningrad contributes to the sizable corpus of "siege literature." It is important to note, however, that in several significant ways the culture of the city endured, often to the benefit of its inhabitants. Leningrad had already been "besieged" by Stalinism, and in that sense had already adapted to an atmosphere of terror. Accordingly, during the Siege, some became only more impervious to fear. Leningraders had a history of feeling either "cut off" or "chosen"; in any case, they had come to accept their special status and to take pride in it. This pride of place emboldened them in their defense of the city. Finally, the tradition and love of high culture in the most "civilized" of Russian cities not only spurred inhabitants to defend Leningrad; its cultural moments, whether written, painted, sculpted, or performed, had the power, for some, to reaffirm humanity and transcend the horrors of war.

Notes

1. Citations here refer to Lidiia Ginzburg, *Chelovek za pis'mennym stolom* (Leningrad, 1989) and Lidiya Ginzburg, *Blockade Diary* (London, 1995).

2. Ginzburg, *Blockade Diary*, 5.

3. Elliot Mossman, ed., *The Correspondence of Boris Pasternak and Olga Freidenberg 1910–1954* (New York, 1982), 203. Historians of the Siege (including Harrison Salisbury in his *The 900 Days: The Siege of Leningrad* [New York, 1969]) have revealed that many of those persecuted under Stalin (e.g., Jews and intellectuals) believed that Hitler's rule could be no worse, and perhaps better. This compares with a similar phenomenon at the outbreak of World War I. Some women welcomed the apocalypse of war and the destruction of the social structure. In the words of Nina Macdonald: "Girls are doing things / ... / All the world is topsy-turvy / Since the War began" (Sandra M. Gilbert, "Soldier's Heart: Literary Men, Literary Women, and the Great War," in M. Higonnet et al., eds., *Behind the Lines: Gender and the Two World Wars* [New Haven, 1987], 220).

4. I refer here to the more social and political, rather than religious, connotation of the term, as an "organic union of believers in love and freedom." See Catriona Kelly and Vadim Volkov, "*Obshchestvennost', Sobornost': Collected Identities*," in Catriona Kelly and David Shepherd, *Constructing Russian Culture in the Age of Revolution: 1880–1940* (Oxford, 1998), 26–27.

5. Ginzburg, *Chelovek za pis'mennym stolom*, 520.

6. Ginzburg, *Blockade Diary*, 6.

7. Research in the post-Soviet period in particular has sought to complement the official Soviet history of the Siege as uniformly valorous. More recently available archival materials, as well as private documents that lay outside the official purview, have broadened and rendered more subtle the assessment of popular mood during the Siege. In addition to the dissenting opinions and subversive behavior noted here, which undermined the sense of communal struggle that many intellectuals experienced and described so eloquently, see, for example, Cynthia Simmons and Nina Perlina, *Writing the Siege of Leningrad: Women's Diaries, Memoirs, and Documentary Prose* (Pittsburgh, 2002); N. A. Lomagin, "Nastroeniia zashchitnikov i naseleniia Leningrada v period oborony goroda, 1941–1942," in Koval'chuk and Shishkin, eds., *Leningradskaia èpopeia: Organizatsiia oborony i naselenie goroda* (St. Petersburg, 1995), 200–259; Richard Bidlack, "The Political Mood in Leningrad during the First Year of the Soviet-German War," *The Russian Review* 59 (January 2000): 96–113; A. R. Dzeniskevich, *Leningrad v osade: Sbornik dokumentov o geroicheskoi oborone Leningrada vo gody Velikoi Otechestvennoi voiny, 1941–1944* (St. Petersburg, 1995), 463–486.

8. A. V. Darinskii and V. I. Startsev, *Istoriia Sankt-Peterburga, XX Vek: Uchebnoe posobie* (St. Petersburg, 1997). This history/regional-studies text received the recommendation of the Committee on Education of the Administration of St. Petersburg (*Komitet po obrazovaniiu Administratsii Sankt-Peterburga*).

9. Elena Hellberg-Hirn, *Imperial Imprints: Post-Soviet St. Petersburg* (Helsinki, 2003), 115–116.

10. Ibid., 318.

11. Bogdan Bogdanović, "The City and Death" (translation of "The Ritual Murder of the City"), in Joanna Labon, ed., *Balkan Blues: Writing out of Yugoslavia* (Evanston, IL, 1995), 36.

12. Hellberg-Hirn, *Imperial Imprints*, 325.

13. Simmons and Perlina, *Writing the Siege of Leningrad*, 30. The previously unpublished excerpts in this volume from Ostroumova-Lebedeva's diary, from which this passage is taken, reveal additional opinions that are not patently patriotic, and even an abstract anti-Semitism that taints, unfortunately, the artist's emblematic sacrifice and generosity in the face of war.

14. Dmitrii Likhachev, "Kak my ostalis' zhivy," *Neva* 1 (1991): 28.

15. Abram Tertz (Andrei Sinyavsky), *A Voice from the Chorus* (translation of *Golos iz khora*) (New Haven, 1995), vi.

16. Ibid., 98.

17. Ginzburg, *Blockade Diary*, 14.

18. Ibid., 21–22.

19. Simmons and Perlina, *Writing the Siege of Leningrad*, 153.

20. Ibid., 24.

21. Ibid., 24. Shaporina here cites the phrase Pushkin employed in *Poltava* to symbolize the hardships that rendered Russia a more resilient nation: "No v iskushen'iakh dolgoi kary / Pereterpev sudeb udary / Okrepla Rus. Tak tiazhkii mlat / Dobria steklo, kuet bulat" (Fortune's harsh blows and long denials/Steeled Rus'. The heavy hammer thus / Shapes iron while it shatters glass. Walter Arndt, trans.).

22. Andrei Sinyavsky, *The Russian Intellegentsia*, Lynn Visson, trans. (New York, 1997), 5–6.

23. On March 6, 1943, "for outstanding service as leader of the Red Army," Stalin was awarded the title of "Marshal." This event was celebrated with a flood of festive ceremonies attended by the party leadership and writers from the front.

24. *Probeg zhizni*, Vol. 9, Chapter 125, in Simmons and Perlina, *Writing the Siege of Leningrad*, 65.

25. Ibid., 68.

26. Dmitrii Likhachev, "Kak my ostalis' zhivy," 21.

27. Daniil Granin, *Tainyi znak Peterburga* (St. Petersburg, 2001), 334.

28. Ginzburg, *Blockade Diary*, 83.

29. Ibid., 84.

30. Ibid., 86.

31. Isaiah Berlin, *Four Essays on Liberty* (New York, 1970), 122.

32. Ibid., 135–136.

33. Ginzburg, *Blockade Diary*, 94.

34. Ginzburg, *Chelovek za pis'mennym stolom*, 521.

35. Simmons and Perlina, *Writing the Siege of Leningrad*, 149.

36. Ibid., 179.

37. Likhachev, "Kak my ostalis' zhivy," 21–22.

38. Ginzburg, *Blockade Diary*, 17.

39. Ibid., 11–12.

40. Ibid., 11.

41. Likhachev, "Kak my ostalis' zhivy," 21.

42. *New York Times*, March 27, 2003, A25.

43. Ibid., A25.

Eight

Cultural Capital and Cultural Heritage: St. Petersburg and the Arts of Imperial Russia

Richard Stites

In the years after 1991, and a bit earlier under glasnost, the reconstructed memory of St. Petersburg's former cultural glories has often been mixed and sanitized in the elitist traditions not only of Soviet cultural conventions but of the Russian intelligentsia itself—especially its critical, curatorial, and historical establishments. The "bad" things—such as serfdom and imperialist wars—were sometimes omitted, and the "good" ones—such as aristocratic high culture—romanticized. St. Petersburg was trying to recover if not cultural hegemony at least equity with Moscow. Not many years ago, the historical and cultural "capital" that the former capital could claim was based upon three main identities: the home of the imperial style, the cradle of revolution, and the site of the Leningrad Blockade. The revolution is not only old news, but also bad news; the memory of the Blockade, long partly blockaded, is still being contested. And so only the grandeur of St. Petersburg imperial culture is left.[1]

What kind of culture was and is being revived or restored, and on what grounds? In other words, what drove and drives the selective memory of the cultural establishment? The study of memory, a major enterprise nowadays, sometimes threatens to overshadow the very objects of those memories.[2] Since events can never be recaptured, since all texts are unstable and all readings are potential misreadings, it may now seem less important to talk about "real" things that actually happened or about real persons who actually lived and died, created, organized, and consumed art and culture than to relate how we remember them. But such a metahistorical approach is simply substituting one epistemologically problematic task for another, since the evidence of memory is also created by the agency of real people creating real texts, rituals, and artifacts. Any discussion of recent choices being made about the presentation of the cultural heritage of St. Petersburg requires knowledge about what can be presented—in other words, about the canon and what lies outside it. I choose as my base point the late eighteenth and early nineteenth centuries, an era whose musical, theatrical, and artistic life is less studied than those of later periods and whose sociocultural underpinning was marked by high serfdom and a flourishing gentry culture, thus susceptible to all sorts of politicized nostalgia and screening. For the sake of making a few points, I will also mention some aspects of the later nineteenth century.[3]

St. Petersburg's exceptionally self-conscious possession of "cultural capital," in the Bourdieuian sense, invites a critical look at heritage practices and the deployment of cultural capital.[4] David Lowenthal's learned inquiry into "the heritage crusade" now raging throughout the world is particularly apt. "What heritage does not highlight," he writes, "it often hides."[5] Throughout the long monumental-memorial-historiographical reign of Soviet cultural managers—in Leningrad and in the nation at large—ideology and elitism rendered memory acutely selective. Of the cultural riches of the past, only what was "good" in elitist and aesthetic terms and "true" in ideological terms could be presented. Since the collapse of that system, the elitism remains in force, and Soviet ideology has been replaced by a new one, that of heritage: preserving, protecting, and exhibiting the culture that best seems to reflect the glories of the city's past. This process necessarily involves the selection and omission of certain works. The heritage mentality is not simply the pious aspiration to show one's best face. It is conditioned by what I elsewhere have called "market fossilism,"[6] the habit of presenting the old and familiar to patrons in order to fill museums and concert halls, an understandable posture given the economic rigors that beset the city and its cultural sites. The heritage approach combines these two impulses, which often conflict. Lowenthal has much to say about museums, though almost nothing about the performing arts. But it is clear that opera houses and concert halls operate like museums in two senses: the interiors are revered as hallowed sites of architecture; and the works are presented like the exhibited pieces in an art gallery.

A Night at the Opera

St. Petersburg is a window to the West through which its cultural leaders must constantly look for inspiration and for connection to the global system of high culture. But it also aspires to be a "window to Russia,"[7] a cultural gateway for foreign visitors. Russian dramatic theater suffers in terms of foreign audiences who have no command of the language. In Paris, the Comédie Française does well because so many visitors know enough French to follow; but far fewer Russian speakers visit St. Petersburg. Opera and ballet have always been more universal; listeners are used to hearing opera in other languages, and in any case visual splendors provide compensation, even when there are no surtitles. Therefore St. Petersburg draws its theatrical renown only from the Mariinsky Theater of Opera and Ballet. Luckily, it is headed by a very gifted and powerful cultural capitalist—in the Bourdieuian as well as the older sense of the word: Valery Gergiev. Gergiev and his orchestra also feature in Aleksandr Sokurov's surrealistic film *Russian Ark*, which, though exhibiting ambiguities about Russia's cultural past and its relation to the West, unfolds in the Winter Palace among tsars, courtiers, and heroes of high culture.[8]

One manifestation of Gergiev's leadership is the cooperative project of the Mariinsky and the Library of Congress to preserve that theater's priceless archive of music and librettos. The American side is headed by James Billington, who is not only the Librarian of Congress but a well-known historian of Russian culture, author of a pioneering book, *The Icon and the Axe* (1961). Preliminary examination of the archive has already uncovered some priceless old manuscript scores of Russian and European composers. The project itself is eminently valuable and a tribute to the concern of both sides in preserving a magnificent cultural heritage. It is also an impressive public relations feat that will call attention to donors, well-wishers, and audiences from all around the world who come to Russia precisely to sample its treasures.

The repertoire of the musical stage, long controlled by Soviet cultural managers, has expanded since the collapse of the USSR and, enjoying a free hand politically, continues admirably to seek new works, with modern music and dance vocabularies. Of nineteenth-century works (1836 to 1917), it has retained or restaged the canonical repertoire established late in that century and featuring the usual masterpieces of Glinka, Tchaikovsky, Borodin, Rimsky-Korsakov, Stravinsky, and a whole range of European works. When it comes to previously neglected operas of the eighteenth and early nineteenth centuries, however, selective memory comes into play. During my last extended visit to St. Petersburg, I witnessed the performance of a work that, to my knowledge, had not been performed in Soviet times.

An opera by Catherine the Great, *Under the Leadership of Oleg*, premiered in 1791 at the Hermitage Theater, with music by the Italians Giuseppe Sarti and Carlo Cannobio, and Polish-born Wasili Paszkiewicz (Vasily Pashkevich), with a libretto by the empress herself, assisted by Mikhail Lomonosov. Possessing a flair for showy effects, Sarti was wont to put on grandiose productions, embellished with hundreds of voices, the ringing of bells, and the roar of cannon to mark royal visits and military victories. Since he specialized in reworking themes of religion, mythology, and history (particularly Russia's past glory), the Soviet Musical Encyclopedia belittled his art as "academic, archaic classicism," a label that Sarti might have been proud of. A "historical representation" for reader, chorus, and orchestra, *Oleg* treats in a rather ponderous and didactic fashion the Kievan Prince Oleg's occupation of Constantinople in 907. This theme no doubt reflected Catherine's Greek Project, the lingering dream of taking Istanbul (Constantinople) from the Ottoman Turks and turning it into a Russian Tsargrad for her grandson Konstantin (so named with that ambition in mind). The music is up to Sarti's high standards, though jointly composed; the clever use of the folk melody "Kamarinskaya" in the peasant wedding scenes was later made famous in Glinka's arrangement. The enormous cast included 600 guardsmen of the Jaeger Regiment.[9]

The revival I saw on November 21, 1997, was astonishing in many ways. Its staging at the St. Petersburg Capella, among the most revered of the capital's musical venues, signified that the work was being honored as one of high prestige, catering to the city's elite. The composition of the audience in this elegant concert hall seemed to confirm as much: a reverent, well-dressed assembly of the intelligentsia. The 1997 public in no way resembled the courtiers and magnates who first saw the opera in the 1790s. Rather it was as if Alexander Benois, a well-known worshiper of eighteenth-century high culture, had brought an entire cénacle of elitists from the turn of a different century to relish the precious heritage of an aristocratic epoch (see Helena Goscilo, this volume). Given the size of the stage, the production was much less elaborate than the original, and it focused on performance art rather than on showy effects. The result was a success. Yet I could not help feeling that, by inducting the librettist, Empress Catherine II, into the charmed circle of Russian theatrical authorship worthy of public presentation, the organizers were bowing to the fashionable trend of reviving the reputation of long-gone monarchs and the opulence that surrounded them. Doing so is legitimate in the context of "heritage" culture. But for the historian of culture, the choice was more of a curiosity than one representing what many Russian opera audiences usually saw on stage in the decades after it was first produced.

A case in point, and one among many, is Aleksei Verstovskii—the most widely-performed opera composer in the reign of Nicholas I, but buried in oblivion during most of the twentieth century. Glinka's contemporary and a theater bureaucrat, Verstovskii maintained that "the dawn of Russian national opera music began in Moscow and not in St. Petersburg [with Glinka's *A Life for the Tsar*]."[10] By "Moscow" Verstovskii was referring to the performance there of his opera, *Askold's Grave* (1835), based on Mikhail Zagoskin's 1833 novel. It recreated a dark and gothic mood in tenth-century Kiev, with sinister doings by moonlight near the grave of Askold, a ruined church, kidnapping, and wizardry. These elements alternated with folkloric scenes of peasant revelry, Viking feasts, and references to the "broad and deep Dnieper River" and to "Kiev, mother of all Russian cities." The Moscow public was so delighted by its folkish and national themes, its choruses and melodies, that within days the tunes were heard on the streets. The opera also ran well in St. Petersburg and in the provinces. By 1859, the *Theatrical and Musical Gazette* could ask: "In what theater, in what corner of Russia didn't they sing this opera?"[11] It remained on stage throughout the next seventy-odd years, and by the early twentieth century, it had played 400 times in Moscow and 200 times in St. Petersburg.

In terms of stage life and the spread of its songs, for many years *Askold* did better than Glinka's *Life for the Tsar*; and the spinoff effect, according to the musicologist S. L. Ginzburg, lasted almost to the end of the Russian monarchy. For a time, at least, Verstovskii's large loyal following probably considered *Askold* the Russian national opera, until its eventual eclipse by

Glinka's *Life for the Tsar,* which premiered a year after *Askold.* Both men were disappointed: Verstovskii because discerning critics preferred Glinka's opera, Glinka because of the continued popularity of Verstovskii's music on stage and off. In recreating or "remembering" the operatic life of the mid-nineteenth century, the historian would have to give proper attention to Verstovskii. Though his music was on the lips of countless Russians, the mass of Russian listeners today and in the future might never know his name, let alone his earlier popularity. Verstovskii's work has been screened out partly because it is undeniably inferior to the work of Glinka, and partly perhaps because he was a director of the Imperial Theater system, Glinka's rival, and, for Petersburgers, a Muscovite to boot. The only performance of *Askold* during the Soviet era and thereafter that I know of, based on fragments of the music, was recorded in Kiev in 1959.[12] The new theater managements are certainly entitled to mount Glinka again and again, but I wonder if any of them will endeavor to stage other works that were extremely popular in the early part of the nineteenth century.

Evenings with the Orchestra

The history of high culture almost everywhere, in the past half-century, at least, has shown that excellence is not enough to promote or even preserve great monuments of cultural performance. Carnegie Hall in New York City was saved by a hair's breadth through the Herculean efforts of violinist Isaac Stern. The old Soviet subsidy system is largely gone, so that now culture has to stand on its own legs in what Lenin used to call "profit and loss accounting." The marketization of the arts has resulted in some terrible pain. The conservatory of music in St. Petersburg goes begging for support to maintain a magnificent collection of old recordings of music inaccessible anywhere in the world.[13] Sadder still is the sight of Petersburg conservatory musicians and students playing violins and xylophones for tips in the St. Petersburg underpasses and on the streets of Helsinki and other European cities. Changing the name of the conservatory and that of the one in Moscow, founded by the Rubinstein brothers, would not help in the least—though it would be an act of simple fairness. Those brothers pale in comparison to Rimsky and Tchaikovsky in terms of musical genius, but they were the main forces in founding the two conservatories in the 1860s.

The plight of classical music in Russia is not unique: throughout Europe and the United States, such music has been relegated to the status of a poor relative and taken off the air by some public radio stations. Many labels finance classical recordings with the profits made by rock musicians.

Concert music in Russia and elsewhere does not possess the same draw as opera and ballet. The Great Hall of the St. Petersburg Philharmonia is among the most impressive concert sites in the world, with its extraordinary acoustics and classical décor. Few visitors realize that this accidental concert hall once and for a long time served as the ballroom of the St. Petersburg Noble Assembly. In tsarist times, the balcony—where Liszt, Shostakovich, and Stravinsky have stood—was used for a dance orchestra.[14] The cream of the capital's nobility first rented the ballroom of the Assembly to the Philharmonic Society in 1836, and from 1847 on a more or less permanent basis. But this venue—which in 1943 served as a virtual emblem of the city's wartime spiritual survival—was still very much a site of aristocratic leisure. The power of the capital's corporate gentry class in the mid-nineteenth century and the grandeur of its headquarters stand in contrast to the then relative insignificance of the Philharmonic Society, which subsequently gave the hall its name.

The St. Petersburg Philharmonia, for all its glorious past, cannot compete with the visual thrills that most visiting audiences seek in the musical theater at the Mariinsky: the edifice itself, with its red velvet plush, ornate carving, glittering chandeliers; and the spectacle presented on stage by bodies in motion, elaborate sets, and brilliant costumes (whether historically accurate or not). The names Kirov and Mariinsky (like the Moscow Bolshoi) have had a magic ring for decades in a way that the Philharmonia has not, despite the eminence of those who have played or conducted there. The impoverished musical public of St. Petersburg may not be enough to sustain the expense required of such a major musical establishment.

A few years ago, in an effort to project the heritage image of the Philharmonia by connecting it to its hallowed past—and thus win audiences and possibly financial support—a live television broadcast from the Great Hall in 1997 commemorated its 150th anniversary as a concert hall in a recreation of an 1847 concert there: Haydn's Symphony No. 88; an aria from Mozart's *Clemenza di Tito*; Beethoven's *Fantasy for Piano, Orchestra, and Chorus*; a solo piano piece by Adolphe Henselt; and Mendelssohn's *Midsummer Night's Dream* music.[15] The program was superb, but it seems to me that the organizers deliberately chose a concert, rather atypical of that era, that included complete versions of canonical works. In the early nineteenth century, most Russian concerts were extremely eclectic and far from the balance and symmetry of modern programs; they offered excerpts and mixed genres, with longer works often divided between the first and second half of the concert. A much more typical program of a Philharmonia concert, given in March 1859, offered in the first half of the evening Beethoven's Fifth Symphony, an aria from Mendelssohn's *Elijah*, the first movement of the Beethoven violin concerto, the "Sanctus" from his *Missa Solemnis*, Wagner's *Tannhäuser* overture, and the finale of Glinka's *Life for the Tsar*; and in the second half the last two movements of the Beethoven concerto, an aria from Glinka's *Ruslan and Liudmila*, a solo piece for the ophicleide, an aria from Halévy's *La Juive*, and the finale of Mozart's *Jupiter Symphony*.[16] Russian audiences of that time were accustomed to this kind of sequence because it was the standard. The 1997 choice of program, which fits modern notions, was, I believe, more related to the compulsive tendency to show only the best moments of the past that is being recaptured than to celebrating a particular anniversary.

There are other ways of attracting attention to the great musical sites of Russian history that are still operating. Two examples: the Capella, which I have described above; and the Engelhardt House. The latter was the original home of the St. Petersburg Philharmonia Society, founded in 1803, and the ancestor of the present Philharmonia. The founding occasion was a performance of Haydn's *Creation*. Although the Philharmonia's concerts had no permanent site, they were mainly performed on the second floor of the Engelhardt House near the corner of Nevsky Prospect and the Catherine (Griboedov) Canal—a building (with a Metro station beneath) that many readers of these pages have walked past a hundred times. Engelhardt House, the main site of Philharmonia concerts up to 1846, witnessed Petersburg audiences' raptures at performances by Franz Liszt, Clara Schumann, and Hector Berlioz—to name only the most famous of the visiting virtuosos and conductors who appeared there in the reign of Nicholas I. In the spirit of cultural versatility, the place also hosted testimonial dinners and masques for high society. Literary scholars best remember the Engelhardt House as the setting for Mikhail Lermontov's play *Masquerade*. Only in 1847, after this building was sold, did the House of Nobility become the regular home of the Philharmonia.[17]

Nowadays the musical offerings in the Capella and the Engelhardt continue, or in some cases revive, the best traditions of nineteenth-century music. But ticket-buying tourists largely neglect them, and only partly because of foreign audiences' preference for opera and ballet. The Engelhardt (now Glinka) concert hall is practically in the dead center of the city—and a block or so away from the Philharmonia itself, of which it is a filial. But its concerts are not well advertised or promoted. This neglect is chiefly the fault of tour guides, who know or care only about the big and famous tourist targets—the ones the tourists themselves are likely to know: the Mariinsky, the Circus, and, of course, the Hermitage. I have more than once heard Intourist guides apologize to their groups for not getting them into the Mariinsky, offering as poor compensation seats in the Engelhardt! The Capella, also in the center, has suffered the same fate, as has the Smolny Cathedral, which offers breathtaking performances of Russian sacred music.[18]

Pictures Not at an Exhibition

If, in the hierarchy of cultural establishments, the Mariinsky towers above the drama theater, as does the Philharmonia over its smaller sisters, then in even greater measure the Hermitage—set in the 1,100-room Winter Palace—far outshines the Russian Museum. In terms of tourist attraction, nothing in Russia except the Moscow Kremlin has greater resonance. The director of the Hermitage, Mikhail Piotrovsky, speaking to an influential group of women in Washington, D.C., in 1999, focused on two glories of his museum: the enormous and varied collection of European art, and the personal items that reflect the splendor of the Romanov dynasty—particularly the works of Carl Fabergé.[19] Piotrovsky's presentation was, in a sense, circular: He stressed those aspects of the Hermitage with which his audience would already be familiar, a perfectly understandable market strategy that is constantly reinforced by tour and museum guides.[20] The tone in all cases is prideful. The Soviets, of course, did the same thing, though with a different political subtext, one designed to underline the immense wealth that was amassed by the privileged few at the expense of the people.

In both eras, the Russian Museum has played second fiddle to the Hermitage. But managers of the recently renovated museum on the Square of the Arts have their own hierarchical agenda. On the walls of the Russian

Museum, the public—Russians and foreign visitors—will find many of the great masterpieces of Russian art, from medieval icons to modern paintings. The curators have carefully selected them for exhibition. In the case of early nineteenth century art, the sampling is extremely limited. But up in the dark recesses near the roof of the museum, and inaccessible to the public, is an attic storehouse that contains an unhung collection of thousands of pictures that are displayed only periodically or never at all.[21] Having spent several months working through this collection, I was amazed at its magnitude and richness. The numbered canvases are stored on racks. By means of an elaborate index file, one can find paintings on such themes as daily life in town and country, peasants at work, blacksmiths, metallurgical foundries, drunken tavern scenes, bourgeois interiors—the whole gamut of urban and provincial life in pictures, good and bad, that caused consternation among some authorities and critics when they were first painted. Tsar Nicholas I himself became outraged at scenes of drunken revelry and said so.[22]

In the attic of the Russian Museum, one can inspect both "minor" works of famous painters and the works of unknowns. These often deal with subjects unpalatable to art museum officials, who always want to exhibit the best to the art-viewing public. Of course, the works of the canonized early realists of the 1840s, and the "accusers" and Itinerants (*Peredvizhniki*) of the late nineteenth century are on public view, and some of these also show drunken priests, female suicides, and overworked children. Privileging works such as Karl Briullov's *The Last Day of Pompeii* and Aleksei Venetsianov's idealized peasant scenes, however, has sanitized the early part of the century. Viewing works like these without seeing the canvases in the attic, visitors witness a prettified and distorted tableau of what life was like and how art portrayed that life in the early nineteenth century. Curatorial strategies in the Russian Museum, which do not differ significantly from those elsewhere, presuppose that the quality of a painting should be the criterion for public showing because that is what the public actually wants to see. And yet in our postmodern age, there is certainly room for a more varied and more historically resonant approach, one that sets the masterpiece beside the inferior work of the same epoch in a way that permits a more nuanced visual understanding of the age. As long as pious and elitist selectivity prevails, such an educational juxtaposition is not likely to take place in the Russian Museum; and the exalted memory of the Age of Pushkin (another pious trope) will remain unsullied by the prose of reality.[23]

Whatever the arguments for curatorial elitism, less forgivable is the practice of falsifying by omission the record of Russian art in exported shows. Just a few years ago, I attended an exhibit of nineteenth century Russian art on loan from the Russian Museum to the White Hall on Senate Square in Helsinki. Vasilii Vereshchagin was one of the featured artists. Anyone who has been to the Russian Museum is not likely to forget the Vereshchagin room, with its striking canvases depicting the Russian campaigns in the steppes and deserts of Central Asia in the 1860s and 1870s. Amid the various scenes of "oriental" voluptuousness and brutality, one item stands out for its balanced view: a matched set of two canvases called Defeat and Victory. One shows two Kirghiz or Kazakh warriors admiring their trophy, the severed head of a Russian soldier. The other depicts corpses of the native warriors piled against the wall of a fort; standing over them and contentedly smoking a cigarette is a Russian soldier, decked out in the costume designed for desert warfare usually associated with the French Foreign Legion. The main message leaping out from this juxtaposition seems fairly clear: War generates violence and cruelty on both sides of the battlefield. A subsidiary theme may be that modern weaponry causes many more casualties than traditional ones. The exhibit in Helsinki, which hundreds of Finns and foreign tourists saw that summer, contained only the first painting of this set.

Let me conclude my remarks on the Russian Museum on a somewhat different note. This building was once the Mikhailovsky Palace, the mid-century residence of Grand Duchess Elena Pavlovna, where a kind of exalted political circle met in the 1850s to talk of coming reform and of the serfs' emancipation. Less well known, perhaps, is that in these same rooms, Elena Pavlovna hosted musical evenings and that her musician-in-chief was the celebrated founder of the St. Petersburg Conservatory, Anton Rubinstein. How this son of a Jewish merchant from the Pale came to move in such lofty Petersburg circles makes for one of the remarkable stories of pre-emancipation Russian history. During his sojourn at the Palace, Rubinstein not only composed what was once one of the most popular recital piano pieces in the world, the Melody in F, but also floated the idea to the Grand Duchess for a conservatory of music. A 1998 television special on the museum,[24] celebrating its upcoming centenary, made a big point about this aspect of the building's history, justly claiming that the St. Petersburg Conservatory was in a sense born at the Mikhailovsky Palace. Rubinstein was its inspiration, Elena Pavlovna its patron. The first rehearsals and classes of the Conservatory took place there. In the tastefully produced television program, the camera lovingly captured the exquisite White Salon, the site of the musical evenings. The entire effect was to broaden and enrich the setting and meaning of the edifice that would eventually house the Russian Museum (1898) and to take viewers back to a moment when the Mikhailovsky Square, as it was then called, was truly a square of the arts—framed by Elena Pavlovna's palace, the Mikhailovsky Theater, and the House of Nobility.

Truth, Beauty, History, Heritage

The period roughly from the 1790s to 1861—a period of high aristocratic culture, whose epicenter was St. Petersburg—also marked the twilight of serfdom, upon which that culture was built. The efforts to revive and make known to the public works of that period that were denied performance or exhibition in Soviet times are admirable. But the revivals—perhaps like all revivals—have been the result of selective memory. In the Soviet era, a tension existed among many cultural historians between their adulation for the art of the Tsarist era and their need to condemn the kind of society that produced it. The denunciatory literature assembled many stories, some true and some exaggerated, about the mistreatment of serf artists, musicians, and actors: overwork, physical punishment, sexual abuse, and the repression of serf talent. Against this emphasis on the dark side, the scholarly and curatorial approach to canonical figures such as Glinka, who also happened to own serfs, downplayed that aspect of their lives and even invested their art with some sort of proto-democratic sensibility.[25] That tension seems to have disappeared, at least judging from post-Soviet program notes and other commentary on the great masters of the early nineteenth century. But erasing the social context of creativity for aesthetic reasons has had the effect of romanticizing the imperial past, thus replacing the celebrated minus signs with pluses and sweetening memories that in fact should more closely resemble the sweet-and-sour taste of reality.

Though heritage practices and history writing differ in their aims, they need not annul each other. Honest historians strive to avoid falsification and to achieve an objectivity that they know can never be attained. Heritage managers are rarely concerned with these matters. Uplift, pride, and sometimes profit are inscribed on their banners. But, as Lowenthal persuasively argues at great length, despite these different approaches, each can inform the other.[26] Great culture, in St. Petersburg or anywhere else, can be enriched in presentation and reception by being acknowledged in a temporal and social context as well as in its accepted place in the narrative of excellence.

Notes

1. On forgetting, see Elena Hellberg-Hirn, "On the Art of Forgetting: the Siege Story," Conference on Selective Memory and Group Identity in Russia and Eastern Europe, Renvall Institute, Helsinki University, August 30, 2001. See also her *Imperial Imprints: Post-Soviet St. Petersburg* (Helsinki, 2003); on the Blockade, 102–115; on nostalgia for palaces and balls among the New Russians, 165–174.

2. Pierre Nora, *Realms of Memory: Rethinking the French Past*, 3 vols. (New York, 1996–1998), 3.

3. Direct observations about the city's cultural life are based on my residence in Russia in 1997–1998. I wish to thank the International Research Exchange Committee (IREX) for a grant that enabled my stay; Serafima Hager of the International Research Initiative of Georgetown University for additional support; and Elena Hellberg-Hirn of the Renvall Institute for inviting me to her project on St. Petersburg culture and memory. I wish to thank also the audiences at the Baltic and East European Graduate School in Södertorn, Sweden, and at Cambridge University for provocative discussion of my ideas. Most of all, I am grateful to the staffs of the St. Petersburg theaters and concert halls I attended and to the art specialists in the Russian Museum.

4. Pierre Bourdieu, *Distinction: A Social Critique of the Judgement of Taste* (Cambridge, MA, 1984).

5. David Lowenthal, *The Heritage Crusade and the Spoils of History* (New York, 1997).

6. Richard Stites, *Russian Popular Culture: Entertainment and Society since 1900* (Cambridge, UK, 1992) 165.

7. A difficult position to maintain, given the magnetism and easy travel access to Moscow. See the stimulating essays in Ewa Bérard, ed., *Saint-Pétersbourg: une fenêtre sur la Russie, 1900–1935* (Paris, 2000).

8. For more on the film and its meanings, see the chapter by Norris in this volume.

9. *Nachal'noe upravlenie Olega* is often mistranslated as "The Early Reign of Oleg." See S. L. Ginzburg, ed., *Russkii muzykal'nyi teatr, 1700–1835 gg: khrestomatiia* (Leningrad, 1941) 150–156 for an excerpt. *Muzykal'naia entsiklopediia*, IV, 801; Vera Krasovskaia, *Russkii baletnyi teatr ot vozniknoveniia do serediny XIX veka* (Leningrad, 1958) 53–54; Tat'iana Dynnik, *Krepostnoi teatr* (Leningrad, 1933) 65, 203–205; Richard Wortman, *Scenarios of Power: Myth and Ceremony in Russian Monarchy*, 2 vols. (Princeton, 1994–2000) I, 138; Stephen Baehr, *The Paradise Myth in Eighteenth-Century Russia* (Stanford, 1991) 48–49, 212. In Simon

Karlinsky's words, *Oleg* was "the most lavishly mounted stage presentation in the history of Russia": *Russian Drama from its Beginnings to the Age of Pushkin* (Berkeley, 1985), 88.

10. Quoted in O. E. Levasheva, "A. N. Verstovskii," *Sovetskaia muzyka* 6 (1949), 72.

11. *Teatral'naia i muzykal'naia gazeta* 8 (1859), 6 quoted in A. N. Verstovskii, *Askol'dova mogila: romanticheskaia opera*, Boris Dobrokhotov, ed. (Moscow, 1963), 5.

12. Mimoza [pseudonym], "Opera nashikh babushek," *Moskovskaia gazeta* (September 20, 1910), 4; S. L. Ginzburg, *Russkii muzykal'nyi teatr*, 286–300 (excerpt from the libretto). The aristocratic officer Mikhail Buturlin, a devotee of Italian opera, asserted that *Askol'd* produced an indescribable furor: *Russkii arkhiv* 5–8 (1897), 541. The full score has not survived: Boris Dobrokhotov, *A. N. Verstovskii* (Moscow, 1949), 40. But see Verstovskii, *Askol'dova mogila*, an arrangement for piano and voices from which a performance was mounted in 1959 by the Taras Shevchenko Academic Theater Orchestra and Opera Company of Kiev: Aleksei Verstovskii, *Askol'dova mogila*, recording in the fonoteka (recording room) of the Glinka State Central Museum of Musical Culture in Moscow. In 2005, the release of a CD containing selections by Verstovsii seems to augur a revival of interest in him.

13. Conversations with Neli and Vasily Kuznetsov, archivists of the Rimsky-Korsakov Conservatory recording collection, 1997–1998.

14. For historical pictures, see Eleanora Fradkina, *Zal Dvorianskogo Sobraniia: zametki o kontsertnoi zhizni Sankt-Peterburga* (St. Petersburg, 1994).

15. St. Petersburg TV, Nov. 25, 1997, a live concert accompanied by commentary and contemporary graphics.

16. Fradkina, *Zal dvorianskogo sobraniia*, 55–56. Fradkina, reflecting both a twentieth-century elitism and a Russian purist version of it, is indignant over the patchiness of the 1859 program she describes. The ophicleide was a mechanical instrument popular at the time.

17. The current name is the Glinka Small Hall, Branch of the St. Petersburg Academic Shostakovich Philharmonia. Concert hall historical placards and program notes for a concert, December, 1997; Malyi zal imeni M. I. Glinki (St. Petersburg, 1997); Evgenii Kuznetsov, *Iz istorii proshlogo russkoi estrady* (Moscow, 1958), 107n.

18. There is a big literature on the history of the Engelhardt and the Capella, once headed by Aleksei L'vov, composer of the tsarist national anthem (1833), who worked side by side with Glinka. For sources, see Richard Stites, *Serfdom, Society, and the Arts in Imperial Russia* (New Haven, 2005).

19. Mikhail Piotrovsky, speech at the Washington Museum for Women in the Arts, November, 1999.

20. A more spectacular example of the Hermitage's outreach is the recent Guggenheim Hermitage Museum in Las Vegas: *Aveniu: iskusstvo i kul'tura za rubezhom* 1 (2001), 16; *Financial Times* (Oct. 7, 2001), 9.

21. Stephen Norris visited the Russian Museum in May 2003 and noted that many pictures of the old capital had been taken from the storage attic and put on display for the exhibit "Sankt-Peterburg: Portret goroda i gorozhan." See his chapter in this volume and that of Helena Goscilo.

22. See Stites, *Serfdom*, chapter 8.

23. The architectural and art historian Grigory Kaganov has also noted that pictures showing the neighborhoods of St. Petersburg that resembled villages and provincial towns

have been neglected in favor of art that focuses on the sectors of that city where the monumentalism of the Empire style prevails. Illustrated lecture at the Renvall Institute, Helsinki University, November 14, 2001.

24. "Russkii Muzei: Avtobiografiia," St. Petersburg TV Channel 2, January 22, 1998.

25. See Stites, *Serfdom*, passim, for references.

26. Lowenthal, *The Heritage Crusade*, passim.

Nine

Strolls Through Postmodern Petersburg: Celebrating the City in 2003

Stephen M. Norris

On October 1, 1991, the residents of Leningrad voted to restore the old name of St. Petersburg to their city. The renaming took place as the Soviet Union was collapsing, and rethinking the past dominated Russian life. Although the symbolism of reverting to the original name eventually carried the day, the debate over St. Petersburg versus Leningrad was contentious, bringing numerous issues to the surface. Many residents recalled Hitler's intentions to rename Leningrad in 1941, while others insisted that Lenin's name shamed the city and the memory of its founder.[1] While the city became St. Petersburg once more, most residents continued to call it Piter, a reference to the founder whose presence continues to cast shadows over its streets.

St. Petersburg's celebration of its tercentenary in 2003 followed a tumultuous decade that confirmed the dominance of Moscow as Russia's center. The hopes that St. Petersburg could lead a post-Soviet Russian Renaissance had been crushed by the city's emergence not as the new cultural center, but as Russia's crime capital. Indeed, one of the best-selling books in the mid-1990s, later made into a forty-two-part television series, was *Banditskii Peterburg (Bandit Petersburg)*.[2] By 2003, the renovated, cleaned-up streets of Russia's imperial capital could not disguise the lingering reminders of St. Petersburg's economic decline, even if its cultural life remained vibrant.

Postmodern St. Petersburg, as Svetlana Boym reminds us, has become something of a "cosmopolitan province," where many have nostalgia not for the past it had, but for the past it *could* have had, one interrupted by 1917.[3]

Aleksandr Sokurov's film *The Russian Ark* (*Russkii kovcheg*), his "personal gift to the Jubilee," best reflected the desire-driven perspective of the tercentenary.[4] *Russian Ark* highlights the dominant theme of Petersburg's tercentenary—the way in which the city itself had become a museum. At the same time, the film also presented the dominant metaphor of the celebrations, a stroll through this museum-city, meant to convey a sense of action in the face of cultural ossification. Desirous nostalgia thus found concrete expression throughout 2003 as a series of strolls through and into the past.

Filming Petersburg

On December 23, 2001, the St. Petersburg filmmaker Sokurov successfully pulled off a remarkable feat. On one of the shortest days of the year, with only four hours of daylight to work with, he filmed a 96-minute one-take tour through Russia's history. Sokurov set his *Russian Ark* in the Hermitage, formerly the site of the tsar's residence and, as William Brumfield has indicated earlier in this volume, one of the few buildings that has retained its magnificence alongside of its multiple meanings. In the film, Sokurov plays an unnamed narrator who travels back in time to a St. Petersburg and Winter Palace in their full glory. Before the narrator realizes that he has made this trip, he encounters the Marquis de Custine, the nineteenth-century French writer who, after spending a month in Russia during 1839, famously described it as a barbaric country. Once the two men discover where they are, they travel through the Hermitage together, entering a different historical epoch in each room they enter. Throughout their journey Custine and the narrator engage in a debate about Russia and St. Petersburg, and their place in the world.[5]

Sokurov's stunning film captures nearly all of the preservations of St. Petersburg discussed in this volume, turning some on their head while recasting others in a different light. As Birgit Beumers has written, "It is the preservation of the past for the present which interests both the Hermitage museum and the film-maker Sokurov."[6] Peter the Great appears only once, in the bowels of the great palace, mercilessly beating one of his subjects (perhaps Menshikov). Catherine the Great, Nicholas I, and Nicholas II, along with the current and past directors of the Hermitage, also make appearances in Sokurov's Petersburg and its ultimate site of power. The film's image of St. Petersburg evokes nostalgia for what the city could have been by imagining what it had been before the decisive year of 1917. Sokurov's brief mention of the effects of the Siege of Leningrad on the Hermitage provides a moment of reflection on the city's survival during the darkest times and a reminder of the tragedy that befell Petersburg and its culture in the twentieth century. The fact that only a single two-minute sequence in the entire film deals with Soviet history essentially erases this era from the historical memory of Petersburg. Instead, Sokurov offers a second glimpse of twentieth-century life in the form of a conversation between Mikhail Piotrovsky (the current director of the Hermitage, playing himself) and his two predecessors. The three men discuss the difficulties of keeping the museum together over the course of the century, only to conclude, "We managed to preserve all this through the catastrophes." *Russian Ark* transforms the Hermitage museum into a metaphor for Petersburg itself, which also, at considerable human cost, has preserved an older culture despite the cataclysmic events of the twentieth century.

Above all, Sokurov's *Russian Ark* evokes this past culture, epitomized in the final scene, where the city's elite slowly leave the Winter Palace after a 1913 ball, the last one held there before the maelstrom of 1914–1921. The scene takes place on the Jordan Staircase and inverts the final scene of Vsevolod Pudovkin's 1927 homage to the Russian Revolution, *The End of St. Petersburg*. Sokurov's film recaptures the Winter Palace as a site of historical memory that predates "the storming of the Winter Palace" and all the contestations of that event ever since October 1917.[7] Sokurov has stated that the Hermitage is one of the major reasons he lives in St. Petersburg, and has declared: "As long as we have the Hermitage, we have a refuge." For Sokurov, the museum is the ultimate symbol of St. Petersburg and all it has represented over the years—a place where art can inspire. In an interview with the *Moscow Times*, he implicitly contrasted his film with Aleksei Balabanov's screen vision of St. Petersburg: "The idea of shooting a film like this one arose more than ten years ago, when the most popular associations with Russia were with the war in Chechnya and the new mafia. I wanted to change that vicious stereotype and suggest a powerful alternative."[8]

Sokurov's film and its images made history as well as wrestled with it: *Russian Ark* had its Russian debut during St. Petersburg's tercentenary celebrations and even had screenings in the Small Hermitage auditorium as part of the "day of museums" in May 2003. The museum remained open for twenty-four hours as the film ran continuously and Petersburgers who had served as extras donned their costumes and strolled through the halls of the Hermitage. One such extra, Vanda Starodubtseva, dressed as a member of the eighteenth-century imperial court, later claimed that "the situation had something mystical about it," adding that "at some moments, I really started believing that not only the costume belongs to that epoch, but that I am living in that century as well."[9] During the night of May 27, when over 22,000 visitors took strolls through the palace, a costumed Marquis de Custine also embarked on a 1.5 km walk through the Hermitage, thereby collapsing history into a single aesthetic moment. Many of the visitors echoed Starodubtseva's comments, stating that they felt a "spiritual euphoria" that enhanced their museum experience.[10]

The film rekindled discussions about St. Petersburg's decline into a lifeless, carefully preserved museum—a charge that the filmmaker vehemently denied. "I disagree with people who call St. Petersburg an open-air museum," he told the *St. Petersburg Times*, "it is not a museum city. Rather, it is a martyr city, originally built on the bones of hundreds of thousands of people. This legacy is still heavily felt."[11] Sokurov may believe that the city evokes a sense of loss, but that image does not always emerge in the film, which omits the city's historical travails. Despite his claims, Sokurov's announcement that the Hermitage provided a refuge and "a source of inspiration and energy to fight on for future life" left many convinced that the city could be seen only as a museum piece, a conclusion reinforced by the film's screening at the Hermitage Theater (thus one could watch Catherine the Great viewing a performance at the very same theater in the eighteenth century, then see a "character" from the film in period costume stroll around the museum).

Russian Ark, though the most widely discussed, was not the only official "tercentenary film." Three other productions bore the slogan "in honor of St. Petersburg's 300th birthday," and deserve to be placed within the culture of the celebrations. The first of these, *Bedroom Key* (*Kliuch ot spal'ni*), by El'dar Riazanov, depicted a love triangle in 1914 St. Petersburg. Famous for his Soviet comedies, Riazanov stated that he wanted to set a comedy of manners in pre-revolutionary St. Petersburg because "that tasty epoch

[had] splendid clothes, architecture, and Vertinskii had started singing. . . . Besides, in the dramatic arts of that time there's a naïveté that you cannot carry over into our day."[12] *Bedroom Key* depicted a Silver Age St. Petersburg, with an ornithologist (played by Sergei Bezrukov), a wealthy industrialist (Nikolai Fomenko), and a decadent poet (Sergei Makovetskii) all competing for the attention of a major's beautiful wife. In evoking the Silver Age and its personages as a symbol of St. Petersburg's past, Riazanov posited a different kind of "modern hero," one that countered the postmodern "hero" of Balabanov's hugely popular gangster films (*Brother* [1997] and *Brother 2* [2000]). "*Brother* is alien to me," claimed Riazanov, "I cannot justify murder without reason."[13] As a response to the 1990s vision of the city as a center of crime, Riazanov instead offered up another cinematic version of St. Petersburg as a museum. Filmed entirely in the city, *Bedroom Key* connects 2003 St. Petersburg to the incomparably grander pre-revolutionary imperial capital.

As part of the celebrations, *Bedroom Key* premiered at Pushkin, formerly Tsarskoe Selo, which had undergone extensive renovations before the tercentenary. Reactions to the film were mixed. Ekaterina Barabash praised the "lovely pre-revolutionary Petersburg" depicted on the screen, but ultimately concluded that "the film is good overall, except for one thing—it's not funny."[14] Zhanna Vasil'eva, writing in *Literaturnaia gazeta*, viewed the film as an attempt to link the vibrant yet decadent culture of the Silver Age with present-day Russia, and found that such an ambitious evocation "flatters the present epoch."[15] For Vasil'eva, the film's major interest resides precisely in its recreation of the lost era when Petersburg poets such as Blok and Akhmatova held sway over Russian culture. Reviews and reactions to the film largely characterized it as Riazanov's celebration of Peter's city in the past,[16] riding the wave of nostalgia associated with postmodern Petersburg, a place of loss permeated by a sense of what could have been.

This theme also emerged in Vitalii Mel'nikov's tercentenary film, *Poor, Poor Paul* (*Bednyi, bednyi Pavel*). Starring Viktor Sukhorukov (the actor playing the non-heroic brother in Balabanov's films) as Tsar Paul I, the film presents the title character sympathetically, rather than the as the madman of Russian pre- and post-revolutionary historiography. Based on the 1908 novel by Silver Age poet Dmitrii Merezhkovskii, Mel'nikov's film depicts elaborate costumes and court rituals filmed at Paul's favorite estate of Gatchina and the newly renovated Engineer's Castle in St. Petersburg. Ignored by his mother,

Catherine II, and surrounded by court intrigues (led by Baron von Pahlen, played by screen legend Oleg Iankovskii), Paul does his best to rule justly and expresses sympathy for the plight of ordinary Russians. Ultimately, however, Sukhorukov's Paul falls victim to conspirators. David Gillespie has argued that the film presents a vision of the past where "Mel'nikov's Pavel loves his people, bursting into tears when he sees the suffering of the destitute, . . . holds the interests of state and the capital St Petersburg before his own personal needs, and talks about modern notions of ruling through trust rather than Russia's well-worn government through coercion and fear."[17] Like *Russian Ark* and *Bedroom Key*, *Poor, Poor Paul* thus depicts a nostalgic Petersburg of the past, one that returns the city to its "original state"—in Mel'nikov's vision, the Petersburg of the eighteenth century.

Although Riazanov's and Mel'nikov's films carried the tercentenary label, the anniversary film that caused the greatest stir after *Russian Ark* was Aleksei Uchitel"s *The Stroll* (*Progulka*). Shot on a steadicam, like Sokurov's film, *The Stroll* follows three young Petersburgers as they walk in real time throughout their city. It begins with a young woman, Ol'ga (Irina Pegova), being dropped off by an unseen male companion on Nevsky Prospect. She sets off on a stroll through St. Petersburg; as she walks, the viewer takes in the sights and sounds of the present-day city, much of it under construction for the tercentenary. Almost immediately a flirtatious young man named Aleksei (Pavel Barshak) approaches her and accompanies her, the two essentially serving as informal tourist guides for the audience. After Aleksei telephones his friend, Petia (Evgenii Tsyganov), and invites him to join them at Palace Square, the rest of the film follows the three as they talk, argue, flirt, reveal secrets, and discuss life in today's Russia. On one level, this is a mobile exhibition of St. Petersburg and its changes since 1991: Current slang, fashions, the use of cell phones, backdrops that feature modern cafés, and Western cars appear on the screen as the trio meanders through the city. Dunia Smirnova, the screenwriter, echoed Sokurov's comments about his *Russian Ark* when she claimed that *The Stroll*'s vision of St. Petersburg represented another antidote to the grim depiction of the city in Balabanov's films.[18]

The film had little impact in the West (particularly by comparison with *Russian Ark*) but it generated an enormous amount of discussion in Russia. Nikita Mikhalkov, perhaps thinking of his star-making turn in Georgii Daneliia's 1963 *I Stroll Around Moscow*, declared *The Stroll* a breakthrough in Russian cinematography. Critics debated its meanings and its importance, some dismissing it as derivative of Daneliia's film, others comparing it unfavorably to *Russian Ark* and other recent Petersburg films, while still others welcomed its triumph at the Vyborg Film Festival as a victory for a "vibrant Petersburg." One writer even suggested that those who criticized the film, along with the powers that be in Russia's cinema, all hailed from the Russian capital, where *The Stroll* had been denied a screening at the Moscow film festival. Thus the traditional Moscow/Petersburg cultural split had a role in the discussion of tercentenary films.[19]

Elena Kutlovskaia, a film critic for *Iskusstvo kino*, also commented that "the capital's [i.e., Moscow's] critics have already had time to reduce the film's reels into torn rags," and though "the spectator votes 'yes,' filling the cinema halls," the "critics for some reason vote 'against,' proposing that the public vacate these same halls." For her, the film offered not a trendy, shallow look at Russian life, but a journey into "love and youth," which may be simultaneously simple and complex, particularly in St. Petersburg.[20] Natal'ia Sirivlia's review in the same journal claimed that the film captures the vibrancy of Petersburg life, but argued that "if it is a film about a city, then it is impossible to live in that city" because of the chaos and noise in which the film frames St. Petersburg.[21] What critics and audiences all focused upon, whether they liked the film or not, was the presentation of Peter's city and the responsiveness of "the stroll" to the meanings of St. Petersburg. As one viewer concluded, "the film, certainly, is interesting, original, not similar to other films . . . the entire film is permeated with the desire to show Piter from a different side—from the side nearest to its inhabitants, i.e., absolutely that which they see every day."[22] Despite these claims, the film shows a city under renovation, and the three characters strolled essentially through a museum city—past important buildings, museums, and historical actors dressed as Peter and Catherine, all of which turn the film itself into a "live museum" of sorts.

Exhibiting Petersburg

As part of the celebrations, the Russian Museum assembled the most comprehensive art exhibit about St. Petersburg ever undertaken. The museum's director, Vladimir Gusev, and his curators collected more than one thousand artworks depicting St. Petersburg (many of which had been kept in the museum's attic, as Richard Stites notes in the previous chapter), to construct a visual panorama of the city over the past three centuries. Eventually five hundred of these works were displayed at the Benois Wing of the gallery, in an exhibition titled "St. Petersburg: A Portrait of the City and Its Citizens." Gusev conceived of the exhibit as a stroll through his beloved city—a "wander[ing] about the town," as he wrote in his introduction to the exhibit—which allowed visitors to admire the architectural, historical, and artistic monuments for which the city is renowned. The wanderer could view "the most important aspect of the city—the rich tapestry of life, not always noticeable and not always comprehensible, exemplifying the small human galaxy known as St. Petersburg."[23] The works on display not only celebrated St. Petersburg as "the main hero" of Russian secular art since 1703, but also provided viewers with an opportunity, as Gusev noted, to take "a historical walk—a free and effortless excursion, not entirely aimless, yet not planned in any strict chronological order or overloaded with didactic routes, themes, and documental information."[24] Gusev thus invited his visitors to amble through the city's visual treasures, as does the Marquis de Custine in *Russian Ark*, in a recreation of the strolls Petersburg preservationists advocated in the early twentieth century, as Julie Buckler argues.

The walk through Petersburg's history that the Russian Museum invited visitors to take was a thematic one—throughout the halls of the Benois Wing, one could explore Aleksei Zubov's engravings of the city as an expression of "Early Petersburg," Mstislav Dobuzhinskii's "unsaintly" images alongside Il'ia Repin's drawings of Nevsky Avenue and Petr Ivanov's panorama of it (as part of a section on "Avenues, Streets, and Courtyards"), and Anna Ostroumova-Lebedeva's canvases near Johann Wilhelm Gottfried's depictions of St. Petersburg's embankments (an entire section of the exhibit was devoted to images of "Rivers, Canals, Islands, and Bridges"). Numerous images of Peter the Great's creation were juxtaposed so as to present "St. Petersburg as a living organism," as Evgeniia Petrova, Deputy Director of the Russian Museum, noted.[25] Rather than striving for a single unified concept of Petersburg, the exhibit combined all the visions of the city that had delighted some and frightened others, who perceived Petersburg as a locus "of architectural ensembles and phantom-like mists and fogs, shrouding the hearts and minds of all who live there."[26]

Several of the mystical works on display focused upon Petersburg's canals as sites where the "old Petersburg" continued to be preserved in the Soviet

FIGURE 9.1. Arnol'd Lakhovskii's "resonant landscape," *Fontanka* (1919).

era. Arnol'd Lakhovskii's 1919 painting *Fontanka*, for example (Fig. 9.1), deliberately presented the city as a beautiful, European one even as Petrograd suffered through the early years of the Civil War and Bolshevik rule. The exhibit
guidebook declared that Lakhovskii's work, "with its lavish play of light and
shade of flickering reflections in the water" depicts "a resonant landscape" that

contrasted dramatically with reality.[27] The exhibit linked Iaroslav Krestovskii's *Hour Before Sunrise* (Fig. 9.2, 1977) to Nikolai Antsiferov's concept of
"the soul of St. Petersburg." The grandson of Vsevolod Krestovskii, who first
depicted the city as slum-ridden, Krestovskii inverts his grandfather's vision
by featuring "a painterly sonnet to the white nights and azure clouds embracing the bell-tower of St. Nicholas's Cathedral and the houses lining the Kri-
uchkov Canal." As the artist claimed, "I wanted to poeticize a place that I
consider to be one of the most beautiful parts of our city."[28] In works such as
these, St. Petersburg no longer is a city of slums and palaces, but a preserved
work of art in its own right that can be viewed not just on a canvas, but by
standing alongside a canal during the White Nights.

Despite the Russian Museum's attempts to showcase St. Petersburg as
an amalgam of visions, certain images of Peter's city did not feature in the
exhibit. Only two of the events traditionally associated with Petersburg had
sections devoted to them: "Revolutionary Petrograd" and "The Siege of
Leningrad." While the canvases displayed in these halls contained paintings by Boris Kustodiev, Dobuzhinskii, Ostroumova-Lebedeva, and numerous lesser-known artists, the remainder of Petersburg's history was
packaged as a series of parades, unveilings of monuments and palaces, and
portraits of famous Petersburgers. Proclaimed "comprehensiveness" proved
to be "careful selectiveness," much like Sokurov's *Russian Ark*.

As in Sokurov's film, the visions of Petersburg on exhibit, while varied in
content, dated primarily from the eighteenth, nineteenth, and early twentieth centuries. Aside from the two sections mentioned above, few Soviet
paintings, and fewer still from the postwar era, were included. In this remarkable celebration, St. Petersburg propagated the long-standing sense of
the city as a snuffbox, as Arkadii Ippolitov phrased it in his prize-winning
essay about the tercentenary.[29] Not surprisingly, Ippolitov published his
skeptical response to the Russian Museum exhibit not in local papers, but
in *Moskovskie novosti* (*Moscow News*). Entitled "All Is Not As It Seems," Ippolitov's review argues that "while the exhibit is billed as a casual stroll [*leg-
kaia progulka*] around the city, it is a stroll outside of time, outside of chro-
nology, outside of any didacticism."[30] Although he praises the exhibit's
organizers for presenting the city in this manner, one that "deviates from
the usual way of showing Petersburg as a certain change in eras," Ippolitov
concludes that the exhibit ultimately showcases what he terms "Petersburg's
main character"—the "melancholy that is so natural to Petersburg, and

FIGURE 9.2. Iaroslav Krestovskii's *Hour Before Sunrise,* capturing "the soul of Petersburg" (1977).

what distinguishes this former capital, built at one person's will [. . .] from other cities."[31] Thus, for Ippolitov, the stroll through St. Petersburg on offer was a journey through the myths and meanings Petersburg had accumulated over the years, but one that evoked a sense of loss, of nostalgia, and of what could have been.[32] The Russian Museum reinforced this image on the day the exhibit opened (May 18), when it also sponsored the Cherry Forest arts festival in the gardens behind the Mikhailovsky Palace. In a scenario that might be called "nostalgia squared," the festival marked the reopening of the gardens, which had closed for repairs, by inviting St. Petersburgers to dress in Chekhovian costumes and to plant cherry-tree saplings.[33]

The Hermitage similarly cleaved to the past in its two major exhibitions devoted to the tercentenary. The first, "Aleksandr Menshikov: First Governor of St. Petersburg," opened at the restored Menshikov Palace on the Neva River, the displayed objects stressing the importance of Menshikov, Peter's right-hand man, as St. Petersburg's "other founder." The theme of origins resonated in the second exhibit—the Museum's largest that year—"In

Honor of St. Petersburg's Founder." The more than eight hundred objects on show, all dating back to Peter and his era, included such famous items as Zubov's panorama of the city, clothes worn by the tsar, and his portrait by Sir Godfrey Kneller.

Alongside these retrospective exhibits promoting Petersburg as the site of Peter the Great's revolution in Russian culture, on May 27, the city's official "birthday," the Hermitage opened its doors for twenty-four hours without charging visitors an entrance fee. "We wanted to give St. Petersburg an original birthday present," announced Piotrovsky.[34] According to the Hermitage press service, 22,000 people took advantage of that gift, and for some the nocturnal visit involved a stroll dramatically different from the one Gusev envisioned for the Russian Museum's exhibit. Many claimed that the walk through the Hermitage deep into the night produced a feeling of "spiritual euphoria" and "nirvana," partly helped, no doubt, by sleep deprivation.[35] Others got to see Sokurov's *Russian Ark*—the director's "gift" to the city—which ran continuously throughout the night. The film, which preserved a vision of Petersburg as the major repository of culture, thus served as a mirror for the audience, who could "enter" the film by tracing Custine's footsteps in the museum. The premier museum in St. Petersburg, in other words, showcased its historical role as a site of culture and preservation to remind visitors of its long-serving significance within the nation.

The absences and repackagings of the past that the major museums presented in 2003 did not go unnoticed and unchallenged in other exhibitions. Art from the 1950s through the 1990s formed the basis of the exhibit "Festival of Nonconformist Art," held at the Free Arts Foundation at Pushkinskaia 10, the center of the Leningrad nonconformist movement that emerged during the 1980s. The works of Timur Novikov (1958–2002), one of the movement's founders, were exhibited there, while the Russian Museum featured only one of his works, the early *Fontanka* (Fig. 9.3, 1980). Novikov's painting follows in the tradition of works such as Arnol'd Lakhovskii's painting of the same name. As the caption below the painting claimed, *"Fontanka* is endowed with profound lyrical feeling."[36] "Image of the City," a retrospective part of the "Festival" at Pushkinskaia 10, which featured Novikov's numerous odes to his city, served as a reminder of the visions of St. Petersburg lacking in both the Russian Museum and Hermitage exhibits. At the same time, Novikov's exhibit and other ones sponsored by the nonconformist group reaffirmed the power of St. Petersburg and its ability to inspire or repel—even artists associated with Pushkinskaia 10 who rejected the tercentenary celebrations felt compelled to hold an exhibit of cartoons, "Wildlife in the City (Not a Jubilee Event) [*Zhivnost' v gorode (eto—ne iubilei)*]." This exhibit featured works by the Petersburg caricature group Nuance that included various animals in non-Petersburg settings (ranging from elephants in the works of Leonid Mel'nik to the crows in Viktor Bogograd's paintings). Despite their attempts to escape the "museumification" of the tercentenary, the official website of the Jubilee appropriated the exhibit, and included the Nuance group and a review of their works.[37]

Some cultural figures insisted that "collusion" with the events at Pushkinskaia 10 reinforced the tercentenary's agenda of preserving the city as a museum piece. According to them, St. Petersburg in the early years of the twentieth century had been an important center for avant-garde and alternative forms of art, whereas the new millennium betrayed "an officially sanctioned desire to turn the city into a museum." Accordingly, in May 2003 Dmitrii Vilneskii, an artist, Aleksandr Skidan, a poet, and Artem Mogun, a philosopher, issued their "Manifesto Against the Museumification of St. Petersburg," which attacked "the official version of the city's cultural policy [. . .] steeped in stagnant conservatism." For the authors, the tercentenary was "distinguished by a conservation of the past, with the only activities being the restoration of old buildings, the installation of memorial plaques, and speculation about [the city's] 'grand history and cultural traditions.'"[38] Novikov's work, which materialized his neo-academist aesthetic, intent on restoring the classical image of St. Petersburg within the contemporary world, did not find approval among those who opposed the tercentenary's tendency toward "museumification." "Neo-academism was indeed an artistic revolution, but a conservative one," claimed Vilenskii, for, as the very term indicates, it espoused "regressive" values.[39]

St. Petersburg photographer Andrei Chezhin and comic artist Dmitrii Mishenin organized the most fully realized artistic rejection of the tercentenary exhibitions in their "Neo-academism is Sadomasochism," a web-based exhibit that appeared during the celebrations. The exhibit, in the words of one reviewer, "couples examples of classical architecture with modern interpretations of the works that involve young women posing tied up and in other sadomasochist compositions."[40] For all the postmodern features of this online exhibit (still up at www.dopingpong.com)—the use of comics, the Internet, and the rejection of "official" art—Chezhin's and Mishenin's

FIGURE 9.3. The "profound lyrical feeling" of Timur Novikov's *Fontanka* (1980).

works could only signify in the context of the myths and images of St. Petersburg and its celebrations.

Strolls with Putin

Russia's President Vladimir Putin also made his mark on the tercentenary celebrations and took his own stroll through the city-museum. A native of Leningrad, Putin first gained notice as a political figure in St. Petersburg under the city's first post-communist mayor, Anatoly Sobchak. After his surprising rise first to the office of prime minister (in 1999) and second to the office of president (in 2000), Putin sought to bring his hometown into his presidency and thus partly restore Petersburg's image as "the second capital." As Tatiana Zakaurtseva and Irina Kochetkova have noted, St. Petersburg has featured as an important part of Putin's foreign policy: "[St. Petersburg's] possibilities as an industrial, trade, and especially cultural center have been used ever more successfully in the development of bilateral and multilateral relations."[41] Russia's president has held high-level meetings, received important state visitors, and promoted the Eurocentric element in his foreign policy. According to Zakaurtseva and Kochetkova, "St. Petersburg's cultural mission in Europe is seen as a symbol of greater 'culturalization' of the political space." St. Petersburg's historical and geographical proximity to Europe, as well as its preserved palaces and parks, has provided Putin with rhetoric for conducting foreign relations.

During the Jubilee, Putin took his guests on a stroll through the museum that is present-day Petersburg. According to some Russian and Western commentators, Putin aspires to be Peter the Great (his acknowledged hero), a role the present-day leader played during May 2003. Putin himself encourages the comparison. When he became director of the FSB, the post-Soviet intelligence agency formed from the KGB, Putin hung a portrait of Peter I in his Lubianka office. Earlier, upon his appointment as prime minister, his aides frequently stated that Putin's model as a leader was Petersburg's founder.[42] To prepare for the tercentenary, Putin allocated forty billion rubles to the city in order to restore St. Petersburg's beauty in the center of the city.[43] The clean-up of historic buildings ate up a large portion of these funds. Putin therefore helped to pay for the renovation of Petersburg as a museum.

Putin also approved the complete renovation of the Konstantin Palace, located outside the city, in Strel'na. Originally built by Peter the Great, the palace had fallen into a state of extreme disrepair after its last tenants, an Arctic school, had left in 1991, when the federal government deemed the institution "unnecessary."[44] Putin created a fund that allowed for private donations to underwrite the reconstruction of the palace, which was intended as a presidential retreat in Russia's second capital. The Konstantin Palace, after over a year of round-the-clock work and $200 million worth of repairs that some journalists implicitly compared to Peter the Great's construction of St. Petersburg,[45] reopened in time for Putin to host world leaders who came to the tercentenary. These meetings, "the central foreign-policy event of the celebrations,"[46] formed part of Putin's overall plan to use St. Petersburg's image as a means of demonstrating Russia's post-Soviet successes. The renovated palace, in the apt words of Andrei Kamakin, ultimately served as Putin's "parade window to Europe,"[47] and bought into the tercentenary's "museumification" of St. Petersburg.

Putin invited his tercentenary guests, including the leaders of Germany, France, the United States, and other countries—more than forty heads of state—on a private tour around Petersburg's newly renovated buildings. The tour began on May 30, when Putin led his guests through St. Isaac's Cathedral and on to the Mariinsky Theater for a performance. The following day the tour continued with events at the restored Konstantin Palace, where the heads of state heard Luciano Pavarotti sing and the German (heavy-metal pioneers) Scorpions play, in addition to watching a film of the palace's restoration.[48] The day's stroll continued with a private tour of Catherine's Palace at Tsarskoe Selo, where German Chancellor Gerhard Schroeder participated with Putin in the opening of the newly renovated Amber Room. The second day also included a walk through the Hermitage and a first look at the exhibit devoted to Peter the Great. It ended with a boat cruise to Peterhof, where U.S. President George Bush joined the guests in time to gaze at gold-painted ballet dancers and an elaborate laser show that rounded off the evening.[49] Like the Russian Museum's exhibit and the Hermitage's screening of *Russian Ark*, Putin's tour presented the entire city as a historical museum for visitors' consumption.

Putin's private stroll through Petersburg took place amid the contentious debates over the U.S.-led invasion of Iraq earlier in 2003. Bush and Schroeder, who had clashed over the invasion, shook hands and spoke briefly at the tercentenary tour, but French President Jacques Chirac, Bush's most vocal European critic, left St. Petersburg before Bush arrived (ostensibly to prepare for a G-8 summit in Evian). After the tour, Bush and Putin held a brief meeting to discuss their disagreements over the conflict. Putin's tercentenary, in other words, continued to rely on St. Petersburg's reputation as a "window onto Europe" and an important tool in Russian foreign policy. Vladimir Chizhov, Russia's deputy foreign minister, best articulated the city's role in that policy when he claimed that the tercentenary summit "had become a symbol of Russia's historic choice in favor of integration into a united Europe without dividing lines."[50]

Behind the scenes of Putin's foreign-policy stroll, however, lurked some uncomfortable facts. In order to take his guests on a tour of Petersburg, Putin ordered parts of the city cordoned off—for anyone in the city during the summit, the sight of soldiers lining the streets only ten feet apart was ubiquitous. Much like the exclusion not only of selective periods in Petersburg's history from Sokurov's film, but also of sundry people from the later narrative of the

Blockade, the tercentenary hardly involved all Petersburgers in its events. Entire neighborhoods on the road between Stre'lna and St. Petersburg witnessed the construction of privacy walls, which blocked "unsightly" houses from the view of visiting dignitaries. Abandoned buildings were razed along the road, and prior to the arrival of the heads of state authorities removed St. Petersburg's homeless.[51] Putin's Petersburg, as exhibited to guests, consisted in part of a present-day Potemkin village dressed up for its role as foreign policy instrument. Just a few blocks from Nevsky, streets and buildings that did not figure into the live museum remained dirty and disorganized. As an open-air museum, the Petersburg "on show" during the tercentenary strolls excluded everyday Piter.

In addition, Russian authorities shut down St. Petersburg's airport for a couple of days, established road signs that warned of traffic blockades and the closing of buildings to accommodate foreign visitors, and in some cases actively encouraged Petersburgers to leave their city during the celebrations. Frustration and fear that the 300th anniversary was turning into a vehicle for Putin to add to his growing personality cult found ironic expression in the comics of Sergei Lemekhov, who depicted hordes of ordinary Russians forced out of Petersburg, exclaiming as they departed: "We won't disturb you! We've had our fun!"[52] For critics like Lemekhov, the official festivities could not disguise contemporary problems such as corruption, a poor economy, and growing divides between social classes. Other commentators went even further in their criticisms of Putin and his use of St. Petersburg—Elena Shestopal, a professor at Moscow State University, claimed that while "Putin likes to compare himself to Peter the Great . . . psychologically he is by much closer to Emperor Paul—a rather tragic figure, contradictory, and slow-witted."[53]

Postmodern Petersburg

Numerous events, publications, and programs supplemented the exhibits, films, and display of dignitaries. Music fans could attend the festival organized by the St. Petersburg rock band DDT (later prevented from performing), listen to a concert thrown by the group Leningrad (Putin and his wife were in the audience), or see Valery Gergiev direct any number of productions at the Mariinsky. The city's role in Russia's history and national identity was the topic of magazines devoted to the holiday, books issued in time for the event, and newspaper accounts of the tercentenary that spanned the political spectrum.

Television viewers could tune into NTV's lavish documentary, titled *Russian Empire*, which claimed that the foundations of imperial Russia could be traced to Peter the Great's decision to build his showcase city. Hosted by the most popular personality then on the air, Leonid Parfenov,[54] who stated that "the empire is still alive today," the program itself essentially stopped with the death of Nicholas II, thus freezing Petersburg's history in a fashion similar to that of Sokurov's film. Near the end of the series, Parfenov walked on the Pskov railroad platform and stated that the last tsar "made a lonely stroll" around the very same platform in February 1917 before deciding to abdicate, after which "the age of thrones and crowns in Russia ended." The program only commented briefly on the Soviet empire, enough to state that its "power would remain tsarist in character." *Russian Empire* presented yet another stroll through Petersburg's past that many saw as a "museumification" of the city—Parfenov himself visited every site mentioned in the program, and told the history of Russia as he walked through places ranging from Paris to Pskov.

Exhibits that asked viewers to stroll through Petersburg's history, films that presented a cyclical vision of Russia's history or offered a view of "the real side" of Petersburg, ghosts of murdered emperors who visited actors or who reminded journalists of their president, renovations of Petrine palaces, strolls by arguing world leaders around cleaned-up tourist sites, rock concerts offered by a group named Leningrad, and television programs that declared the Russian Empire alive and well: Taken together, this bizarre mix of events and images associated with St. Petersburg's tercentenary offered a concrete instance of the Russian postmodernism as defined by Mark Lipovetsky: an embrace of chaos and a belief that postmodern Russians live in an "afterlife of culture."[55] According to Lipovetsky, Russian postmodernism differs from Western versions in that it embraces the modernist heritage that disappeared with the advent of Stalinist cultural policies. While Russian cultural figures turn to the past for inspiration, they also work within a period of chaos. Russian postmodernists, Lipovetsky contends, "have been saturated with explosive dialogic energy, rooted not only in age-old ties and traditions but in their ruptures, breaks, voids."[56] The combination of cultural energy, the uses of the past, and the rupture provided by the end of communism led many in St. Petersburg (from museum directors to artists and filmmakers) to preserve Petersburg as the repository of "traditional values," a museum of sorts. The process of transition from Soviet to Post-Soviet society has entailed efforts to connect the past to the future and has produced an increasing concern with the past in the present,[57] as amply demonstrated in the tercentenary celebrations.

Postmodern Petersburg has again become a focus for discussions about Russian history and Russia's place in the world. As Elena Hellberg-Hirn maintains, "A truly postmodern condition of total relativity, a mosaic of unrelated or amalgamated cultural fragments and the freedom of self-definition" are the "gifts that the city of *Leninburg* has to offer in the new millennium."[58] As the city refashioned itself for its tercentenary by cleaning off the buildings of the past, and as Petersburgers and visitors alike strolled through the city in 2003, they did so in a fashion similar to Sokurov's narrator and Custine in *Russian Ark*. St. Petersburg, as the exhibits, commentaries, films, and even Russia's president all indicated, exists today as a nostalgic museum.

Notes

1. See Solomon Volkov, *St. Petersburg: A Cultural History* (New York, 1995), 542–550.

2. For more on Petersburg's post-Soviet reputation as a crime capital, see Jennifer Ryan Tishler, "Menty and the Petersburg Myth: TV Cops in Russia's 'Crime Capital,'" *Journal of Criminal Justice and Popular Culture* 10/2 (2003): 127–141.

3. Svetlana Boym, *The Future of Nostalgia* (New York, 2001), 121–171; (her emphasis). My use of the term "nostalgia" falls into the category Boym calls "reflective nostalgia," or a belief that "dwells on the ambivalences of human longing and belonging (xviii)." This sort of longing for the past is not one that "impedes democracy," causes a "memory disorder," or seeks to restore the Soviet era, as many recent commentators have claimed about post-Soviet nostalgia. Rather it is a retrospective longing described wonderfully by Serguei Oushakine in his "'We're Nostalgic but We're Not Crazy': Retrofitting the Past in Russia," *Russian Review* 66 (July 2007): 451–482. I thank Serguei for sharing his article with me before its publication. For the dissenting views above, see Maria Ferretti, "Memory Disorder: Russia and Stalinism," *Russian Politics and Law* 41/6 (November/December 2003): 38–82; and Sarah Mendelson and Theodore Gerber, "Soviet Nostalgia: An Impediment to Russian Democracy," *The Washington Quarterly* 29/1 (Winter 2006): 83–96.

4. Elena Hellberg-Hirn, *Imperial Imprints: Post-Soviet Petersburg* (Helsinki, 2003), 324–325, refers to the film as Sokurov's "personal gift," but also as "heavily sponsored, tourism-promoting, technically brilliant kitsch."

5. The film has already generated several excellent articles: see Tim Harte, "A Visit to the Museum: Aleksandr Sokurov's *Russian Ark* and the Framing of the Eternal," *Slavic Review* 64/1 (Spring 2005): 43–58; Kriss Ravetto-Biagioli, "Floating on the Borders of Europe: Sokurov's *Russian Ark*," *Film Quarterly* 59/1 (Fall 2005): 18–26; Dragan Kujundzic, "After 'After': The Arkive Fever of Alexander Sokurov," *Quarterly Review of Film and Video* 21/3 (July—September 2004): 219–239; Ernest Zitser, "After the Deluge: *Russian Ark* and the (Ab)uses of History," *NewsNet: News of the American Association for the Advancement of Slavic Studies* 43/4 (2003): 17–22; Oleg Kovalov, "Russian Context: Sokurov's 'Russian Ark' in the Context of Russian Culture," *Rossica* 10/11 (Spring/Summer 2003): 100–102; Birgit Beumers, "'And the Ship sails on . . .': Sokurov's Ghostly Ark of Russia's Past," *Rossica* 9 (Winter 2003): 56–59; and Jamey Gambrell, "The Museum as Time Machine," *Art in America* 91/7 (July 2003): 29–30.

6. Online review of the film at http://www.kinokultura.com/reviews/Rark.html, accessed August 2007.

7. For more on the memory of the Revolution and the ways in which the Bolsheviks attempted to refashion the storming of the Winter Palace, see Frederick Corney, *Telling October: Memory and the Making of the Bolshevik Revolution* (Ithaca, NY, 2004).

8. Galina Stoliarova, "Shooting the Hermitage Through the Ages," *The Moscow Times*, 25 April 2003.

9. Titova, "Hermitage Comes Alive for Night Crowds," *St. Petersburg Times* 29, May 2003; online at http://www.sptimesrussia.com/index.php?action_id=2&story_id=10159, accessed August 2007.

10. Hellberg-Hirn, *Imperial Imprints*, 356–57.

11. Quoted in Galina Stoliarova and Peter Morley, "Feasts for Culture Vultures," *St. Petersburg Times* "White Nights Tercentenary Edition," 21.

12. Evgeniia Leonova, "El'dar Riazanov: 'Delaiu, chto khochu i imeiu pravo'"; interview with film.ru at http://www.film.ru/article.asp?ID=3656, accessed August 2007. "Vertinskii" refers to Aleksandr Vertinskii (1889–1957), who became famous for his love songs and renditions of gypsy tunes. See Richard Stites, *Russian Popular Culture: Entertainment and Society Since 1900* (New York, 1992), 14–15.

13. Ibid.

14. Ekaterina Balabash, "Kak Riazanov sam sebia u sebia ukral," online review at http://www.film.ru/article.asp?ID=3586, accessed August 2007.

15. Zhanna Vasil'eva, "Kliuch ot spal'ni, gde skelety lezhat," *Literaturnaia gazeta* 11 (19–25 March 2003), online at: http://old.lgz.ru/archives/html_arch/lg112003/Polosy/art9_3.htm, accessed August 2007.

16. For a representative sample of audiences' responses to the film, see the online listserv discussion of the film at http://www.kino.ru/forum.php?id=1482#times. Most of the respondents on this forum compared the film unfavorably to Riazanov's Soviet classics.

17. David Gillespie, "Poor, Poor Paul Review," at http://www.kinokultura.com/reviews/R44pavel.html, accessed August 2007.

18. David MacFadyen, review of *The Stroll* on the online journal *KinoKultura*: http://www.kinokultura.com/reviews/R74stroll.html, accessed August 2007.

19. See David MacFadyen's review of the film on *KinoKultura* (http://www.kinokultura .com/reviews/R74stroll.html, accessed August 2007); the view of the film as a triumph for Petersburg over Moscow comes from Ivan Miasoedov, "Triumfal'naia 'Progulka,'" *Novye izvestiia* August 18, 2003 (online at http://www.newizv.ru/print/?id_news=580, accessed August 2007).

20. Elena Kutlovskaia, "Vdol' po Piterskoi," *Iskusstvo kino* 10 (2003); online at www.kinoart .ru/magazine/10-2003/repertoire/Kutlo310, accessed August 2007.

21. N. Sirivlia, "Po ulitsam khodila . . ." *Iskusstvo kino* no. 10 (2003), online at http:// www.kinoart.ru/magazine/10-2003/repertoire/sirivlao110/.

22. The comments appeared on a listserv devoted to the film: see it and others like it at www.kino.ru/forum.php?id=1689&offset=0.

23. Vladimir Gusev, Introduction to *St. Petersburg: A Portrait of the City and Its Citizens* (St. Petersburg, 2003), 7.

24. Ibid.

25. Ibid., 12.

26. Ibid. On the range in verbal and visual depictions of the city, see Goscilo's chapter in this volume.

27. Gusev, *St. Petersburg: A Portrait*, 92–93.

28. Ibid., 99.

29. Arkadii Ippolitov, "Gorod v farforovoi tabakerke" in E. D. Shubina, *Moi Peterburg* (Moscow, 2003), 210–215.

30. Arkadii Ippolitov, "Vse ne to, chem kazhetsia," *Moskovskie novosti* 2003, online at http://www.mn.ru/print.php?2003-24-54, accessed August 2007.

31. Ibid.

32. For another view of the exhibit, one that criticizes it for its exclusion of contemporary Petersburg and everyday Petersburgers, see Anna Tolstova, "Chelovek-nevidimka," *Afisha* 5 (19 May—1 June 2003), 85. Tolstova concludes that the exhibit ultimately is "a parade portrait of the city."

33. I thank Helena Goscilo for the suggestion of these events as "nostalgia squared."

34. Quoted in Galina Stoliarova and Peter Morley, "Feasts for Culture Vultures," *St. Petersburg Times* "White Nights Tercentenary Edition," 21.

35. Titova, "Hermitage Comes Alive for Night Crowds."

36. Gusev, *St. Petersburg: A Portrait*, 100.

37. Online at http://www.300online.ru/print/4584.html, accessed August 2007. For examples of the Nuance group's work, see their official website: http://cartoon.spb.ru.

38. See Aliona Bocharova, "On the Cutting Age of Art," *St. Petersburg Times* (White Nights Tercentenary Edition,) 18.

39. Quoted in Ibid.

40. Ibid.

41. Tatiana Zakaurtseva and Irina Kochetkova, "St. Petersburg in Russia's Foreign Policy," *International Affairs* 49/5 (2003): 198.

42. Andrew Meier, *Black Earth: A Journey Through Russia After the Fall* (New York, 2003), 93. The filmmaker Igor Shadkin, who observed that Putin had a portrait of Peter in his office when he worked for Sobchak, also noted that he had a bust of Lenin. See Andrew Jack, *Inside Putin's Russia* (New York, 2004), 68.

43. Valentina Matvienko, Putin's spokesperson (and later governor of St. Petersburg), gave this figure at a May 2003 press conference.

44. Claire Bigg, "Fit for a Tsar, or a President," *St. Petersburg Times* (White Nights Tercentenary Edition), 6.

45. See Andrei Kamakin, "Paradnoe okno v Evropu," *Itogi* May 13, 2003; online at http://www.itogi.ru/Paper2003.nsf/Article/Itogi_2003_05_13_11_3434.html, accessed August 2007. Kamkin writes that the "renaissance in Strel'na began in November 2001, . . . then construction began, and such an accelerated tempo the country had not seen in a long time."

46. Zakaurtseva and Kochetkova, "St. Petersburg in Russia's Foreign Policy," 193.

47. Kamakin, "Paradnoe okno v Evropu."

48. The overall staging prompted European Commission President Romano Prodi to remark that the relationship between Russia and the EU was "like vodka and caviar."

49. The description of Putin's tour comes from Simon Saradzhyan and Natalia Yefimova, "Putin Shows Off Hometown to World," *St. Petersburg Times* 872 (June 3, 2003), 1.

50. Vladimir Chizhov, "From St. Petersburg to Rome," *International Affairs: A Russian Journal of World Politics, Diplomacy and International Relations* 49/5 (2003), 8.

51. See "Bronze Horseman, White Knight," *Transitions Online* May 26, 2003; "The Secret Policeman's Ball," *The Economist* 367/8326 (May 31, 2003); and Jack, *Inside Putin's Russia*, 294–295 for details of the behind-the-scenes maneuvers prior to the visit.

52. The comic appeared in the St. Petersburg cultural journal, *Sobaka* 5/28 (2003), 146–147.

53. Shestopal's comments appeared in an interview by Igor Bederov, "Tsar' bolota, skoree Pavel, chem Petr," *Novaia gazeta*, February 9, 2004.

54. Before he was fired in June 2004 for airing an interview with the widow of a Chechen separatist leader.

55. Mark Lipovetsky, *Russian Postmodernist Fiction: Dialogue with Chaos* (Armonk, New York, 1999). See also Eliot Borenstein's introduction to Lipovetsky's book, "Postmodernism, Duty Free." The dizzying number of images and events associated with the tercentenary certainly conforms to the "postmodern condition" as defined by most theorists, one where "we are subject everywhere to a sensory overload of images, in magazines and advertisements, on the TV, in the cityscape, etc.," to use the words of Christopher Butler. See his *Postmodernism: A Very Short Introduction* (Oxford, 2002), for a useful critique of postmodernism.

56. Lipovetsky, *Russian Postmodernist Fiction*, 247.

57. I borrow these concepts from Michael Burawoy and Katherine Verdery, eds., *Uncertain Transition: Ethnographies of Change in the Postsocialist World* (Lanham, MD, 1999), 4; and C. M. Hann, ed., *Postsocialism: Ideals, Ideologies, and Practices in Eurasia* (London, 2001), 7.

58. Hellberg-Hirn, *Imperial Imprints*, 13. See also her epilogue about the tercentenary celebrations, "Ten Days That Did Not Shake the World."

Contributors

William Craft Brumfield is Professor of Russian Studies at Tulane University. He is the author of numerous books and articles on Russian architecture, including *The Origins of Modernism in Russian Architecture; A History of Russian Architecture;* and *Lost Russia: Photographing the Ruins of Russian Architecture.*

Julie Buckler is Professor of Slavic Languages and Literatures at Harvard University. She is the author of two books, *Mapping St. Petersburg* and *The Literary Lorgnette: Attending Opera in Imperial Russia.*

Steven Duke manages the Education Abroad office at Virginia Tech. He received a Ph.D. in history at Indiana University, and his articles about education and non-Russian residents of St. Petersburg have appeared in publications such as the *Journal of Baltic Studies, Nordost-Archiv,* and *Kritika.*

Helena Goscilo, Professor of Slavic at the University of Pittsburgh, writes primarily on gender and culture in Russia. The twenty-odd volumes that she has authored or (co-)edited include *Dehexing Sex: Russian Womanhood During and After Glasnost; Russian Culture in the 1990s; Politicizing Magic: An Anthology of Russian and Soviet Fairy Tales* (with M. Balina and M. Lipovetsky); *Gender and National Identity in 20th Century Russian Culture* (with Andrea Lanoux); *Poles Apart: Women in Modern Polish Culture* (with Beth Holmgren); and *Encyclopedia of Contemporary Russian Culture* (with Tatiana Smorodinskaya and Karen Evans-Romaine). Her current projects include *Fade From Red: Screening the Cold War Ex-Enemy During the Nineties* (with Bozenna Goscilo), a co-edited collection of articles on paternity and filiation in Soviet and post-Soviet film (with Yana Hashamova), a volume on glamour and celebrities (with Vladimir Strukov), and augmentation of the web site *Stalinka* (with Susan Corbesero and Petre Petrov).

Vladimir Khazan is a professor in the Department of Russian Studies at Hebrew University. He is the author of numerous works, including *Peterburg v poezii russkoi emigratsii* and *Osobennyi evreisko-russkii vozdukh*.

Stephen M. Norris is Associate Professor of History and Director of Film Studies at Miami University (Ohio). He is author of *A War of Images: Russian Popular Prints, Wartime Culture, and National Identity, 1812–1945* and co-editor (with Zara Torlone) of another volume with Indiana University Press, *Insiders and Outsiders in Russian Cinema*. His current projects include *People of Empire: Lives of Culture and Power in Russian Eurasia, 1500–Present* (co-edited with Willard Sunderland) and a book about post-Soviet historical films.

Cynthia Simmons is Professor of Slavic and Eastern Languages at Boston College. She is the author of numerous publications on contemporary literature and cultural studies in Russia, Croatia, and Bosnia-Herzegovina. Her books include *Writing the Siege of Leningrad: Women's Diaries, Memoirs, and Documentary Prose* (with Nina Perlina) and *Their Father's Voice: Vassily Aksyonov, Venedikt Erofeev, Eduard Limonov, and Sasha Sokolov*.

Richard Stites is Professor of History at Georgetown University. He is the author of numerous works on Russian history and culture, including *Serfdom, Society, and the Arts in Imperial Russia: The Pleasure and the Power*; *Russian Popular Culture: Entertainment and Society Since 1900*; and *Revolutionary Dreams: Utopian Vision and Experimental Life in the Russian Revolution*.

Zara Torlone is Assistant Professor of Classics at Miami University (Ohio). She is the author of the forthcoming book *Et in Arcadia Gallus: Eclogues and Elegy* and co-editor of the forthcoming Indiana University Press volume, *Insiders and Outsiders in Russian Cinema*. Her book *Russia and the Classics: Poetry's Foreign Muse* will appear in 2009.

Index

Page numbers in italics refer to illustrations.

Milton Keynes UK
Ingram Content Group UK Ltd.
UKHW050930180724
445758UK00005B/133